INQUIRY AND GENRE

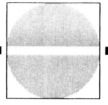

INQUIRY AND GENRE

WRITING TO LEARN IN COLLEGE

David A. Jolliffe

DePaul University

ALLYN AND BACON

Boston ▪ London ▪ Toronto ▪ Sydney ▪ Singapore

Vice President: Eben W. Ludlow
Editorial Assistant: Linda M. D'Angelo
Marketing Manager: Lisa Kimball
Senior Editorial-Production Administrator: Susan Brown
Editorial-Production Service: Matrix Productions
Designer: silk
Cover Administrator: Linda Knowles
Composition Buyer: Linda Cox
Manufacturing Buyer: Suzanne Lareau

Credits appear on page 207, which constitutes a continuation of the copyright page.

Copyright © 1999 by Allyn & Bacon
A Pearson Education Company
160 Gould Street
Needham Heights, Mass. 02494
www.abacon.com

Library of Congress Cataloging-in-Publication Data

Jolliffe, David A.
    Inquiry and genre : writing to learn in college / David A.
Jolliffe.
        p.   cm.
    Includes index.
    ISBN 0-02-361133-2
    1. English language—Rhetoric.   2. Report writing.   3. Study
skills.   I. Title.
PE1408.J755   1998
808'.042—dc21   98-8062
                                                                               CIP

Printed in the United States of America

10   9   8   7   6   5   4   3   2   02   01   00   99   98

Brief Contents

Contents

Inquiry as Clarification   24

The Clarification Project, the Reflective Reading Response, and Three Potential Clarifying Techniques   32

Inquiry for Information   72

7

The Information Project, the Informative Report, and the Art of Careful Conversation 86

8

Exploration: Raising Questions and Resisting Closure 106

9

The Exploration Project and the Exploratory Essay 118

PART

II

The Trim-and-Target Method for Rewriting Prose 181

Preface to Instructors

Like many people who embraced the enterprise of college composition as their professional vocation in the late 1970s, I have always found the notion of "writing as a mode of learning" attractive, but I have wondered over the years how to put that concept into play in my teaching. Like many people who have directed and taught in large university composition programs, I have always found the notion of composition as a "service course" disconcerting, but I have pondered over the years what legitimate, useful "service" a writing course should perform for college and university students—in other words, what "transfers" from first-year composition to other courses in the college curriculum? Like many people in higher education, I have been concerned by accusations, leveled usually by journalists and politicians, that colleges and universities are isolated from the world in an ivory tower, but I have considered over the years how composition could effectively rebut these charges, hastily conceived as they sometimes are.

Inquiry and Genre: Writing to Learn in College emerges from all three of these concerns. First and most important, in this book students are taught a writing-to-learn system, a structure called the Inquiry Contract, that can help them come to terms with complicated, college-level subjects as they learn about effective writing. Second, the Inquiry Contract is an extremely "serviceable" concept in that it teaches students how inquiry and writing are related, a concept that certainly transfers to courses beyond first-year writing. It guides students through a series of five related, sequenced writing projects, and it teaches them how different genres are appropriate for the purposes their compositions are accomplishing and the audiences they are addressing. The system is ideally suited for use in first-year writing courses, first-year or sophomore seminars, writing-intensive courses throughout the curriculum, and senior-level capstone courses. The Inquiry Contract, in other words, helps to expand the concept of the "service course" beyond the traditional view of composition as the "proper format, correct sentence structure, and good grammar" course. The writing course that uses the Inquiry Contract can—indeed, should—still teach format, arrangement, style, and usage, but it can do so in the context of a challenging intellectual inquiry.

Third, in the version of the Inquiry Contract proposed in this text, students have the opportunity to extend their writing into arenas outside the alleged "ivory tower" of the campus. Students are taught to recognize not only that the type of inquiry in which they are engaged and the genre of writing they produce are related but also that written genres have their proper places: Some are most appropriate for use within the academy, but some can—indeed, should—be employed in forums open to the general public. *Inquiry and Genre* thus embodies the belief that learning to write in college carries with it the possibility, perhaps even the responsibility, of writing as public service, functioning beyond the bounds of college.

The book is divided into two parts. In Part One, students learn about the Inquiry Contract. They examine how inquiry and genre are related, and they move through the five related projects in the contract, producing a different genre for each one: a proposal, a reflective reading response, an informative report, an exploratory essay, and a working document. Throughout Part One, students have the opportunity to put their emerging ideas into written form in a series of in-progress tasks, and they have the chance to follow the work of three student writers completing different projects in their own Inquiry Contracts. At the end of Part One, both students and instructors can examine variations on the Inquiry Contract that might be useful in different writing-intensive courses. In Part Two, students learn a relatively simple, ten-step method for revising their compositions. This system, the *Trim-and-Target Method* of revising, is designed on the assumption that the major problem of much writing in college is overcomplication and lack of structure and focus.

I wish to thank the reviewers for their comments: Chris M. Anson, University of Minnesota; L. Bensel-Meyers, University of Tennessee; James C. McDonald, University of Southwestern Louisiana; Carol Rutz, Carleton College; and Penny L. Smith, Gannon University.

INQUIRY AND GENRE

PART I The Inquiry Contract

- Next, in the *Clarification Project,* you clarify for yourself what you already think, feel, know, and believe about the subject, and you write a genre called a *reflective reading response.*
- In the next project, the *Information Project,* you learn something new about the subject and write an *informative report* telling your readers what you learn.
- In the next-to-last project, the *Exploration Project,* you explore your subject by raising questions about it, proposing more than one answer to every question you raise, and hypothesizing about what kinds of people would advocate the different answers you suggest. For this project, you write an *exploratory essay* about your subject.
- Finally, in the *Working Documents Project,* you produce a composition designed to change people's minds and possibly their actions in regard to your subject—in other words, to think and/or act in a different way than they currently do with regard to your subject.

Part One explains the Inquiry Contract and illustrate its genres with models, written by students. Because it's important to get your project started quickly, instructions for drafting the Contract Proposal follow immediately after this preview in Chapter 2. Then Chapter 3 defines inquiry and explains how inquiry and writing are related. Chapters 4 and 5 introduce the Clarification Project, explaining how you can use writing to clarify your ideas and feelings about a subject early in the process of inquiring into it. Chapters 6 and 7 present the Information Project, examining writing as informative and exploring how to produce a genre that conveys information. Chapters 8 and 9 set out the Exploration Project, illustrating the processes involved in exploring your subject and teaching the exploratory essay, a genre that can capture the richness of your subject. Chapters 10 and 11 offer the Working Documents Project, the culmination of the Inquiry Contract, analyzing how writers try to get a certain group of readers to think and act in a specific way in regard to the subject at hand. An Appendix to Part One, located right after Chapter 11, explains variations on the Inquiry Contract compositions—different kinds of papers you can write besides reflective reading responses, informative reports, exploratory essays, and working documents. The appendix also describes several sample Inquiry Contracts for classes in the humanities; the social sciences, business; and education; and the natural and life sciences and engineering.

Throughout Part One, you will find an array of In-Progress Tasks, designed to help you "think on paper" in a learning journal as you move through your project. It's important to do these tasks when you encounter them. It's better to focus your ideas on the pages of a learning journal, or in a similarly named computer file, while your ideas are form-ing than to try to recall what you were thinking about at some later time.

Part Two offers a ten-step process, called the *Trim-and-Target Method,* for *rewriting* initial drafts to produce efficient and effective prose, an ability central to completing all the projects in Part One and to writing in a great many other intellectual, professional, and social groups.

2 The Contract Proposal: Getting Started on Your Inquiry Project

Because this book is designed to help you learn about careful inquiry and effective writing, it's important for you to begin thinking about a subject that you would like to explore and write about. Throughout the book, you will have several opportunities to write about this subject in projects designed to accomplish different purposes for different sets of readers.

This is the first of these projects. After reading this chapter, you should write a one-page statement proposing a subject that you will write four more papers about—a reflective reading response, an informative report, an exploratory essay, and a persuasive, "working document." Let's call this one-page statement your *Contract Proposal.* You can examine one student's Contract Proposal at the end of this section.

Consider this statement a planning document, a "thinking-aloud-on-paper" project. Don't feel that you must commit yourself to a subject to the point that you might be trapped in it as your work progresses. Your ideas about this subject will grow and change as you proceed through your Inquiry Contract. In consultation with your instructor, you should feel free to make changes in the subject you are inquiring into at any point in the course.

To begin this project, think of a realm of subject matter that meets two requirements. First, you should be genuinely interested in it, interested enough to have gained some knowledge about it, perhaps through your own readings, discussions with others, or experiences. Second, you should remain sincerely curious about it, curious enough so that you are willing to learn more about this domain as opportunities to do so present themselves.

In other words, think of a subject about which you are a budding expert. You can't quite write an in-depth article about this subject yet, but you wouldn't mind doing so someday. The talk show producers don't call you now to be their featured guest about this area of knowledge, but some day they might.

As you brainstorm possible subjects for your Inquiry Contract, perhaps it would help you to hear about some subjects that students in previous college and university writing classes have written about in their Inquiry Contracts:

- One student had spent many wonderful afternoons listening to her grandmother's stories about how she and friends had conserved food, fuel, and supplies at home to help the U.S. military efforts in World War II. The student capitalized on the curiosity that these stories sparked and wrote an Inquiry Contract about the roles women in the United States have played in wars.
- One student was an avid tennis player and was dissatisfied with the methods his local tennis association used to seed players in tournaments. This student wrote an Inquiry Contract that examined the history of this seeding system and then proposed a new, improved one for the tennis association to use.
- One student was a distance runner and was just beginning to take yoga classes in an effort to improve her running performance. She wrote an Inquiry Contract on the relationship between exercise and meditation.
- One student was a veteran of the U.S. Army and was studying finance. He wrote an Inquiry Contract that examined the relationship between the stock market and the defense contracting industry.
- One student was living in a predominantly Jewish neighborhood for the first time in her life and was curious about the concept of *kosher* food. She wrote an Inquiry Contract that examined the traditions and current practices of Jewish dietary laws.
- One student was planning to become an elementary teacher and had begun doing some reading about the types of school where she might eventually teach. She wrote an Inquiry Contract about the history and current status of charter schools in her area.
- One student had played sports in high school but did not plan to do so in college. He wrote an Inquiry Contract on the professionalization of college sports.

In each case, these students selected a subject about which they were curious and knew *something*, but not everything. They developed very rich, very informative Inquiry Contracts. You can find even more Inquiry Contracts sketched out in the Appendix to Part One that follows Chapter 11.

Throughout Part One, you will encounter the work of three of my former students, Jamie, Katie, and Jeanette, who were in a writing class in which all students were asked to develop Inquiry Contracts about aspects of a single, general subject matter: the nature and purposes of education, and particularly the relationship between getting a bachelor's degree and preparing for a specific job. Here are several of the questions that Jamie, Katie, Jeanette, and other students in the class took up in their papers:

- What are the reasons you came to college?
- How do your reasons resemble or differ from other people's?
- What do you think the primary purpose of a college education is? What do you think some of its other purposes are?
- How do your perceptions of the nature and purposes of a college education differ from those of other members of your family, your friends, the people in your neighborhood, or members of your ethnic or national culture?
- How well educated will you be to fulfill the responsibilities of a job when you leave college?
- How many jobs will you be likely to hold during the remainder of your working life? How many times can you expect to change jobs?
- What skills exactly will your jobs demand of you? How familiar will you need to be with technology and computers? How important will it be to communicate with people in languages other than your native language, to work cooperatively with people from many other cultures, and to be willing to live and work in another culture yourself?

Throughout Part One, we will refer to this general subject as our *sample domain,* and we will examine how Jamie, Katie, and Jeanette take up different aspects of it in their papers. Your own Inquiry Contract may certainly involve your working with an aspect of this sample domain, if you and your instructor agree. On the other hand, with your instructor's permission, you may propose some other subject to inquire into and write about.

Once you have thought about your subject and perhaps discussed several possibilities with your instructor, friends, or classmates, write a *one-page* document that has three brief sections, each no longer than a paragraph.

In the first section, address the following questions: Why are you interested in this subject? What motivated you to get started inquiring into this subject? (Note: Though you may have some genuine, personal motivation to work with this subject, it's perfectly acceptable to say that your instructor assigned you the topic.)

In the second section, address the following question: What are *two* things you feel, think, believe, or know about the subject right now? (Note: If you can definitely answer this question, that's excellent. But don't worry if you don't know anything about it at all. Just get something down on paper or in a computer file—initial feelings and impressions, things you've heard but not checked out, and so on. It's important to situate yourself in relation to the subject matter right from the outset.)

In the third section, address the following question: What are *two* questions that you have about the subject that you could reasonably address in your inquiry? (Note: Again, if you have definite questions in mind, that's fine. But don't worry if your questions are relatively general and indeterminate. It's simply important for you to begin posing questions about the domain.)

One last introductory note about the Contract Proposal: It's a good idea to have a folder or notebook where you can keep all the materials concerning your Inquiry Contract. Keep the Contract Proposal near the front of it. You will continually refer to the proposal—and probably continually revise it—as you proceed with your project.

Here is Jeanette's Contract Proposal. In Chapter 9 and in Part Two you will have the chance to study the exploratory essay that was part of Jeanette's Inquiry Contract, and in Chapter 11 you will find her working document, an electronic brochure. As you work on your own Contract Proposal, it might be helpful to see how she started her project.

Jeanette Doane

Contract Proposal

31 January 1997

Gender Biases in Schools

1   Both past personal experience and recent observations have made me very aware of the gender issues that exist in today's schools. Whether or not it is intentional, male and female teachers tend to treat boys and girls very differently in class. In light of the huge advances in the struggle for equal rights, why does society still maintain that male students are skilled in math and science, while female students excel in humanities and the fine arts? Living in an age that supposedly glorifies individualism and diversity, we as a society should be far beyond the constraints of traditional gender roles. One only has to look around, however, to see that this is not the case. How can we teach children that they should "dare to be different" when they are constantly reminded that boys and girls have different strengths and abilities? In this project, I hope to fully explore both traditional and current trends in education with respect to gender differences. Why are teachers, parents, and students still caught up in archaic thinking, and more importantly, what can all involved parties do to ensure that both male and female students receive quality educations?

2   Through my experiences with the educational system and some reading I have done on gender differences, I feel that I have a pretty good grasp on how gender discrimination occurs. Obviously, I plan to research this even further. I also plan to study how the progress that has been made in the educational system came about, and compare how female students in the past were treated compared to those of the present. I know that conditions are a lot better how, but I want to see what I can do to make them even better.

3   At this point, I can say that I need to read as much as I can about the issue in order to come up with any realistic suggestions for changing the methods by which female children are educated. I have already done some reading as well as some net surfing, and I have discussed the topic with an advisor in the Women's Center. I think that once I find out why thinking on gender discrimination in schools has been somewhat stagnant, I might be able to come up with some suggestions for teachers to keep in mind when dealing with their students.

Now, start writing your own Contract Proposal.

3 Writing, Inquiry, and Learning, Plus a Primer on Effective Writing Processes

HOW WRITING AND INQUIRY ARE RELATED

Welcome to college writing. As a veteran teacher of college writing courses, I bet I know what's going through your minds as you begin to read this book. Though many ideas may be swirling around, at least three may surface as you think about the writing course ahead of you. First, you may think, "Why do I have to take this course? I learned how to write in high school. Why do I have to take *another* writing course?" Second, you may admit, "Okay, so I do have some problems as a writer, but if someone would just teach me how not to make any mistakes with grammar and sentence structure, I'd be okay. Really, my grammar's my only problem." Third, you may think, "Why can't I just get on with my regular classes? I came to college to learn *about* things—the important facts, theories, and concepts of my major field, and the information and ideas from other disciplines that will help me become a well-rounded person. I'm not going to learn *about* anything in a writing course—all I'm going to learn is *how to* do something."

These are excellent questions: Why are you taking a writing course? Isn't good writing just a matter of writing good sentences and not making any grammatical mistakes? And what does a writing course have to do with the rest of your career as a student?

At the risk of sounding like a know-it-all, let me offer some answers. First, ideally you did learn to write well in high school. That will make writing in the college years a bit easier for you. But the fact is that writing in high school and writing in college are different because the subjects you study in college are more difficult than the subjects you studied in high school. Good writing is always *about* something, and as the things you are writing about become more complicated, you must improve as a writer to be able to state and develop your complex ideas clearly and correctly.

Second, this intricate ability to write fully, clearly, and intelligently about difficult subjects involves knowing more than the rules of sentence structure and the principles of "good grammar." This is not to say that writing complete sentences and avoiding errors are not important. *These things are vitally important.* Though you might have lived or worked in communities where people spoke and wrote imprecisely or incorrectly, you should realize that doing well in college and succeeding in life beyond it will almost always require you to use standard English. Thus, if your experience as a writer has led you to be an *unaware* writer—that is, if you often are not sure that your sentences are good and complete, and you frequently guess about which phrase, word, or punctuation mark to use—then your college writing course should help you become a more informed, more aware, more correct writer. But don't believe anyone who tells you that "grammar is your only problem." It's an extremely rare person who writes very well but who commits errors of grammar and usage. Good writing involves coming up with interesting ideas, stating them clearly and efficiently, supporting them with convincing evidence, dividing a composition into manageable parts, developing each part appropriately just as you develop the whole piece, *and* using language that is correct and pleasing to your readers. Good writing is a huge job.

Third, a college writing course is an ideal opportunity to learn *about* something. A writing course is rarely just a *how-to* experience. When you think about your writing course in the same way you think about your other college courses—as an opportunity to learn about something—you see that it offers you the chance to learn about the relationship between your writing and difficult paths of study that await you in college and beyond. What's more, you see your college writing course as a place where any problems you may have with writing standard English can be addressed as part of a larger project involving writing and learning.

WHAT YOU CAN LEARN IN A COLLEGE WRITING COURSE

I think you can learn five important concepts.

WRITING MEANS WORKING IN AN INTELLECTUAL COMMUNITY

First, you learn that in your college career and in your life outside school, you will belong to many groups of people who work collectively to learn about a subject and to create knowledge about it. Within these groups—let's call them *intellectual communities*—there are certain topics, certain specific subject matters, that people think it's important to read and write about. In some of these communities, the specific topics you will read and write about will be prescribed for you. For example, when you take a course in the history of the religions in the United States, you will read and write about that history. If after you graduate you work for an engineering firm like the one I work at occasionally, you will read and write about how to accomplish tasks related to building and maintaining electric generating plants. In other communities, what you read and write about may be more open-ended. Indeed, in some courses, the subjects you read and write about may be solely up to you. When you are given this leeway, do not take the attitude that it's really not important what subjects you choose. You will learn more about writing, and your writing will improve more, if you write about something that matters to you and your readers. When you write about a subject that demands careful inquiry, you benefit from working in an intellectual community with classmates and colleagues who are as curious and conscientious as you are.

WRITING MEANS INTERACTING WITH OTHER PEOPLE'S WORK

The second thing you can expect to learn about in a college writing course is related to the first. As you and your classmates learn about writing by inquiring into an issue that really interests you, you will encounter many writers' compositions as works-in-progress and have the chance to offer suggestions for revision and improvement, just as many of your colleagues will read and comment on your own drafts. You will come to understand that effective writing is always a transaction: Not only do your central and supporting ideas have to make sense to you, but, more important, they have to be taken in and understood by other readers. Thus, you will learn that for any subject or issue you investigate by reading, discussing, and writing about it, certain ideas, attitudes, and beliefs exist that people generally hold about it. Think of these ideas, attitudes, and beliefs as the *starting points* of effective writing. You will have to learn what people who are reading your composition already assume about your subject or issue. You may not always need to show directly that you are aware of these starting points, but a composition is usually improved when its writer at least hints that she knows what her reader's *status quo* thinking on the subject at hand is.

DIFFERENT WRITING SITUATIONS DEMAND DIFFERENT STRATEGIES AND EVIDENCE

Third, in the process of learning about writing by pursuing an inquiry project, you will discover that different writing situations require you to use different strategies and offer varying kinds of evidence. Once again, think of writing as a transaction: Your job as a writer is to understand and acknowledge what your readers already know and believe about your subject matter and to move them from maintaining their own positions to accepting your ideas and arguments. In some situations, you can tell stories from your own experiences, and these stories will lead your readers to accept your ideas. In other situations, you can offer a line of reasoning, and this logical process will encourage your readers to accept what you have to say. In still other situations, you can provide whatever facts and "hard" evidence you might be able to marshal, and these data will lead your readers to see the world the way you want them to. There are not many absolute rules about what works to move readers to accept your ideas and arguments—you have to be able to assess what kind of transaction the particular writing situation calls for.

COMPOSITIONS SERVE A VARIETY OF PURPOSES

Fourth, as you begin to write compositions that show the results of your inquiry, you will learn that texts accomplish different purposes, varying according to whom you want your texts to interact with and what you want your readers to *do* in relation to your writing. With some texts, you may simply want to clarify a complicated issue for yourself and a few other readers whom you know very well. With other texts, you may want to let some readers have specific information that they need to know. With other texts, you may want to raise questions and, rather than trying to answer all of them yourself, simply suggest that other people might be interested in pursuing answers to them. With still other texts, you may have in mind specific readers whose opinions you want to change or whose actions you want to influence.

STRUCTURE AND FORMAT ARE FLEXIBLE—THERE IS NO SINGLE KIND OF COMPOSITION

Fifth, as you assimilate all of this "writer's knowledge," you will learn that your decisions about the actual structure of your writing will be influenced by the intellectual community within which you want your texts to interact and by the kind of interaction you want your text to be part of. For some readers and purposes, it will be appropriate for you to have an introductory paragraph that captures attention and states the central idea, several paragraphs that support this idea, and then a paragraph that concludes the composition. For other readers and purposes, however, this structure will be completely inappropriate. For most readers and purposes, you will want to adhere carefully to the rules of sentence structure and correct usage. But in some situations, because you want to identify yourself with a certain group of readers, you will choose to use unusual sentences and perhaps even unorthodox words and phrases. Remember that the rules of English structure and use—rules that some people view as absolute and inflexible—can be bent according to your writing situation.

Given all that you have to learn, therefore, who says that a college writing course is easy and you really should not have to take it if you learned to write well in high school? No one in his right mind would claim this. To summarize, look at what you should expect to learn in college writing:

- Your writing is a part—perhaps the most important part—of your participation in various intellectual communities, groups of people who investigate subjects and try to create new knowledge about them. Within these communities, certain topics and subject matters are most important to members.
- For each of these important subject matters, there are certain key ideas, attitudes, and beliefs that members of the community generally hold. As you write to interact with this community, you need to learn what these "starting points" are and how to build upon, amplify, and alter them.
- In writing away from these starting points, you will learn that different writing situations require that you use different kinds of reasoning and evidence as part of the transaction that writing represents.
- Within the inquiry that you are conducting, you can accomplish several purposes with your writing: clarification, information, exploration, conviction, persuasion, and so on.
- While you should learn and plan to use good structures for paragraphs and sentences and correct practices of grammatical usage, you should realize that the "rules" of English are human artifacts, not holy writ. You should adapt your language to the writing situation.

I hope this book will help you learn all five of these things. It is designed to assist students who want to learn about writing well by inquiring deeply into challenging subjects by reading, discussing, and writing about them. The readers of this book, ideally, are serious students who want to learn how writing well will help them succeed as college students and as committed professionals and workers outside college.

WRITERS AND THEIR INQUIRY PROGRAMS

When dedicated students and professionals in a field begin a writing project, they are curious about some important question or vital issue. Sometimes they encounter this question or issue as part of their assigned study or work, and other times they come across it just through personal observation, reading, and thought. If they are wise, they realize that they cannot learn everything they need to know about this issue or answer all potential questions about it quickly. So they develop an inquiry program, a structured sequence of activities. In this program, they read about their subject, think about it, discuss it with other people, put their thoughts down on paper or computer disk, get people to respond to this early writing, rethink the issue or questions, read and discuss some more, write more fully, get more responses, and so on. At some point, these students and professionals have to produce finished compositions that they submit for evaluation or action. When they do, their compositions emerge from an inquiry program, a structure that enables them to produce writing that is thoughtful and well prepared, writing they can be proud of.

Students in introductory college writing courses can learn to do these things. They can learn how writing extensively about a subject allows them to *engage* with ideas, data, and theories in a more detailed way than simply reading about and discussing them. They can learn that writing extensively about a subject requires them to *analyze* ideas, data, and theories, to take the subject apart in ways that only writing demands. They can consider how writing extensively about a subject requires them to *synthesize,* to put together various threads of their thinking, in ways that no other kind of learning requires. Ideally, your work with an Inquiry Contract will help you learn to write effectively as you develop these abilities of *engagement, analysis,* and *synthesis.*

A STRUCTURE FOR WRITING AND INQUIRY

This book offers a structure, the *Inquiry Contract,* to help you construct your program, to build connections between writing and learning. Not only is this contract useful in college writing courses, but it is also valuable in other courses in which you need to give structure to your studies, reading, and writing.

If you have completed the Contract Proposal described earlier, you have taken the first step in negotiating an agenda for an inquiry-and-writing project. The remainder of Part One is devoted to "unpacking" the Inquiry Contract, to explaining how you can learn about writing, learn by writing, and learn how to write well by inquiring into a challenging subject. Here briefly is how the Inquiry Contract proceeds:

- For any subject that you want to inquire into and write about, you first write a *Contract Proposal,* as described earlier (pp. 6–10).
- After you have written your Contract Proposal, you consult it by yourself or, better, meet with your instructor, writing inquiry group (more about this later), or tutor. Your goal in this individual brain-

storming session, group meeting, or conference is to sketch out *initial*—not necessarily binding—plans for you (and possibly your group members) to write a sequence of compositions about the subject.

- Next, you take up the *Clarification Project*, described in Chapters 4 and 5. In this project, you clarify for yourself (or for *yourselves*, if you are working on the first composition in a group) what you already feel, think, believe, and know about the subject. The composition that results from the Clarification Project is a *reflective reading response*.

- Next, you do the *Information Project*, described in Chapters 6 and 7. In this project, you learn something new about your subject. You may do so, of course, by reading something about it, but there are other ways to learn about a subject. One way is to interview someone who has a clear perspective, based on experience, with the domain of knowledge you are inquiring into and writing about. The composition that emerges from the Information Project is an *informative report* of what you learn, directed to a specific group of readers, perhaps your writing-as-inquiry group.

- Next comes the *Exploration Project*, described in Chapters 8 and 9. In this project, you examine your subject by taking a portion of what you have generated already about it and raising questions about it. You should not feel compelled to *answer* all of these questions. The important goal is to generate questions and offer at least *more than one* answer to every question you come up with. The composition that results from the Exploration Project is called an *exploratory essay*.

- Finally, you undertake the *Working Documents Project*, described in Chapters 10 and 11. In this project, you present and develop a central idea, incorporating material you have produced in the reflective reading response in the Clarification Project, the informative report in the Information Project, and the exploratory essay in the Exploration Project. The Working Documents Project calls for you to write a document designed to change people's minds and perhaps influence their actions in regard to your subject. Chapter 11 describes how to write an "opinion-piece" editorial column, an open letter, and a brochure.

In your initial planning session, you should at least start to make notes for the Clarification Project. You may, in addition, be able to make some plans about the other compositions that follow it. But rather than locking yourself into some unchangeable plan, why not plan to review your Contract Proposal as you proceed through the inquiry, revising it as necessary each time you finish the composition and plan the next one?

The Contract Proposal, after all, is short and easy to revise. If you allow the proposal to change as necessary as your project proceeds, you may discover that the reflective reading response from the Clarification Project points you toward information you need to discover for the informative report in the Information Project, that the information in the informative report directs you to an area you want to investigate in the exploratory essay in the Exploration Project, and that the central idea in whatever composition you produce for the Working Documents Project will emerge from all your previous pieces.

GENRES, READERS, AND YOUR INQUIRY CONTRACT

In the Inquiry Contract, notice how different kinds of composition grow out of each project: a contract proposal, a reflective reading response, an informative report, an exploratory essay, and some kind of working document like an opinion-piece editorial column, an open letter, or a brochure. People who study and teach writing refer to different kinds of compositions as *genres,* a French word meaning "types" but used in academic communities to refer specifically to types of written texts and other artistic products.

A genre is closely related to the kind of work you want a piece of writing to do—the purpose you intend to accomplish with it, the readers you envision interacting with it, the types of action or thinking you hope it will eventually bring out. If you want an awards committee to consider you for a scholarship, you should not write a love poem or a humorous anecdote. Instead, you should write a letter about yourself, trying to convince the committee that you are a worthy candidate and to persuade them to give the scholarship to you. If you want people in your school to think or behave differently about a controversial issue, you should not write a letter to your best friend about it. Instead, you should write an editorial column and submit it to the school newspaper.

Notice that for each of the genres in the Inquiry Contract and, for that matter, each of the other genres just mentioned—the love poem, the letter to the awards committee, the letter to your best friend, and the editorial column—a specific reader or set of readers is strongly suggested. Every piece of writing, of course, is meant to be read by somebody. In some cases, that somebody is simply you yourself. But more frequently, the potential readers of the pieces you write are those people with whom you want your writing to interact and who are *capable* of doing so. In each of the following chapters that introduce the projects (Chapters 4, 6, 8, and 10), I will discuss more carefully how potential readers of your genres must influence the content, organization, and style of your writing.

Traditionally, composition courses have taught students to produce one genre more than any other: the five-paragraph theme, also known as the 500-word theme or just "the theme." It has an introductory paragraph with a thesis statement at the end of it; three paragraphs, each with a topic sentence at the beginning, that support the thesis statement; and then a concluding paragraph that summarizes the three points and restates the thesis.

The theme is a useful genre in many academic fields. It is particularly valuable when you have to organize and write essay examinations in a relatively short time. But it is not appropriate for all writing situations, and its capacity to interact with readers—to motivate people to adopt some new kind thinking or action—can be limited. Chapter 9 will help you learn how to write a theme and to decide which writing situations it would be appropriate for, but the Inquiry Contract does not require you to write any themes. Indeed, part of the goal of the Inquiry Contract is to help student writers understand that writing in college and beyond requires them to use many different genres, of which the theme is only one.

KEEPING A LEARNING JOURNAL AND ORGANIZING A WRITING-AS-INQUIRY GROUP

To get a good start on your Inquiry Contract, it would be wise to do two things from the outset. First, you should start immediately keeping a learning journal—a separate computer diskette, portfolio, or notebook—that you use *only* for the work you do on your writing-as-inquiry project. Your instructor may direct you to use this journal in specific ways during class sessions, and a great many of the In-Progress Tasks throughout the book ask you to write in your learning journal. As you produce your Inquiry Contract projects, you will return to your learning journal time and again to reshape your proposal and to generate ideas and find material for future papers.

Now would also be an ideal time to establish as *writing-as-inquiry* group, either on your own or with your instructor's guidance. (Note: Your instructor may have his or her own plans for establishing groups, so if you form your own, please get your instructor's permission first.) A writing-as-inquiry group should consist of three or four people, no more or no less. They should all be members of the same section of the writing course you are taking. It is often difficult for people taking different sections of the same course to work together in a group. You should plan to meet with your writing-as-inquiry group at least once a week for an hour. Your work with the group can accomplish two important functions. First, you can use your group members as sounding boards to discuss what you are planning to write about, why you have chosen to write about it, and how you plan to present and develop your ideas and organize your composition. Second, once you have actually started writing the compositions for your Inquiry Contract, at least once a week someone should bring a draft of a composition to the group for its reactions, commentary, and suggestions for revision.

The group's feedback can take many forms, but I prefer to use a set of directions developed by the WordShop Corporation, a group of writing instructors based in Tacoma, Washington. In the WordShop method, a group session operates as follows. One person, "the writer," is designated to bring his or her draft to the group. The writer reads the draft aloud to the other members and they simply listen. When the writer has finished, the other members write freely and informally for three minutes, describing their general impression of the writer's draft. Then the writer announces, "Now I'm going to read my paper a second time," and does so. This time, the other members take a blank sheet of paper and make three columns, one headed by a plus sign, one by a minus sign, and one by a question mark. As they listen to the second reading, the members make notes in the columns about the features of the draft that they like, those they think are not successful, and those about which they would like additional details, information, or explanation from the writer. After the second reading, each of the members orally goes over his or her columns of notes with the writer so that he or she can plan a revision.

A PRIMER ON EFFECTIVE WRITING PROCESSES

As you write the compositions in your Inquiry Contract, you will probably put into practice some principles about writing that began to emerge about thirty years ago in writing courses, first in Great Britain and then in the United States and all over the world. This new style of teaching writing came to be known collectively as the *process movement*. Its main goal was to teach students that effective and successful writing does not happen magically, all at once, on the first draft. Instead, successful writing emerges as writers take the opportunity to think about their task, to generate and organize their ideas, to draft, to get feedback on their work, to revise (perhaps many times), and finally to produce a version of their composition that they are willing to submit for inspection and evaluation.

All of you probably have had some experience with a process approach to writing in earlier writing courses. You may know, based on your experience, that one's writing process cannot be described simply as a matter of stages or steps: Developing a successful process does not mean "first you prewrite, and then you draft, and then you revise." Often you are revising while you are drafting, planning additional sections while you are revising, and so on.

Even though you are probably familiar with a process approach, let's review some of the basic terminology that can be used to talk about the process of writing as it develops in your Inquiry Contract. Seven terms are helpful in this task. Remember, though, that these are not linear, chronological steps:

- *Investigating* is the general name for the activities people undertake to discover information and generate a fund of knowledge about which they will write.
- *Planning* occurs when a writer determines what reader or readers the composition must interact with and what purpose or purposes the composition can accomplish and then decides accordingly what to say and how to say it.
- *Inventing* is the general term for the activities a writer undertakes to extract information from the "database" of his or her memory, experience, or notes and in some cases to categorize and evaluate this information to write about it.
- *Drafting* is the process by which writers simply get something written on paper or diskette so they can begin to develop their writing and move toward producing a completed product.
- *Consulting* is the activity of seeking the help of a "fresh" reader and asking him or her to respond to what's good about a draft, what is questionable, and what definitely needs change and improvement.
- *Revising* is the name for the activities during which the writer returns to his or her drafts, rereads and rethinks it, and decides whether to make changes to improve it.
- *Editing* is the final cleanup of a text before the writer must submit it for the instructor's, his or her peers', or the public's inspection and evaluation. Editing occurs when the writer goes over the text very slowly, looking for lapses in standard English usage, obvious gaffes, misspelled words, missing or incorrect punctuation, and so on.

Your instructor may explain distinctions among these terms, assign a project that will help you understand them, and even introduce new terminology for describing writing processes. But let me offer three final ideas about a process approach to writing. First, bear in mind that drafting is, by its very nature, a relatively messy activity, one that produces a text that inevitably needs more work. It's very rare for any writer to produce a presentable text on the first draft. Second, many writers feel as though they can, or should, avoid consulting with other readers. Some people feel that consulting is "cheating." It's not, and it should only be construed as such if your consultant reader actually writes or rewrites part or all of your composition for you. Third, bear in mind that revising and editing are not the same thing. Revising is a more wide-ranging process of reseeing, rethinking, and rewriting part or all of the draft. Editing is the cleanup of a draft before it is handed in.

 ## In-Progress Task

With these preliminary notions of writing as inquiry, writing-as-inquiry groups, and effective writing processes in mind, reread your Contract Proposal and then write in your learning journal for twenty to thirty minutes in response to the following questions:

- When the general public considers the subject I'm working with, what are the issues, questions, or concerns that they think are important to discuss?
- In discussions of my subject, what are some of the *status quo* assumptions that appear to go unsaid but nonetheless seem almost universally believed? For example, in the case of the sample domain described earlier (pp. 7–8), especially its aspects dealing with the nature and purposes of a college education, what do most people tend to believe about *access* to higher education and the *amount* of it that is best for people to have? Considering the aspects of the sample domain about education and employment, what do most people believe an education *should* do to prepare a person for the world of work?
- In texts that people produce about my subject, what kinds of *outcomes* or *results* do they expect the texts to have with readers? Do writers about my subject usually expect a reader simply to consider their ideas, to believe in them strongly, to take some specific action? What?
- When people write texts about my subject, what *kinds* of genres do they usually produce? Editorials? Articles? Reports? Letters? Posters? What? How does the *kind* of text they generally produce influence how the writers go about producing the text?

In-Progress Task

After you have written your Contract Proposal, meet either with your writing-as-inquiry group or, if it's not formed yet, with at least *two* other people in the class. Pass around your Contract Proposals and read one another's. Discuss how you learned the two things you know about your subject and why you think the two questions you have posed are worth answering.

4 Inquiry as Clarification

An important first step in your project is to clarify for yourself what you feel, think, believe, and know about your subject as you begin to inquire into it. Such clarification is necessary because it begins a process of asking yourself questions that you will eventually have to address head-on as Inquiry Contract proceeds: What do you *really* know about the subject? What do you *need* to learn about it? What do you *want* to learn about it? What is the *status quo* on the subject—that is, what do most people think and feel about it? How does the *status quo* match your thinking? At this moment, can you propose any specific ideas concerning your subject about which you would like to convince people? Do you have an initial idea of how you would like people to think or behave differently in relation to your subject?

No writer can answer all these questions before inquiring into a subject. Indeed, the purpose of writing as inquiry is to understand and address them. But all good writers pose such questions. All good writing proceeds from a writer's questions, and the first big question you need to ask is this: Where are *you* in relation to this subject? This big question begins the process of clarification.

The next chapter will describe three ways for you to produce a reflective reading response, the genre that grows out of your work with clarification. But before we examine them, let's think about what it means to clarify thoughts and feelings to prepare to write papers. Let's work with three techniques for clarification:

- First, consider what your feelings and ideas are, in relation to the feelings and ideas of important people and institutions in your life.
- Second, think about trying to separate the important reactions you might have to the subject you are writing about—reactions of feeling, thought, belief, and knowledge.
- Third, learn to "read" the world around you: not just books and articles but also discussions, lectures, movies, concerts, demonstrations—in sum, all public events.

WHERE DO OUR THOUGHTS AND FEELINGS COME FROM?

Probably all of us have had personal experiences, some perhaps involving work, relations with family and friends, or community service, that have shaped our lives, our feelings, our ideas. Because we associate these feelings and ideas with our specific experiences, we tend to hold a strong sense of ownership—our feelings and ideas are solely ours, we think.

To a certain extent, that's true, but let's look more closely at where our thoughts and feelings come from. All of us live our lives under the influence of people, media, and institutions that shape our thoughts. It's always our goal to live as Polonius advises his son, Laertes, in *Hamlet:* "To thine own self be true." But that's hard to do. The mass media—television, movies, magazines, newspapers, and so on—shape our thoughts more than we usually realize. Our families—our parents and grandparents, our spouses, our children, occasionally even our aunts, uncles, and cousins—often want us to think in special ways about certain subjects, and sometimes they tell us directly what they want us to think, feel, and believe. Our friends and coworkers also influence our thinking. So do clubs and organizations we belong to, political parties who want our vote and support, and charitable causes we work for. Our churches, synagogues, and mosques and their leaders—locally, regionally, nationally, and even internationally—count on our believing in certain ways about issues touching our faith.

Even though the go-it-alone individual is held up as a standard in American popular culture, we should not feel too embarrassed if it turns out that what we think is "my own special way of thinking" really isn't. Your own particular view of a subject may actually be your adaptation of others' views, combinations of thoughts, feelings, beliefs, and ideas that other people have led you to embrace. That's perfectly okay—that's where all intelligent people get their ideas. They hear about them, learn them, experience them via contact with important people and institutions in their lives, and then they add these ideas and perspectives to their own lives. Intelligent people make other people's ideas "their own."

Think, for example, about one aspect of the sample domain in this book: the nature and purposes of a college education. When I discuss this subject with other people, I frequently express a perspective that I know I initially got from other people but that I have now adapted to make "my own." Because I grew up in a small town in West Virginia where, at the time, relatively few people went to college, I learned as a teenager from my parents that attending college is a rare privilege and that you should try to milk the experience for all it's worth, learning as much as you possibly can about as many things as interest you, not just about what you will need to know to get a job after you graduate. This was my parents' idea at the time, not really mine. The small college I attended reinforced this perspective by requiring its students not only to take a set of core courses and their major courses but also to complete a number of practicum experiences in several fields: citizenship, fine arts, health and recreation, and multiculturalism. The idea that going to college offered me the privilege of a liberal education was becoming *my* idea.

I became a teacher, and as the years passed it struck me that more and more people graduating from high school considered it their right to go to college and saw the principal purpose of a college education as being to prepare them for a career, a perspective that contrasted with my developing idea about the privilege of a liberal education. My own emerging perspective was reinforced, however, during the summer of 1988, when I taught at a university in the People's Republic of China. My idea about liberal education clashed with the government's perspective on higher education in that nation. In the People's Republic, only 3 percent of high school students go on to a university, so most Chinese students recognized what a privilege it is to attend. However, there is not much opportunity for Chinese university students either to select their own majors or to get a liberal education. The national educational leaders determine how many professionals will be needed in different fields in the coming years. On the basis of these calculations, most students are assigned their majors and are tracked directly into government-sanctioned jobs after graduation. I returned from China even more convinced that the prospect of getting a broad, liberal education in American colleges and universities is one of the rarest privileges on Earth. The idea that I had originally learned from my parents was now, after modifications and adaptations, my idea.

It's okay, then, to have ideas and perspectives that you have appropriated from other people and institutions. What's not okay is be *unaware* of the way that all these people and institutions shape our thoughts. The more you are aware of where your thoughts, beliefs, feelings, and ideas come from, the more you are able to say, "Wait a minute, do I *really* feel/think/believe/know that?"

 ## In-Progress Task

In your learning journal or some other location, write for about fifteen minutes responding to the following statement: "When I think about or discuss subject X [fill in the subject you wrote your Contract Proposal about], one idea or perspective that I'm sure I initially learned from someone else was this: [here, explain the idea or perspective]. But here is how I have adapted this idea or perspective so that it is 'mine' now: [here, explain your adaptation of the idea or perspective]." After you have written for about fifteen minutes, take five minutes and read someone else's response.

CAREFULLY EXAMINING TRICKY VERBS

Above, I deliberately turned *feel/think/believe/know* into one long verb. I recommend that you now reverse this process and try to *separate* the reactions you might have to challenging subjects that you inquire into and write about. Look at each verb—*feel, think, believe,* and *know*—separately and carefully. Though some people treat them as synonyms, they do not mean exactly the same thing. There is, to be sure, some overlap in meanings, and separating them might require drawing some fine distinctions, but it is good for writers engaging in inquiry to separate the definitions, at least as an early step in clarifying where they stand with a subject.

- When we say we *feel* a certain way about a subject, we mean that our emotions, our intuitions, our "gut reactions" shape our responses to it. We do not have definite ideas about it, and we probably do not have "hard" evidence to support our positions.
- When we say we *think* a certain way about a subject, we mean that we have tried to be rational and to come to a position about it logically. We may not be completely certain about all details concerning the subject, and we may want to spend more time considering it, but we can state at least some of our ideas.
- When we say we *believe* something about a subject, we mean that we are convinced of the rightness and credibility of a statement, perspective, or position on it. Some kind of reasoning or evidence, either our own or that provided by others, convinces us to believe.
- When we say we *know* something about a subject, we are so completely swayed by reasoning or evidence that we can state assuredly that what we know is the case.

Once again, consider the aspect of the sample domain about the nature and purposes of a college education. Here are some statements about things that I feel, think, believe, and know about one issue within this domain. I list these statements to demonstrate the process of separating these tricky verbs. Remember that this exercise is not an exact science.

I am doing this—and you should also do so—simply as a step toward clarifying positions on this issue, as a move toward forcing some distinctions among the definitions of these verbs.

Here's the issue: Leaders of college and universities talk occasionally abut redesigning both curricula and academic calendars so that traditional students can complete their bachelor's degrees in three years rather than four (or five, as is sometimes necessary). I recognize the administrators' motives in proposing three-year degree plans. Here are my other responses:

- I *feel* that it is ultimately not a good idea because college students enjoy many opportunities to mature, intellectually and socially, over four years, and students who graduate after three years might not be mature enough to handle the demands of life beyond the university. Notice that this is an intuitive, gut-level response.

- I *think* that fewer students would actually be interested in getting their degrees in three years than many administrators predict. My reasoning is this: Faced with an uncertain economy after they graduate, many students would rather spend another year in college than try to find a job in an unpredictable job market. Notice that, although I have tried to be logical and rational, I cannot be sure that my position is correct. But I think it is.

- I *believe* a three-year degree plan would hinder students' efforts to get a broad, liberal education. There are only so many days, weeks, and months in an academic year, and if a college or university takes its regular four-year bachelor's degree curriculum and condenses it into three years, what gets omitted are those courses, perhaps unrelated to either your major or graduation requirements, that a student simply wants to take because he or she would like to learn what gets taught in them. My calendar-oriented reasoning is pretty reliable here, so my belief in this proposition is strong.

- I *know* a three-year degree plan could save some college students a lot of money. A student would save one-quarter of his or her total college costs by finishing a degree in three years rather than four. The numbers don't lie. I *know* these savings will accrue.

Don't expect to generate your own *feel, think, know,* and *believe* reactions quickly and easily. Good writers *gradually* discover what they feel and think and believe and know about the world, and part of the way they do so is by writing about challenging subjects. As you begin your writing-as-inquiry project, you may find that you cannot easily separate what you feel, think, believe, and know. Your perceptions of the subject may seem to jumble together. That's perfectly all right. That's the way the mind works; that's the way clarification proceeds. But you will inquire more thoroughly, and write more clearly, if you try to force yourself to make the distinctions embedded in these tricky verbs.

 ## In-Progress Task

In your learning journal or some other place, write for five minutes in response to each of the following four prompts:

- Concerning some particular issue about X [the subject I describe in my Contract Proposal], I *feel*. . . .
- Concerning this issue, I *think*. . . .
- Concerning this issue, I *believe*. . . .
- Concerning this issue, I *know*. . . .

READING THE WORLD

One excellent way to become aware of how your feelings and thoughts are being shaped by the world around you, and a good exercise for separating what you feel, think, believe, and know about any subject is to *read the world* and reflect *in writing* about your reading.

I realize that what I have just suggested may send up some red flags. Here's another English teacher, you may be saying, preaching that all you have to do is read good books and you will know everything there is to know. But hear me out—that's not what I'm saying. To clarify a subject for yourself, you need to read the *world* as your text, and you need to read the many different kinds of texts you find in the world in a way that may be unlike any you have experienced before. You need to think in new, different ways about two terms: *read* and *text*. Let's consider them in reverse order, examining *text* first.

Certainly books and articles are texts, and reading good books and articles is one activity that contributes to your awareness of where your thoughts, feelings, and beliefs come from. But books are not the only texts you should read. Think of the word *text* very broadly. Think about books, magazines, and newspapers as texts but also think about movies, television programs, meetings, conventions, conversations with friends, personal interactions that you observe but don't participate in, lectures, experiments, observations—think about all these things as *texts* that you can read and reflect on.

How are all these things texts, you might ask? Events like these are texts because each of them leads you, the observer, to construct your own version of reality by re-creating it in language. Like books and articles, texts like movies, television programs, conventions, lectures, and so on, have elements in common with printed texts. They have

- *plots*—crafted, created versions of "what happened?";
- *major characters*—narrators, protagonists, antagonists, passive spectators, actors, and receivers of the action;
- *themes*—major, central ideas that they illustrate with real examples and scenes.

Reading these kinds of nonprint events as texts thus means that when you observe them, you make sense of them by putting into language answers to the following questions:

- What happened in this event?
- Who were the major players and what were their roles?
- What were the major ideas that got played out in this event?

Notice that you need not wait until you have finished reading a book, article, or event to think about it as a text. Separate parts of these larger texts can be treated as texts in their own right. A single chapter of a book is a text, as is a section of an article, a movement of a symphony, a scene in a move, a presentation at a conference. So long as you can divide it into a separate part, for the purposes of reading and reflecting about it, you can treat any portion of a longer text as a text in its own right.

To get a sense of the many texts that surround us when we inquire into challenging subjects, let's examine for a moment the aspect of the sample domain about the changing nature of work that faces college graduates in the early twenty-first century. Certainly, there are abundant books and articles you could read about this subject. One of the most interesting books I have found is *The Work of Nations* (New York: Vintage Books, 1991) by Robert B. Reich, who was secretary of labor in the first administration of President Bill Clinton. You can find an excerpt from this book in Chapter 6. Reich explains how people's jobs—and how they are trained for them—will have to change as our society moves from a collection of regional and national production-oriented economies to a global, information-oriented economy. In addition to Reich's book, you can read an array of articles on this subject in journals, newspapers, and magazines ranging from the *New York Times* (e.g., Bob Herbert's article, "America's Job Disaster," December 1, 1993), to *Harper's* (e.g., Paul Krugman's article, "The Myth of Competitiveness," June 1994), to *Smithsonian* (e.g., Edwin Kleister Jr.'s article, " 'Germany Prepares Kids for Good Jobs: We're Preparing Ours for Wendy's,' " March 1993).

But books and articles are not the only kinds of texts that will help you clarify your ideas and feelings about the changing nature of work. If your institution has a career counseling center (and most colleges and universities do), browse through the materials, including computer databases, available there. Ask yourself, "What's happening at this center? Who are the major players? What role do they want me to play here? What's the central idea that supports the work of the center?" Attend a job fair—they are usually held in late winter and early spring on most campuses—even if you are not graduating for three or four years, and observe carefully what happens at it. Ask yourself the same kinds of questions about the "plot," "character," and "themes" of this job fair. What kind of plot could you see yourself acting out in relation to finding a job after you graduate? Who or what would work *for* you in this activity? Who or what would work *against* you? What important ideas or themes do the people running the job fair suggest you should think about as you prepare for entering the job market?

The job fair is not the only kind of nonprint text you can read about this subject. Here are some others: Attend lectures given by professional in a field you are thinking about working in after you graduate. Talk to people who hold jobs like those that interest you, and, if possible, visit them at their workplace. Observe the kinds of collaboration that go on with other workers; notice how computers and other forms of technology figure in their jobs; look carefully for instances in which people from different cultures must communicate with each other and try to determine how such communication works. Again, ask questions about what's happening, who plays what roles, and what ideas emerge in the workplace.

 ## In-Progress Task

Reread your Contract Proposal. For the subject you are inquiring into, select one nonprint text—a performance or event—that you have "read" recently. In your learning journal, describe this text and write a paragraph or two in response to each of the following questions:

- What happened at/in/during this event?
- Who were the major players? What did they do? What was my role in this event?
- What important idea was made real and concrete during this event or performance?

5 The Clarification Project, the Reflective Reading Response, and Three Potential Clarifying Techniques

In this chapter, you will work on a project, the second one in the Inquiry Contract, that puts Didion's and Forster's ideas to work. It's called the Clarification Project, and as you complete it you will learn about a genre called the reflective reading response. You will also learn three techniques that you can use to produce this genre, putting into writing your efforts to clarify what you feel, think, believe, and know about your subject.

Before proceeding, we need to consider how the Clarification Project, the reflective reading response, and the three techniques can work not only in your Inquiry Contract but also in other classes and projects that require extensive writing. As you will see, the basic notion of the Clarification Project and the potential uses of the three techniques extend beyond your current writing class. Any time you decide to "read the world," as Chapter 4 puts it, to write, study, and learn, you can use the techniques explained in this chapter to clarify for yourself what you feel, think, believe, and know. In other words, you can use the material in this chapter once to complete the Clarification Project, but you can also use it in other classes and in projects outside school that require you to read, observe, think, and study. An In-Progress Task at the end of this chapter will illustrate how to use the techniques in settings other than your writing class.

The Clarification Project

For this project, write a reflective reading response, a composition in which you consider and try to clarify what you currently feel, think, believe, and know about the subject you have chosen to inquire into. Your goal is not only to find out what you already feel, think, believe, and know but also to begin to collect your thoughts about *what else* you would like or need to know about this subject.

The most important reader for this composition is you yourself. It is difficult to consider what you feel, think, believe, and know about your subject until you get some material down on paper or diskette. Though you are the primary reader, other readers—your instructor or members of your writing-as-inquiry group—may also read your entry so that they can discuss your work with you.

This project has two stages. First, find and read carefully a written text—about the length of a magazine article or a book chapter—that introduces important ideas about your subject. Look for a text that "primes the pump" of your Inquiry Contract, that raises vital issues you can react to. In the following pages, you will find three such texts about aspects of our sample domain:

- "Five Ways to Wisdom" is about the aspect of the sample domain that examines the nature and purposes of a college education. Written by the journalist Otto Friedrich and originally published in *Time* magazine, the article sets out and explains five potential uses of a college education that beginning students might consider.
- "What We Expect: Preparing for College—A Statement by 12 Deans" is also about the same aspect of the sample domain. It was written by several deans of liberal arts at small colleges and universities. Originally published in a magazine read by high school principals, the article provides an insight into what these deans think should be a student's ideal preparation for college and university study.
- "The Three Jobs of the Future" is about the aspect of the sample domain that looks at the relation between education and the changing world of work. Written by former secretary of labor Robert B. Reich, this chapter from his book *The Work of Nations: Preparing Ourselves for 21st-Century Capitalism* describes three new types of occupations that Americans will find themselves filling in the next century: routine production services, in-person services, and symbolic-analytic services.

You may use one of these texts to work on stage one of the Clarification Project, or you may find a text of your own.

Second, using one of the three techniques explained later, *reading affectively, reading paraphrastically,* or *reading dialectically,* write as steadily as you can for forty-five minutes to an hour about the text and your subject.

After the three readings, you will find three reflective reading responses written by a student. Each of the entries demonstrates one of the techniques, and each can serve as a model for your own composition.

In your own reflective reading response, write well-developed thoughts in complete sentences, but don't be too concerned about the form of the composition. The most important part of this project is to get your ideas down on paper or diskette.

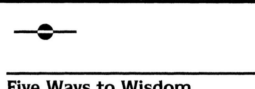

Otto Friedrich   **Five Ways to Wisdom**

Otto Friedrich is a journalist and writer who works for *Time Magazine.* His books on history and biography include *Before the Deluge: A Portrait of Berlin in the 1920's* and *Clover: The Tragic Love of Clover and Henry Adams.*

Opening day! In front of the brick dormitory, the dust-streaked family car lurches to a halt with its load of indispensable college supplies: one Sony stereo with headphones, two gooseneck lamps, five pairs of blue jeans, two down parkas (one old, one new), one pair of Rossignol skis . . . and one nervous freshman wondering whether anybody will like him. The older students have an easier time of it, needing only to unpack what they left in storage over the summer: more lamps, more blue jeans, boots, bicycles, one unused thesaurus donated by an out-of-date uncle. . . .And now, from any reopening dormitory window on any campus from Chapel Hill to Santa Cruz, can be heard the thrumming, insistent sound of the contemporary campus: *Tattoo You . . . Vacation . . . Hold Me . . .*

These are the rites of initiation. Orientation meetings on subjects like time management. Tryouts for the glee club or the football team. Beer bashes. Join the struggle to save Lebanon; join the struggle to save Israel. At Princeton the freshmen and sophomores meet each other in a traditional series of games and rope pulls known as Cane Spree, which custom decrees that the freshmen lose. At Gettysburg College, the rituals of getting acquainted are even more folksy: a "shoe scramble" determines who will dance with whom. At Carleton, there is a fried-chicken picnic and square dancing on the grassy area known as the Bald Spot.

Along with the social games, though, a lot of intellectual choices have to be made, courses picked, books bought. Will it be the class known as "Slums and Bums" (Urban Government) or "Nuts and Sluts" (Abnormal Psychology)? The students joke about these things because they know the choices are serious; their future lives depend on them, and so does much else besides. It has been said that every nation has only a few years in which to civilize an onrushing horde of barbarians, its own children.

The barbarian hordes beginning their classes this month may be the largest in U.S. history, a tribute to both parental prodigality and the ideal of universal education. Though the crest of the 1950s baby boom has passed the college years, a larger percentage of high school graduates now goes to college (61%, vs 40% a generation ago), and the number of older and part-time students keeps increasing (34% of students are over 25). All in all, the number of Americans who are signing up for some form of higher education this fall totals a mind-boggling 12.5 million. Mind-boggling not only because of the quantity, but because there is very little agreement on what they are learning or should be learning.

Under the dappling elms of Harvard, which likes to think that it sets the national tone in such matters, President Derek Bok traditionally welcomes each graduating class into "the company of educated men and women." The phrase goes trippingly on the tongue, but what does it mean? Does any such community exist? Are the millions of people now engaged in earning diplomas really being educated?

The statistics of growth, unfortunately, are also the statistics of glut. When the 2.4 million college students of 1949 swelled into today's 12.5 million, the educational system was all but overwhelmed. The most prestigious institutions took easy pride in the numbers they turned away, but the states, somewhat idealistically committed to a policy of open admissions, had to double the number of public colleges, from some 600 to more than 1,250. Most of the new schools were two-year community colleges that featured remedial and vocational classes.

The overall quality of education almost inevitably sank. "Every generation since Roman days has decried the weakening of educational standards," sighs one Midwestern university dean, but the statistics provide sad evidence that there has been a genuine decline. Average scores in reading on the Scholastic Aptitude Tests (SATs) have dropped from 466 out of a possible 800 in 1968 to 424 in 1981, when the decline leveled out; mathematics scores over the same period sank from 492 to 466. A study conducted at the University of Wisconsin reported that at least 20% of last year's entering freshmen "lack the skill to write [acceptably] and 50% are not ready to succeed in college algebra."

"They don't know how to write, they don't read, they have little contact with culture," says Professor Norman Land, who teaches art history at the University of Missouri, in a typical complaint. "Every so often I give them a list of names, and they can identify Timothy Leary or The Who but not Dante or Vivaldi. They haven't received an education: they've just had baby sitting." Nor are the criticisms entirely about intellectual shortcomings. "I think students are becoming less reflective, less concerned about fellow human beings, more greedy, more materialistic," says Alexander Astin, professor of higher education at U.C.L.A. "They're interested in making money and in finding a job that gives them a lot of power and a lot of status."

College officials tend to blame student shortcomings on the high schools, which undeniably need reform and renewal, but the high schools can blame the elementary schools, the elementary schools the family at home, and everybody blames TV. Wisconsin's President Robert O'Neil, however, argues that the colleges are "in part to blame." Says he: "Having diluted the requirements and expectations, they indicated that students could succeed in college with less rigorous preparation." Mark H. Curtis, president of the Association of American Colleges, is more caustic: "We might begin to define the educated person as one who can overcome the deficiencies in our educational system."

The traditional curriculum, such as it was, virtually disintegrated during the campus upheavals of the 1960s, when millions of students demanded and won the right to get academic credit for studying whatever they pleased. There were courses in soap operas and witchcraft. Even more fundamental, and even more damaging, was the spread of the "egalitarian" notion that everybody was entitled to a college degree, and that it was undemocratic to base that degree on any differentiations of intellect or learning. "The idea that cosmetology is just as important as physics is still with us but is being challenged," says Curtis.

"Quality," argues Chester E. Finn Jr., professor of education and public policy at Vanderbilt, "is almost certainly going to turn out to be the foremost national education concern of the 1980s, much as equity was the premier issue of the 1960s and 1970s." The counterrevolution has actually been well under way for some time. In 1978 Harvard announced with great fanfare a controversial new core curriculum, and in 1980 Stanford inaugurated an elaborate system of seven tracks that would carry every student through the basics of Western civilization. "A miracle has happened among Stanford undergraduates," Charles Lyons, director of the Western-culture program, proudly told the faculty senate last spring. "They do talk about Plato at dinner and about Shakespeare on the lawns."

Other colleges followed suit. Amherst now requires all freshmen to take an interdisciplinary program called Introduction to Liberal Studies. At Washington University in St. Louis, the science and math requirements, which were cut in half during the heady days of student power, have been restored to the old levels (four semester-long courses). "The students were evading the real purpose of their education," says Associate Dean Harold Levin, adding, in the language of deans everywhere, "The product we were turning out was not what we wanted." All told, according to a survey of 272 universities and colleges last spring, 88% are engaged in revising their curriculums, and 59% of these are increasing their programs of required courses in general education. That, presumably, will improve the "product."

While the educators reorganize their methods, the fundamental goals of the process—truth, knowledge, the understanding of the world—remain somewhere just beyond the horizon. It was said of Goethe, after his death in 1832, that he was the last man to know everything worth knowing. Today's cliché is that 90% of all scientists in the history of the world are alive now. Yet their knowledge has become hopelessly fragmented; the specialist in recombinant DNA feels no more obligation to understand laser surgery than to hear the latest composition by Pierre Boulez.

As scientific specialties spawn subspecialties, the rapidly growing mass of information has confused the arts and humanities as well. Historical research now presupposes a mastery of old tax records and population movements, and anyone who ventures into such popular fields as American literature or impressionist art must wade into a rising tide of studies, analyses, psychographic portraits and sheer verbiage. In addition, all the political trends of the past two decades have tended to multiply the demands for studies in fields once ignored: Chinese history, the languages of Africa, the traffic in slaves, the thwarted ambitions of women.

Not everyone is overawed by the so-called knowledge explosion. "What happens," says Computer Scientist Joseph Weizenbaum of M.I.T., "is that educators, all of us, are deluged by a flood of messages disguised as valuable information, most of which is trivial and irrelevant to any substantive concern. This is the elite's equivalent of junk mail, but many educators can't see through it because they are not sufficiently educated to deal with such random complexity." To many experts, the computer seems a symbol of both the problem and its solution. "What the computer has done," according to Stephen White of the Alfred P. Sloan Foundation, "is to provide scope for analytical skills that never before existed, and in so doing it has altered the world in which the student will live as well as the manner in which he will think about the world. . . .No adult is truly civilized unless he is acquainted with the civilization of which he is a member, and the liberal arts curriculum of 50 years ago no longer provides that acquaintance."

Acquaintance seems a bare minimum, and even that is difficult enough to attain in a world where millions cannot read and millions more read mainly falsehoods or formulas. Yet the basic questions of education still reach deep into every aspect of life: What is it essential to learn—to know—and why? Everyone seems to have his own answer, but there are interesting patterns among those answers. They can be organized into five main ideas:

I: Education Means Careers

Today's most popular answer is the practical one, on which students are most likely to agree with parents virtually impoverished by tuition bills: an education should enable a student to get a better job than he would otherwise be able to find or fill. In a Carnegie Council poll, 67% of students cited this as an "essential" purpose of their education. A 9.8% unemployment rate makes this purpose seem all the more essential. Michael Adelson, 23, who studied psychology at U.C.L.A., has been unable to find a job in this field for a year and a half, and he now wishes he had chosen engineering. He calls his bachelor of arts degree "completely useless."

The idea that education has a basically social purpose derives more or less from Plato. In his *Republic*, the philosopher portrayed a utopia governed by an intellectual elite specially trained for that purpose. This form of education was both stern and profoundly conservative. Children who attempt innovations, warned Socrates, acting as Plato's narrator, will desire a different sort of life when they grow up to be men, with other institutions and laws. And this "is full of danger to the whole state." To prevent any innovations, Socrates forthrightly demanded censorship so that students could not "hear any casual tales which may he devised by casual persons." When asked whose works he would ban, Socrates specifically named Homer. The poet's crime, he said, was to provide "an erroneous representation of the nature of gods and heroes."

Political pressure of this kind has never been far from the campus, but the overwhelming influence of U.S. education has been not politics but economics: the need for a technologically trained managerial caste. The very first Land Grant Act, in 1862, handed out 30,000 acres per Congressman for the building of state colleges at which "the leading object shall be . . . to teach such branches of learning as are related to agriculture and the mechanic arts." These needs keep changing, of course, and over the decades the U.S. economy demanded of its universities not only chemists and engineers but lawyers and accountants and personnel analysts, and then, after Sputnik's shocking revelation of the Soviet lead in space, yet more engineers.

Students naturally respond to the economy's needs. The Rev. Theodore Hesburgh, president of Notre Dame, complained last year that "the most popular course on the American college campus is not literature or history but accounting." This criticism reflects the fact that less than half the nation's swarm of college students go to liberal arts colleges; the rest are seeking not just jobs but entry into the middle class.

There are now thousands of Ph.Ds unable to find anyone willing to pay them for the hard-earned knowledge of Renaissance painting or the history of French monasticism, but any Sunday newspaper overflows with ads appealing for experts in electromagnetic capability, integrated logistics support, or laser electro-optics. Says George W. Valsa, supervisor of the college-recruiting section at Ford: "We are not ready to sign a petition to burn down liberal arts colleges, but don't expect us to go out and hire many liberal arts graduates." Ford does hire nearly 1,000 graduates a year, and most of them are engineers or M.B.A.s.

This is not the old argument between the "two cultures" of science and the humanities, for science too is often forced to defer to technical and vocational training. In 1979, according to one Carnegie study, 58% of all undergraduates pursued "professional" majors (up from 38% a decade earlier), in contrast to 11% in social sciences, 7% in biological sciences, 6% in the arts and 4% in physical sciences. Rich and prestigious private universities can resist this rush toward vocational training, but public and smaller private colleges are more vulnerable. "The bulk of the institutions will have to give in to a form of consumerism," says U.C.L.A.'s Astin, "in that they need applications and will therefore have to offer students what they want."

Says Paul Ginsberg, dean of students at Wisconsin: "It's becoming increasingly difficult to persuade a student to take courses that will contribute to his intellectual development in addition to those that will make him a good accountant." Quite apart from the pros and cons of professional training, the idea of educating oneself in order to rise in the world is a perfectly legitimate goal. But Ginsberg has been receiving letters from high school freshmen asking about the prospects for professional schools and job opportunities when they graduate from college seven years hence. Says he: "I don't know at what point foresight ends and panic sets in."

II: Education Transmits Civilization

Jill Ker Conway, president of Smith, echoes the prevailing view of contemporary technology when she says that "anyone in today's world who doesn't understand data processing is not educated." But she insists that the increasing emphasis on these matters leaves certain gaps. Says she: "The very strongly utilitarian emphasis in education, which is an effect of Sputnik and the cold war, has really removed from this culture something that was very profound in its 18th and 19th century roots, which was a sense that literacy and learning were ends in themselves for a democratic republic."

In contrast to Plato's claim for the social value of education, a quite different idea of intellectual purposes was propounded by the Renaissance humanists. Intoxicated with their rediscovery of the classical learning that was thought to have disappeared during the Dark Ages, they argued that the imparting of knowledge needs no justification—religious, social, economic, or political. Its purpose, to the extent that it has one, is to pass on from generation to generation the corpus of knowledge that constitutes civilization. "What could man acquire, by virtuous striving, that is more valuable than knowledge?" asked Erasmus, perhaps the greatest scholar of the early 16th century. That idea has acquired a tradition of its own. "The educational process has no end beyond itself," said John Dewey. "It is its own end."

But what exactly is the corpus of knowledge to be passed on? In simpler times, it was all included in the medieval universities' *quadrivium* (arithmetic, geometry, astronomy, music) and *trivium* (grammar, rhetoric, logic). As recently as the last century, when less than 5% of Americans went to college at all, students in New England establishments were compelled mainly to memorize and recite various Latin texts, and crusty professors angrily opposed the introduction of any new scientific discoveries or modern European languages. "They felt," said Charles Francis Adams Jr., the Union Pacific Railroad president who devoted his later years to writing history, "that a classical education was the important distinction between a man who had been to college and a man who had not been to college, and that anything that diminished the importance of this distinction was essentially revolutionary and tended to anarchy."

Such a view was eventually overcome by the practical demands of both students and society, yet it does not die. In academia, where every professor is accustomed to drawing up lists of required reading, it can even be played as a game. Must an educated man have read Dostoevsky, Rimbaud, Tacitus, Kafka? (Yes.) Must he know both Bach's *Goldberg Variations* and Schoenberg's *Gurrelieder?* (Perhaps.) Must he know the Carnot Cycle and Boole's Inequality? (Well . . .) And then languages—can someone who reads only Constance Garnett's rather wooden version of *Anna Karenina* really know Tolstoy's masterpiece any better than some Frenchman can know Shakespeare by reading André Gide's translation of *Hamlet?* Every scholar likes to defend his own specialty as a cornerstone of Western civilization, and any restraints can seem philistine. George Steiner approvingly quotes, in *Language and Silence,* a suggestion that "an acquaintance with a Chinese novel or a Persian lyric is almost indispensable to contemporary literacy." On a slightly more practical level, intellectual codifiers like to draw up lists of masterworks that will educate any reader who is strong enough to survive them—thus Charles Eliot's famous five-foot shelf of Harvard Classics and all its weighty sequels.

It was the immensely influential Eliot, deeply impressed with the specialized scholarly and scientific research performed at German universities, who proclaimed in 1869, upon becoming president of Harvard, the abolition of its rigid traditional curriculum. Basic education should be performed by the high schools, Eliot declared; anyone who went on to college should be free to make his own choice among myriad elective courses. The students chose the practical. "In the end, it was the sciences that triumphed, guided by the hidden hand of capitalism and legitimated by the binding ideology of positivism," Ernest Boyer and Martin Kaplan observe in *Educating for Survival*. Before long, however, the inevitable counterrevolution against the elective system began; there was a "core" of certain things that every student must learn. Columbia established required courses in contemporary civilization; the University of Chicago and St. John's College duly followed with programs solidly based on required readings of classic texts.

St. John's, which is based in Annapolis, Md., and has a smaller campus in Santa Fe, N. Mex., is a remarkable example of an institution resolutely taking this approach. Ever since 1937, all of St. John's students (683 this fall on both campuses) have been required to read and discuss a list of 130 great books drawn heavily from the classics and philosophy but also from the ranks of modern novelists like Faulkner and Conrad. The students must take four years of math, three of a laboratory science, two of music and two years each of Greek and French. That is just about it. This modern liberal arts version of the *trivium* and *quadrivium* includes no such novelties as psychology (except what can be learned in the works of Freud and William James) and no sociology (except perhaps Jane Austen).

St. John's is aware of the obvious criticism that its approach is "elitist" and even "irrelevant" to the real world. But President Edwin De Lattre's mild voice turns a bit sharp when he retorts, "If knowing the foundations of one's country—the foundations of one's civilization—if understanding and learning how to gain access to the engines of political and economic power in the world—if knowing how to learn in mathematics and the sciences, the languages, the humanities—if having access to the methods that have advanced civilizations since the dawn of human intelligence . . . If all those things are irrelevant, then boy, are we irrelevant!" De Lattre is a philosopher by training, and he offers one definition that has an ominous but compelling reverberation in the thermonuclear age: "Don't forget the notion of an educated person as someone who would understand how to refound his or her own civilization."

III: Education Teaches How to Think

Aristotle was one of those who could found a civilization, and while he thought of education as both a social value and an end in itself, he ascribed its chief importance to what might be considered a third basic concept of education: to train the mind to think, regardless of what it is thinking about. The key is not what it knows but how it evaluates any new fact or argument. "An educated man," Aristotle wrote in *On the Parts of Animals*, "should be able to form a fair offhand judgment as to the goodness or badness of the method used by a professor in his exposition. To be educated is in fact to be able to do this."

The Aristotelian view of education as a process has become the conventionally worthy answer today whenever college presidents and other academic leaders are asked what an education should be. An educated man, says Harvard President Bok, taking a deep breath, must have a "curiosity in exploring the unfamiliar and unexpected, an open-mindedness in entertaining opposing points of view, tolerance for the ambiguity that surrounds so many important issues. and a willingness to make the the the best decisions he can in the face of uncertainty and doubt. . . ."

"The educated person," says University of Chicago President Hanna Holborn Gray, taking an equally deep breath, "is a person who has a respect for rationality, and who understands some of the limits of rationality as well, who has acquired independent critical intelligence, and a sense not only for the complexity of the world and different points of view but of the standards he or she would thoughtfully want to be pursuing in making judgments."

This is an approach that appears to attach more importance to the process of learning than to the substance of what is learned, but it does provide a way of coping with the vast increase of knowledge. "The old notion of the generalists who could comprehend all subjects is an impossibility, and it was even in past ages," says Chicago's Gray. "Renaissance humanism concentrated on social living and aesthetic engagement but left out most of science. To know all about today's physics, biology and mathematics, or even the general principles of all these fields, would be impossible." To make matters still more difficult, the fields of knowledge keep changing. Says Harvard's Henry Rosovsky, dean of the faculty of arts and sciences: "We can't prepare students for an explosion of knowledge because we don't know what is going to explode next. The best we can do is to make students capable of gaining new knowledge."

The old Aristotelian idea, combined with a contemporary sense of desperation about coping with the knowledge explosion, helped inspire a complete reorganization—yet again—of Harvard's curriculum. At the end of World War II, Harvard had curtailed Eliot's electives and launched a series of general education courses that were supposed to teach everyone the rudiments of science and the humanities. But by the 1960s, when rebellious students seized an administration building, that whole system had broken down. "At the moment," a saddened Dean Rosovsky later wrote to his colleagues, "to be an educated man or woman doesn't mean anything. . . . The world has become a Tower of Babel."

Out of Rosovsky's unhappiness came what Harvard somewhat misleadingly calls its core curriculum. Inaugurated in 1979, after much faculty debate and amid considerable press attention, this core turned out to be a rather sprawling collection of 122 different courses, ranging from Abstraction in Modern Art to Microbial and Molecular Biology. Students are required to select eight of their 32 courses from five general areas of knowledge (science, history, the arts, ethics and foreign cultures).

Harvard's eminence exerts a wide influence, but other first-rate institutions, like Columbia, Chicago, and Princeton, point out that they have taught a more concentrated core and steadfastly continued doing so throughout the 1960s. "It makes me unhappy when people think that Harvard has done some innovative curriculum work," says Columbia College Associate Dean Michael Rosenthal (a Harvard graduate). "They have millions of courses, none of which, you could argue, represents any fundamental effort to introduce people to a kind of thinking or to a discipline."

But that is exactly what Harvard does claim to be doing. "The student should have an understanding of the major ways mankind organizes knowledge," says Rosovsky. "That is done in identifiable ways: in sciences by experiment, conducted essentially in mathematics; in social science through quantitative and historical analysis; in the humanities by studying the great traditions. We are not ignoring content but simply recognizing that because of the knowledge explosion, it makes sense to emphasize the gaining of knowledge."

If anyone objects that it is still perfectly possible to graduate from Harvard without having read a word of Shakespeare, Rosovsky is totally unfazed. Says he: "That's not necessary."

IV: Education Liberates the Individual

The current trend toward required subjects—a kind of intellectual law-and-order—reflects contemporary political conservatism. It implies not only that there is a basic body of knowledge to be learned but also that there is a right way to think. It implies that a certain amount of uniformity is both socially and intellectually desirable.

Perhaps, but the excesses of the 1960s should not be used to besmirch reforms that were valuable. They too derived from a distinguished intellectual tradition. Its founding father was Jean-Jacques Rousseau, who argued in his novel *Emile* that children are not miniature adults and should not be drilled into becoming full-grown robots. "Everything is good as it comes from the hand of the Creator," said Rousseau; "everything degenerates in the hands of man."

Isolated from the corrupting world, Rousseau's young Emile was given no books but encouraged to educate himself by observing the workings of nature. Not until the age of twelve, the age of reason, was he provided with explanations in the form of astronomy or chemistry, and not until the social age of 15 was he introduced to aesthetics, religion, and, eventually, female company. That was how Emile met Sophie and lived happily every after. It is a silly tale, and yet there is considerable power to the idea that a student should be primarily educated not to hold a job or to memorize literary monuments or even to think like Aristotle, but simply to develop the potentialities of his own self—and that everyone's self is different.

While there is probably not a single university that has not retreated somewhat from the experimentation of the 1960s, and while the rhetoric of that decade is now wildly out of fashion, a few small institutions have tried to keep the faith. For them, education is, in a sense, liberation, personal liberation. At Evergreen State College in Washington, which has no course requirements of any kind and no letter grades, a college spokesman describes a class on democracy and tyranny by saying, "We will try to find out who we are, and what kind of human beings we should become." At Hampshire College, founded in Massachusetts in 1970 as a resolutely experimental school, students still design their own curriculums, take no exams and talk of changing the world. "I don't see myself as giving a body of knowledge or even 'a way of learning.' " says Physics Professor Herbert Bernstein, "but as involved in something beyond that—to help people find their own path and the fullness of who they are."

The times have not been easy for such colleges. Not only do costs keep rising, but many students now prefer conventional courses and grades that will look impressive on job applications. Antioch, which expanded into an unmanageable national network of 32 experimental institutions, stumbled to the verge of bankruptcy in the 1970s, and is drastically cutting costs to survive. But the spirit of Rousseau flickers on. Rollins, which has sometimes been dismissed as a Florida tennis school, is trying to organize a conference for such like-minded colleges as Bard, Bennington, Sarah Lawrence, and Scripps on how best to pursue the goal of "making higher education more personal and developmental rather than formalistic."

Even when the enthusiasts do bend to the current pressures for law-and-order, they tend to do it in their own dreamy way. At Bard, where President Leon Botstein decided last year that all students should attend an incisive three-week workshop on how to think and write, the students pondered such questions as the nature of justice. What color is justice? What shape is it? What sound does it make? What does it eat? "I can't think of anything," one student protested at the first such writing class. "Don't worry about it," the teacher soothingly answered. Among the students' offerings: "Justice is navy blue, it's square. It weaves in and out and backs up . . . Justice is black and white, round . . . It has the sound of the cracked Liberty Bell ringing." Workshop Director Peter Elbow's conclusion: "We're trying an experiment here, and we're not pretending that we have it under control or that we know how it works."

V: Education Teaches Morals

The U.S. Supreme Court has forbidden prayers in public schools, but many Americans cling to the idea that their educational system has a moral purpose. It is an idea common to both the Greeks and the medieval church ("O Lord my King," St. Augustine wrote in his *Confessions,* "whatsoever I speak or write, or read, or number, let all serve Thee"). In a secular age, the moral purpose of education takes secular forms: racial integration, sex education, good citizenship. At the college level, the ambiguities become more complex. Should a morally objectionable person be allowed to teach? (Not Timothy Leary, said Harvard.) Should a morally objectionable doctrine be permitted? (Not Arthur-Jensen's claims of racial differences in intelligence, said student protesters at Berkeley.)

Many people are understandably dismayed by such censorship. But would they prefer ethical neutrality? Should engineers be trained to build highways without being taught any concern for the homes they displace? Should prospective corporate managers learn how to increase profits regardless of pollution or unemployment? Just the opposite, according to *Beyond the Ivory Tower,* a new book by Harvard's Bok, which calls for increased emphasis on "applied ethics." (Writes Bok: "A university that refuses to take ethical dilemmas seriously violates its basic obligations to society.")

Religious colleges have always practiced a similar preaching. But some 500 schools now offer courses in the field. The Government supports such studies with a program known as EVIST, which stands for Ethics and Values in Science and Technology (and which sounds as though a computer had already taken charge of the matter). "The modern university is rooted in the scientific method, having essentially turned its back on religion," says Steven Muller, president of Johns Hopkins. "The scientific method is a marvelous means of inquiry, but it really doesn't provide a value system. The biggest failing in higher education today is that we fall short in exposing students to values."

Charles Muscatine, a professor of English at Berkeley and member of a committee that is analyzing liberal arts curriculums for the Association of American Colleges, is even harsher. He calls today's educational programs "a marvelous convenience for a mediocre society." The key goal of education, says Muscatine, should be "informed decision making that recognizes there is a moral and ethical component to life." Instead, he says most universities are "propagating the dangerous myth that technical skills are more important than ethical reasoning."

Psychiatrist Robert Coles, who teaches at both Harvard and Duke, is still more emphatic in summing up the need: "Reading, writing, and arithmetic. That's what we've got to start with, and all that implies, at every level. If people can't use good, strong language, they can't think clearly, and if they haven't been trained to use good, strong language, they become vulnerable to all the junk that comes their way. They should be taught philosophy, moral philosophy and theology. They ought to be asked to think about moral issues, especially about what use is going to be make of knowledge, and why—a kind of moral reflection that I think has been supplanted by a more technological education. Replacing moral philosophy with psychology has been a disaster, an absolute disaster!"

Each of these five ways to wisdom has its strengths and weaknesses, of course. The idea that education provides better jobs promises practical rewards for both the student and the society that trains him, but it can leave him undernourished in the possibilities of life away from work. The idea that education means the acquisition of a cultural heritage does give the student some grasp of that heritage, but it can also turn into glib superficialities or sterile erudition. The idea that education consists mainly of training the mind does provide a method for further education, but it can also make method seem more important than knowledge. So can the idea that education is a form of self-development. And the teaching of ethics can unfortunately become a teaching of conventional pieties.

To define is to limit, as we all learned in school, and to categorize is to oversimplify. To some extent, the five ways to wisdom all overlap and blend, and though every educator has his own sense of priorities, none would admit that he does not aspire to all five goals. Thus the student who has mastered the riches of Western civilization has probably also learned to think for himself and to see the moral purposes of life. And surely such a paragon can find a good job even in the recession of 1982.

Are there specific ways to come nearer to achieving these goals? The most obvious is money. Good teachers cost money; libraries costs money; so do remedial classes for those who were short-changed in earlier years. Only mediocrity comes cheap. Those who groan at the rising price of college tuition (up as much as $7,000 since 1972) may not realize that overall, taking enrollment growth into account, college budgets have just barely kept up with inflation. Indeed adjusted for inflation, four years of college today costs less than a decade ago, and faculty salaries in real dollars declined about 20% during the 1970s. Crocodile tears over the costs of higher education come in waves from the federal government, which has so far held spending to roughly 1981 levels, and proposes deep cuts (e.g., nearly 40% in basic grants) by 1985. This is an economy comparable to skimping on the maintenance of an expensive machine.

But money alone will not solve all problems, as is often said, and this is particularly true in the field of education. If improving the quality of American education is a matter of urgent national concern—and it should be—then what is required besides more dollars is more sense: a widespread rededication to a number of obvious but somewhat neglected principles. That probing research and hard thinking be demanded of students (and of teachers too). That academic results be tested and measured. That intellectual excellence be not just acknowledged but rewarded.

These principles admittedly did serve the system that educated primarily those few who were born into the governing classes, but the fact that elitist education once supported elitist politics does not mean that egalitarian politics requires egalitarian education. Neither minds nor ideas are all the same.

All that the schools can be asked to promise is that everyone will be educated to the limit of his capacities. Exactly what this means, everyone must discover for himself. At the community college minimum, it may have to mean teaching basic skills, at least until the weakened high schools begin doing their job properly, as philosopher Mortimer Adler urges in his new *Paideia Proposal.* This calls for a standardized high school curriculum in three categories: fundamental knowledge such as history, science, and arts; basic skills such as reading and mathematical computation; and critical understanding of ideas and values. These essentials must really be taught, not just certified with a passing grade. Beyond such practical benefits, though, and beyond the benefits that come from exercising the muscles of the mind, higher education must ultimately serve the higher purpose of perpetuating whatever it is in civilization that is worth perpetuating. Or as Ezra Pound once said of the craft that he later betrayed, "The function of literature is precisely that it does incite humanity to continue living."

This is the core of the core idea, and surely it is by now indisputable that every college student improves by learning the fundamentals of science, literature, art, history. Harvard's Rosovsky may be right in suggesting that it is "not necessary" to have read Shakespeare as part or the process of learning how to think, but he is probably wrong. Not because anyone really *needs* to have shared in Lear's howling rage or because anyone can earn a better salary from having heard Macbeth declaim "Tomorrow and tomorrow and tomorrow . . . " But he is enriched by knowing these things, impoverished by not knowing them. And *The Marriage of Figaro* enriches. *The Cherry Orchard* enriches. *The City of God* enriches. So does a mastery of Greek, or of subnuclear particles, or of Gödel's theorem.

In a sense, there really is no core, except as a series of arbitrary choices, for there is no limit to the possibilities of learning. There are times when these possibilities seem overwhelming, and one hears echoes of Socrates' confession, "All I know is that I know nothing." Yet that too is a challenge. "We shall not cease from exploration," as T. S. Eliot put it, "and the end of our exploring/Will be to arrive where we started/And know the place for the first time." The seemingly momentous years of schooling, then, are only the beginning.

Henry Adams, who said in *The Education of Henry Adams* that Harvard "taught little and that little ill," was 37 when he took up the study of Saxon legal codes and 42 when he first turned to writing the history of the Jefferson and Madison Administrations, and 49 when he laboriously began on Chinese. In his 50s, a tiny, wiry figure with a graying beard, the future master of Gothic architecture solemnly learned to ride a bicycle.   ∎

What We Expect
Preparing for College—
A Statement by 12 Deans

This statement comes from a 1984 national educational conference on the relationship between high school and college.

Most freshmen entering highly competitive colleges arrive on campus with top ranked secondary school averages and impressive SAT scores. Some, from their first day in class, do well, fulfilling our high expectations for them. Others falter educationally, not sure why they are in college, or how to study, or what to study, or why. Some college students take several semesters to begin gaining full advantage of the opportunities for learning that surround them; some never gain that advantage.

Secondary school teachers and administrators see the same problem from their perspective, and some have shared their concerns with us. We think a major reason some students succeed and others are not as successful lies in the kind and character of their secondary school preparation, not in their test scores and grades.

We are sharing our observations for two purposes. First, we want to offer high school students guidance in their selection of courses. Second, we want to assist parents, faculty, administrators, and school boards as they seek to offer high school students an education that will serve them well in a challenging world. We believe that the pluralism of American higher education, beneficial though it is, confuses some college-bound students. Even among the institutions we serve, the requirements for admission and for graduation vary widely, as do the available majors and areas of specialization. Despite these differences, we, as academic deans, share a belief in a basic set of priorities for college-bound students.

Our concern here is with preparation for college-level work, and not with the requirements for admission to a college. Our concern is with the special skills, attitudes, and motivation which students bring to college that let them participate effectively in the learning experiences open to them. Securing admission to college is important; more important is whether the student is prepared to make the best use of that opportunity.

We hope students—especially those who plan to attend selective colleges—will accept our advice. We hope, too, that our views will form the basis of a new cooperative effort between colleges and secondary schools leading to the improvement of education at both levels. Toward that end, we began the preparation of this statement by talking with many secondary school educators. We applaud other such efforts.

We find that students who benefit most from our educational programs are those who enter with certain identifiable attitudes and skills—

such as persistent curiosity, broad intellectual interests, skill at analytical and critical thinking, a concern for exploring and applying values, an ability to manage time responsibly, and a willingness to work hard.

The development of such attributes is, of course, only partially within the influence of secondary schools. We believe, however, that the content and expectations of secondary school courses can be shaped to enhance those characteristics that students will later need. Critical thinking skills can be improved, for example, by the regular practice of writing papers that require analysis and interpretation of material. They can be improved, too, by examinations that require students to assess and integrate information and ideas, rather than repeating only what they have memorized. Students who must master demanding course material within a series of deadlines can learn to manage time responsibly and appreciate the rewards of hard work.

Participation in well-managed extracurricular and cocurricular activities can, as well, help students develop constructive attitudes and sharpen useful skills. Writing for the school newspaper, participating in forensic and theatrical activities, playing in musical organizations or on athletic teams can, if purposefully performed, contribute forcefully to the development of characteristics valuable to college students. We believe that most college-bound students have the capacity to complete the academic program we recommend and have ample time to participate in useful, substantial cocurricular and extracurricular activities.

We believe strongly that our incoming students need to be well grounded in seven specific subject areas. These are the arts, English language, foreign language, history, literature, mathematics, and science. In fact, we recommend that in these areas students go beyond the typical minimum requirements both for secondary school graduation and for admission to college. Competence in each of these areas is crucial for productive study at the college level.

We do not believe our colleges should be expected to provide general remedial work to overcome basic deficiencies in preparation. Some college students, by extra effort, do overcome inadequate preparation in these essential areas; for other students, however, an initial experience of inadequacy in the basics inhibits their intellectual growth during their entire college years. The stronger the secondary school preparation is, the more easily a college student can begin immediately to experience the benefits of serious academic pursuits.

Without being prescriptive or intrusive, we want to indicate briefly what we mean by solid preparation in each of the seven vital subject areas.

The arts: The arts provide a uniquely valuable mode of seeing ourselves and the world around us. In a bureaucratic and technological age, the arts present a necessary balance, a sensitive link to that which makes us more fully human. Students should be familiar with the work of some major artists. They should develop an awareness of artistic sensibility and judgment and an understanding of the creative process. Students should select one or two semester-long courses, taught in an exacting manner in the areas of music, theatre, and/or art.

English language: Students must have a command of English grammar and well developed compositional skills. Students should take courses in several subject areas that require closely reasoned compositions involving both concrete and abstract thought, as well as some fundamental library research activities. Courses that develop student abilities to use writing to form and exchange ideas and to write and speak English with clarity and style are among the most important courses they can take.

Foreign language: Competency in a foreign language, modern or classical, through the third or fourth year of a demanding secondary school program develops a student's language resourcefulness in a world community that increasingly expects that capacity. Such competency improves the comprehension of a student's native language and culture, and enhances the student's understanding of humankind. Such competency, which is most efficiently gained at an early age, also provides a good basis for further language study in college and adds to students' scholarly capability by freeing them from dependency upon translations.

History: The study of American history and culture and of Western traditions, from the ancient world to the present, is important to an understanding of the contemporary world. Familiarity with a non-Western culture (or cultures) adds substantially to that comprehension. Further, an appreciation of good government and civic responsibility is characteristically rooted in an understanding of history. An appreciation of historical perspective is, itself, an important educational objective. Indeed, serious conversation is not possible when students are ignorant either of major historical events, movements, and people or of the general mode of historical discussion and explanation. Such references are fundamental to much of higher education. At least two years of historical study at the secondary school level are highly valuable.

Literature: The study of traditional literary texts adds greatly to a student's understanding of humankind and human associations. Systematic literary study can also better prepare a student for the reading of contemporary literature. The experience of reading, for example, the comedies and tragedies of ancient Greek playwrights, the Judaic and Christian scriptures, the writings of Shakespeare, and the work of more recent writers of enduring reputation, provides an excellent foundation for further literary inquiry and a fine context for study in many fields. The student is best prepared by confronting excellent works in all the major genres—plays, novels, essays, poetry, and short fiction. Some combination of four years, of strong English language courses and literature courses is expected.

Mathematics: The field of mathematics grows ever more important. Quantitative analysis is crucial to understanding the complexities of the modern world. Valuing and decision-making activities often require quantitative judgments. The use of algebra, calculus, and statistics is now commonplace in the study of many disciplines in college. Computer literacy is useful even in the humanities. Sufficient preparation for this range of mathematical applications normally requires four years of secondary school study, resulting in a readiness for beginning college calculus.

Science: The study for one year each of biology, chemistry, and physics is highly desirable; at the very least, a student should take one year or two of these sciences and perhaps two years of one science. Familiarity with the basic sciences has long been a hallmark of the educated person and is now a common, practical necessity. To understand the relationships among science, technology, and public policy makes crucial some knowledge of the basic issues, nomenclature, and methods of science—not the least because the survival of humanity is at stake.

Circumstances may make it difficult for some students to take the maximum number of academic courses available in each of the seven subject areas. Some students may have to exercise choices—depending upon the strengths of the particular secondary school program, the aspirations of the individual students, and even the peculiarities of scheduling. Yet, despite these considerations, we stress that students should remain determined to complete a strong academic program and not substitute other courses for those that are fundamental and exacting.

The excitement of higher learning is more easily gained by those students who arrive on campus properly equipped for the challenge. Successful college students regularly cite with admiration secondary school teachers who helped prepare them well. Those students do, in fact, find the learning experience at each level of their education to be part of the same grand adventure.

George Allan, *Dean of the College*, Dickinson College.
Mary Maples Dunn, *Dean of the Undergraduate College*, Bryn Mawr College
Frances D. Ferguson, *Vice President for Academic Affairs*, Bucknell University
Andrew T. Ford, *Dean of the College*, Allegheny College
Robert M. Gavin, Jr., *Provost*, Haverford College
Thomas J. Hershberger, *Dean of Faculty*, Chatham College
John W. Hunt, *Dean of the College of Arts and Science*, Lehigh University
William A. Jeffers. Jr., *Dean of the College*, Lafayette College
David B. Potts, *Dean of the College*, Gettysburg College
Richard P. Traina, *Dean of the College*, Franklin and Marshall College
Richard I. Van Horn, *Provost*, Carnegie-Mellon University
Harrison M. Wright, *Provost*, Swarthmore College   ■

Robert B. Reich **The Three Jobs of the Future**

The usual discussion about the future of the American economy focuses on topics like the competitiveness of General Motors, or of the American automobile industry, or, more broadly, of American manufacturing, or, more broadly still, of the American economy. But, as has been observed, these categories are becoming irrelevant. They assume the continued existence of an American economy in which jobs associated with a particular firm, industry, or sector are somehow connected within the borders of the nation, so that American workers face a common fate; and a common enemy as well: The battlefields of world trade pit our corporations and our workers unambiguously against theirs.

No longer. In the emerging international economy, few American companies and American industries compete against foreign companies and industries—if by *American* we mean where the work is done and the value is added. Becoming more typical is the global web, perhaps headquartered in and receiving much of its financial capital from the United States, but with research, design, and production facilities spread over Japan, Europe, and North America; additional production facilities in Southeast Asia and Latin America; marketing and distribution centers on every continent; and lenders and investors in Taiwan, Japan, and West Germany as well as the United States. This ecumenical company competes with similarly ecumenical companies headquartered in other nations. Battle lines no longer correspond with national borders.

So, when an "American" company like General Motors shows healthy profits, this is good news for its strategic brokers in Detroit and its American investors. It is also good news for other GM executives worldwide and for GM's global employees, subcontractors, and investors. But it is not necessarily good news for a lot of routine assembly-line workers in Detroit, because there are not likely to be many of them left in Detroit, or anywhere else in America. Nor is it necessarily good news for the few Americans who are still working on the assembly lines in the United States, who increasingly receive their paychecks from corporations based in Tokyo or Bonn.

The point is that Americans are becoming part of an international labor market, encompassing Asia, Africa, Latin America, Western Europe, and, increasingly, Eastern Europe and the Soviet Union. The competitiveness of Americans in this global market is coming to depend, not on the fortunes of any American corporation or on American industry, but on the functions that Americans perform—the value they add—within the global economy. Other nations are undergoing precisely the same transformation, some more slowly than the United States, but all participating in essentially the same transnational trend. Barriers to cross-border flows of knowledge, money, and tangible products are crumbling; groups of people in every nation are joining global webs. In a very few years, there will be virtually no way to distinguish one national economy from another except by the exchange rates of their currencies—and even this distinction may be on the wane.

Americans thus confront global competition ever more directly, unmediated by national institutions. As we discard vestigial notions of the competitiveness of American corporations, American industry, and the American economy, and recast them in terms of the competitiveness of the American work force, it becomes apparent that successes or failures will not be shared equally by all our citizens.

Some Americans, whose contributions to the global economy are more highly valued in world markets, will succeed, while others, whose contributions are deemed far less valuable, fail. GM's American executives may become less competitive even as GM's American production workers become less so, because the functions performed by the former group are more highly valued in the world market than those of the latter. So, when we speak of the "competitiveness" of Americans in general, we are talking only about how much the world is prepared to spend, *on average*, for services performed by Americans. Some Americans may command higher rewards; others, far lower. No longer are Americans rising or falling together, as if in one large national boat. We are, increasingly, in different, smaller boats.

2

In order to see in greater detail what is happening to American jobs and to understand why the economic fates of Americans are beginning to diverge, it is first necessary to view the work that Americans do in terms of categories that reflect their real competitive positions in the global economy.

Official data about American jobs are organized by categories that are not very helpful in this regard. The U.S. Bureau of the Census began inquiring about American jobs in 1820, and developed a systematic way of categorizing them in 1870. Beginning in 1943, the Census came up with a way of dividing these categories into different levels of "social-economic status," depending upon, among other things, the prestige and income associated with each job. In order to determine the appropriate groupings, the Census first divided all American jobs into either business class or working class—the same two overarching categories the Lynns had devised for their study of Middletown—and then divided each of these, in turn, into subcategories.[1] In 1950, the Census added the category "service workers" and called the resulting scheme America's "Major Occupational Groups," which it has remained ever since. All subsequent surveys have been based on this same set of categories. Thus, even by 1990, in the eyes of the Census, you were either a "managerial and professional specialty," in a "technical, sales, and administrative support" role, in a "service occupation," an "operator, fabricator, and laborer," or in a "transportation and material moving" occupation.

This set of classifications made sense when the economy was focused on high-volume, and standardized production, in which almost every job fit into, or around, the core American corporation, and when status and income depended on one's ranking in the standard corporate bureaucracy. But these categories have little bearing upon the competitive positions of Americans worldwide, now that America's core corporations are transforming into finely spun global webs. Someone whose job falls officially into a "technical" or "sales" subcategory may, in fact, be among the best-paid and most influential people in such a web. To understand the real competitive positions of Americans in the global economy, it is necessary to devise new categories.[2]

Essentially, three broad categories of work are emerging, corresponding to three different positions in which Americans find themselves. The same three categories are taking shape in other nations. Call them *routine production services, in-person services,* and *symbolic-analytic services.*

Routine production services entail the kinds of repetitive tasks performed by the old foot soldiers of American capitalism in the high-volume enterprise. They are done over and over—one step in a sequence of steps for producing finished products tradeable in world commerce. Although often thought of as traditional blue-collar jobs, they also include routine supervisory jobs performed by low- and mid-level managers—foremen, line managers, clerical supervisors, and section chiefs—involving repetitive checks on subordinates' work and the enforcement of standard operating procedures.

Routine production services are found in many places within a modern economy apart from older, heavy industries (which, like elderly citizens, have been given the more delicate, and less terminal, appelation: "mature"). They are found even amid the glitter and glitz of high technology. Few tasks are more tedious and repetitive, for example, than stuffing computer circuit boards or devising routine coding for computer software programs.

Indeed, contrary to prophets of the "information age" who buoyantly predicted an abundance of high-paying jobs even for people with the most basic of skills, the sobering truth is that many information-processing jobs fit easily into this category. The foot soldiers of the information economy are hordes of data processors stationed in "back offices" at computer terminals linked to world-wide information banks. They routinely enter data into computers or take it out again—records of credit card purchases and payments, credit reports, checks that have cleared, customer accounts, customer correspondence, payroll, hospital billings, patient records, medical claims, court decisions, subscriber lists, personnel, library catalogues, and so forth. The "information revolution" may have rendered some of us more productive, but it has also produced huge piles of raw data which must be processed in much the same monotonous way that assembly-line workers and, before them, textile workers processed piles of other raw materials.

Routine producers routinely work in the company of many other people who do the same thing, usually within large enclosed spaces. They are guided on the job by standard procedures and codified rules, and even their overseers are overseen, in turn, by people who routinely monitor—often with the aid of computers—how much they do and how accurately they do it. Their wages are based either on the amount of time they put in or on the amount of work they do.

Routine producers usually must be able to read and to perform simple computations. But their cardinal virtues are reliability, loyalty, and the capacity to take direction. Thus does a standard American education, based on the traditional premises of American Education, normally suffice.

By 1990, routine production work comprised about one-quarter of the jobs performed by Americans, and the number was declining. Those who dealt with metal were mostly white and male; those who dealt with fabrics, circuit boards, or information were mostly black or Hispanic, and female; their supervisors, white males.[3]

In-person services, the second kind of work that Americans do, also entail simple and repetitive tasks. And like routine production services, the pay of in-person servers is a function of hours worked or amount of work performed; they are closely supervised (as are their supervisors), and they need not have acquired much education (at most, a high school diploma, or its equivalent, and some vocational training).

The big difference between in-person servers and routine producers is that *these* services must be provided person-to-person, and thus are not sold worldwide. (In-person servers might, of course, work for global corporations. Two examples: In 1988, Britain's Blue Arrow PLC acquired Manpower Inc., which provides custodial services throughout the United States. Meanwhile, Denmark's ISS-AS already employed over 16,000 Americans to clean office buildings in most major American cities.) In-person servers are in direct contact with the ultimate beneficiaries of their work; their immediate objects are specific customers rather than streams of metal, fabric, or data. In-person servers work alone or in small teams. Included in this category are retail sales workers, waiters and waitresses, hotel workers, janitors, cashiers, hospital attendants and orderlies, nursing-home aides, child-care workers, house cleaners, home health-care aides, taxi drivers, secretaries, hairdressers, auto mechanics, sellers of residential real estate, flight attendants, physical therapists, and—among the fastest-growing of all—security guards.

In-person servers are supposed to be punctual, reliable, and tractable as routine production workers. But many in-person servers share one additional requirement: They must have a pleasant demeanor. They must smile and exude confidence and good cheer, even when they feel morose. They must be courteous and helpful, even to the most obnoxious of patrons. Above all, they must make others feel happy and at ease. It should come as no surprise that, traditionally, most in-person servers have been women. The cultural stereotype of women as nurturers—as mommies—has opened countless in-person service jobs to them.[4]

By 1990, in-person services accounted for about 30 percent of the jobs performed by Americans, and their numbers were growing rapidly. For example, Beverly Enterprises, a single nursing-home chain operating throughout the United States, employed about the same number of Americans as the entire Chrysler Corporation (115,174 and 116,250, respectively)—although most Americans were far more knowledgeable about the latter, including the opinions of its chairman. In the United States during the 1980s, well over 3 million *new* in-person service jobs were created in fast-food outlets, bars, and restaurants. This was more than the *total* number of routine production jobs still existing in America by the end of the decade in the automobile, steelmaking, and textile industries combined.[5]

Symbolic-analytic services, the third job category, include all the problem-solving, problem-identifying, and strategic-brokering activities we have examined in previous chapters. Like routine production services (but *unlike* in-person services), symbolic-analytic services can be traded worldwide and thus must compete with foreign providers even in the American market. But they do not enter world commerce as standardized things. Traded instead are the manipulations of symbols—data, words, oral and visual representations.

Included in this category are the problem-solving, -identifying, and brokering of many people who call themselves research scientists, design engineers, software engineers, civil engineers, biotechnology engineers, sound engineers, public relations executives, investment bankers, lawyers, real estate developers, and even a few creative accountants. Also included is much of the work done by management consultants, financial consultants, tax consultants, energy consultants, agricultural consultants, armaments consultants, architectural consultants, management information specialists, organization development specialists, strategic planners, corporate headhunters, and systems analysts. Also: advertising executives and marketing strategists, art directors, architects, cinematographers, film editors, production designers, publishers, writers and editors, journalists, musicians, television and film producers, and even university professors.

Symbolic analysts solve, identify and broker problems by manipulating symbols. The simplify reality into abstract images that can be rearranged, juggled, experimented with, communicated to other specialists, and then, eventually, transformed back into reality. The manipulations are done with analytic tools, sharpened by experience. The tools may be mathematical algorithms, legal arguments, financial gimmicks, scientific principles, psychological insights about how to persuade or to amuse, systems of induction or deduction, or any other set of techniques for doing conceptual puzzles.

Some of these manipulations reveal how to more efficiently deploy resources or shift financial assets, or otherwise save time and energy. Other manipulations yield new inventions—technological marvels, innovative legal arguments, new advertising ploys for convincing people that certain amusements have become life necessities. Still other manipulations—of sounds, words, pictures—serve to entertain their recipients, or cause them to reflect more deeply on their lives or on the human condition. Others grab money from people too slow or naïve to protect themselves by manipulating in response.

Like routine producers, symbolic analysts rarely come into direct contact with the ultimate beneficiaries of their work. But other aspects of their work life are quite different from that experienced by routine producers. Symbolic analysts often have partners or associates rather than bosses or supervisors. Their incomes may vary from time to time, but are not directly related to how much time they put in or the quantity of work they put out. Income depends, rather, on the quality, originality, cleverness, and, occasionally, speed with which they solve, identify, or broker new problems. Their careers are not linear or hierarchical; they rarely proceed along well-defined paths to progressively higher levels of responsibility and income. In fact, symbolic analysts may take on vast responsibilities and command inordinate wealth at rather young ages. Correspondingly, they may lose authority and income if they are no longer able to innovate by building on their cumulative experience, even if they are quite senior.

Symbolic analysts often work alone or in small teams, which may be connected to larger organizations, including worldwide webs. Teamwork is often critical. Since neither problems nor solutions can be defined in advance, frequent and informal conversations help ensure that insights and discoveries are put to their best uses and subjected to quick, critical evaluation.[6]

When not conversing with their teammates, symbolic analysts sit before computer terminals—examining words and numbers, moving them, altering them, trying out new words and numbers, formulating and testing hypotheses, designing or strategizing. They also spend long hours in meetings or on the telephone, and even longer hours in jet planes and hotels—advising, making presentations, giving briefings, doing deals. Periodically, they issue reports, plans, designs, drafts, memoranda, layouts, renderings, scripts, or projections—which, in turn, precipitate more meetings to clarify what has been proposed and how to get agreement on how it will be implemented, by whom, and for how much money. Final production is often the easiest part. The bulk of the time and cost (and, thus, real value) comes in conceptualizing the problem, devising a solution, and planning its execution.

Most symbolic analysts have graduated from four-year colleges or universities; many have graduate degrees as well. The vast majority are white males, but the proportion of white females is growing, and there is a small, but slowly increasing, number of blacks and Hispanics among them. All told, symbolic analysis currently accounts for no more than 20 percent of American jobs. The proportion of American workers who fit this category has increased substantially since the 1950s (by my calculation, no more than 8 percent of American workers could be classified as symbolic analysts at midcentury), but the pace slowed considerably in the 1980s—even though certain symbolic-analytic jobs, like law and investment banking, mushroomed. (I will return to this point later.)[7]

3

These three functional categories cover more than three out of four American jobs. Among the remainder are farmers, miners, and other extractors of natural resources, who together comprise less than 5 percent of American workers. The rest are mainly government employees (including public school teachers), employees in regulated industries (like utility workers), and government-financed workers (American engineers working on defense weapons systems and physicians working off Medicaid and Medicare), almost all of whom are also sheltered from global competition.

Some traditional job categories—managerial, secretarial, sales, and so on—overlap with more than one of these functional categories. The traditional categories, it should be emphasized, date from an era in which most jobs were as standardized as the products they helped create. Such categories are no longer very helpful for determining what a person actually does on the job and how much that person is likely to earn for doing it. Only some of the people who are classified as "secretaries," for example, perform strictly routine production work, such as entering and retrieving data from computers. Other "secretaries" provide in-person services, like making appointments and fetching coffee. A third group of "secretaries" perform symbolic-analytic work closely allied to what their bosses do. To classify them as "secretaries" glosses over their very different functions in the economy. Similarly, "sales" jobs can fall within any one of three functional groups: some salespeople simply fill quotas and orders: others spend much of their time performing in-person services, like maintaining machinery; and some are sophisticated problem-identifiers no different from high-priced management consultants. "Computer programmers" (one of the more recent additions to the standard list of occupations) are as varied: They might be doing routine coding, in-person troubleshooting for particular clients, or translating complex and functional specifications into software.

That a job category is officially classified "professional" or "managerial" likewise has little bearing upon the function its occupants actually perform in the world economy. Not all professionals, that is, are symbolic analysts. Some lawyers spend their entire working lives doing things that normal people would find unbearably monotonous—cranking out the same old wills, contracts, and divorces, over and over, with only the names changed. Some accountants do routine audits without active involvement of their cerebral cortices. Some managers take no more responsibility than noting who shows up for work in the morning, making sure they stay put, and locking the place up at night. (I have heard tell of university professors who deliver the same lectures for thirty years, long after their brains have atrophied, but I do not believe such stories.) None of these professionals is a symbolic analyst.[8]

Nor are all symbolic analysts professionals. In the older, high-volume economy, a "professional" was one who had mastered a particular domain of knowledge. The knowledge existed in advance, ready to be mastered. It had been recorded in dusty tomes or codified in precise rules and formulae. Once the novitiate had dutifully absorbed the knowledge and had passed an examination attesting to its absorption, professional status was automatically conferred—usually through a ceremony of appropriately medieval pageantry and costume. The professional was then authorized to place a few extra letters after his or her name, mount a diploma on the office wall, join the professional association and attend its yearly tax-deductible meeting in Palm Springs, and pursue clients with a minimum of overt avarice.

But in the new economy—replete with unidentified problems, unknown solutions, and untried means of putting them together—mastery of old domains of knowledge isn't nearly enough to guarantee a good income. Nor, importantly, is it even necessary. Symbolic analysts often can draw upon established bodies of knowledge with the flick of a computer key. Facts, codes, formulae, and rules are easily accessible. What is much more valuable is the capacity to effectively and creatively *use* the knowledge. Possessing a professional credential is no guarantee of such capacity. Indeed, a professional education which has emphasized the rote of acquisition of such knowledge over original thought may retard such capacity in later life.

4

How, then, do symbolic analysts describe what they do? With difficulty. Because a symbolic analyst's status, influence, and income have little to do with formal rank and title, the job may seem mysterious to people working outside the enterprise web, who are unfamiliar with the symbolic analyst's actual function within it. And because symbolic analysis involves processes of thought and communication, rather than tangible production, the content of the job may be difficult to convey simply. In answering the question "What did you do today, Mommy (or Daddy)?" it is not always instructive, or particularly edifying, to say that one spent three hours on the telephone, four hours in meetings, and the remainder of the time gazing at a computer screen trying to work out a puzzle.

Some symbolic analysts have taken refuge in job titles that communicate no more clearly than this, but at least sound as if they confer independent authority nonetheless. The old hierarchies are breaking down, but new linguistic idioms have arisen to perpetuate the time-honored custom of title-as-status.

Herewith a sample. Add any term from the first column to any from the second, and then add both terms to any from the third column, and you will have a job that is likely (but not necessarily) to be inhabited by a symbolic analyst.

Communications	Management	Engineer
Systems	Planning	Director
Financial	Process	Designer
Creative	Development	Coordinator
Project	Strategy	Consultant
Business	Policy	Manager
Resource	Applications	Adviser
Product	Research	Planner

The "flat" organization of high-value enterprise notwithstanding, there are subtle distinctions of symbolic-analytic rank. Real status is inversely related to length of job title. Two terms signify a degree of authority. (The first and second column's appellation is dropped, leaving a simpler and more elegant combination, such as "Project Engineer" or "Creative Director.") Upon the most valued of symbolic analysts, who have moved beyond mere technical proficiency to exert substantial influence on their peers within the web, is bestowed the highest honor—a title comprising a term from the last column preceded by a dignified adjective like Senior, Managing, Chief, or Principal. One becomes a "Senior Producer" or a "Principal Designer" not because of time loyally served or routines impeccably followed, but because of special deftness in solving, identifying, or brokering new problems.

Years ago, fortunate and ambitious young people ascended career ladders with comfortable predictability. If they entered a core corporation, they began as, say, a second assistant vice president for marketing. After five years or so they rose to the rank of first assistant vice president, and thence onward and upward. Had they joined a law firm, consulting group, or investment bank, they would have started as an associate, after five to eight years ascended to junior partner, and thence to senior partner, managing partner, and finally heaven.

None of these predictable steps necessitated original thought. Indeed, a particularly creative imagination might even be hazardous to career development, especially if elicited questions of a subversive sort, like "Aren't we working on the wrong problem?" or "Why are we doing this?" or, most dangerous of all, "Why does this organization exist?" The safest career path was the surest career path, and the surest path was sufficiently well worn by previous travelers so that it could not be missed.

Of course, there still exist organizational backwaters in which career advancement is sequential and predictable. But fewer fortunate and ambitious young people dive into them, or even enter upon careers marked by well-worn paths. They dare not. In the emerging global economy, even the most impressive of positions in the most prestigious of organizations is vulnerable to worldwide competition if it entails easily replicated routines. The only true competitive advantage lies in skill solving, identifying, and brokering new problems.

[1]See Alba Edwards, *U.S. Census of Population, 1940: Comparative Occupation Statistics, 1870–1940* (Washington D.C.: U.S. Government Printing Office, 1943).

[2]Because much of the information about the American work force must be gleaned from the old categories, however, the only way to discover who fits into which new category is to decompose the government's data into the smallest subcategories in which they are collected, then reorder the subcategories according to which new functional group they appear to belong in. For a similar methodology, see Steven A, Sass, "The U.S. Professional Sector: 1950–1988," *New England Economic Review,* January–February 1990, pp. 37–55.

[3]For an illuminating discussion of routine jobs in a high-technology industry, see D. O'Connor, "Women Workers in the Changing International Division of Labor in Microelectronics," in L. Benerici and C. Stimpson (eds.), *Women, Households, and the Economy* (New Brunswick, N.J.: Rutgers University Press, 1987).

[4]On this point, see Arlie Russell Hochschild, *The Managed Heart: The Commercialization of Human Feeling* (Berkeley: University of California Press, 1983).

[5]U.S. Department of Commerce, Bureau of Labor Statistics, various issues.

[6]The physical environments in which symbolic analysts work are substantially different from those in which routine producers or in-person servers work. Symbolic analysts usually labor within spaces that are quiet and tastefully decorated. Soft lights, wall-to-wall carpeting, beige and puce colors are preferred. Such calm surroundings typically are encased within tall steel-and-glass buildings or within long, low, postmodernist structures carved into hillsides and encircled by expanses of well-manicured lawn.

[7]Sass's definition of "professional worker" overlaps significantly with my definition of symbolic analyst (although, as I will explain, not all symbolic analysts are professionals, and not all professionals are symbolic analysts). Sass finds that by 1988 professional workers comprised 20 percent of the American labor force. See Sass, op cit.

[8]In the remainder of this [article], when discussing symbolic analysts, I shall, on occasion, illustrate my point by referring to lawyers, management consultants, software engineers, and other professionals, but the reader should understand that this is a shorthand method of describing only the symbolic and analytic work undertaken by such professionals. ■

THE GENRE OF THE REFLECTIVE READING RESPONSE

Genres do not just develop out of the clear blue. Writers invent genres to accomplish purposes in specific situations. Writers invent genres because writing is absolutely necessary in some situations. The reflective reading response has emerged as a genre in the past several centuries as people from many walks of life sense the need to write about their thoughts, observations, and experiences *while their ideas are still fresh* so that they can get them down on paper and think about them at greater length. Many of the great thinkers in European and American culture wrote regularly in journals, reflecting on their reading, not only of printed texts but also of the world around them. The groundbreaking naturalist Charles Darwin wrote such responses in his journal in the nineteenth century. The famous novelist and essayist Joan Didion does so today.

As you prepare to write your reflective reading response for the Clarification Project, notice that this genre differs slightly, but importantly, from two similar ones, the personal diary entry and the scholar's notebook entry. A reflective reading response asks you, the thinker, to reflect on the subjects you are inquiring into and writing about. A reflective reading response is not exactly like a personal diary entry, in which you write about life's events and consider almost solely how they affect you personally and emotionally. A reflective reading response is not exactly like a scholar's notebook entry, in which you mostly write ideas, fact, figures, and observations as objectively as you can.

A reflective reading response, in fact, exists someplace between a scholar's notebook entry and a personal diary entry. As with a notebook, you record ideas, facts, and observations as objectively as you can in a reflective reading response. As with a diary, you ponder what these ideas, facts, and observations mean to you. The difference is that, in a reflective reading response, your reflections are primarily intellectual rather than personal or emotional, as they usually are in a diary. Writers of reflective reading responses do not discount personal or emotional reactions to their subjects, but they do compare and contrast their intellectual and their personal responses. In other words, writers of reflective responses do not simply feel or think about their subjects. They *feel* and *think* about the subject they are inquiring into.

Students frequently ask how long a reflective reading response should be. That's a difficult question, since with this genre you are essentially writing to yourself. In many classes, I encourage students to write reflective reading responses in their learning journals for twenty minutes a time, three times a week. Most students, in twenty minutes of concentrated writing, can produce one and a half to three pages of handwritten, double-spaced writing, or one to two pages of word-processed, double-spaced writing. Using these rough estimates as a guideline, you might expect the reflective reading response you write for the Clarification Project to run about four to six handwritten, double-spaced pages or three to five word-processed, double-spaced pages. But don't be too concerned about length. Wrap yourself around the ideas and the writing will usually come.

THREE TECHNIQUES FOR WRITING THE REFLECTIVE READING RESPONSE

Here, in brief, are the three techniques you can use to write a reflective response for the Clarification Project and for other writing-as-inquiry projects. As you read these descriptions, recall the special definitions of *read* and *text* explained in Chapter 4.

- You can read a text *affectively,* addressing the questions "How does this text make me feel? Why does it make me feel this way?"
- You can read a text *paraphrastically,* taking the organization of an entire text, portions of it, even individual paragraphs and sentences, as a pattern for your own thoughts and ideas.
- You can read a text *dialectically* by asking yourself what questions the text raises, looking for how the text answers those questions, and then considering how closely the text's answers match the way *you* would answer the questions on the basis of your own thinking and experience.

Think for a moment about how these may be new methods of reading for you. One way to look at the act of reading is to think of a text as something that has a "right" answer. This is not a productive attitude for completing the Clarification Project successfully. Do not think that literary works do not have themes or that works of nonfiction do not have main points. They usually do. Do not think, also, that anyone's interpretation of a work's theme or main point is as good as anybody else's. That's just not true. Simply realize that it is hard to succeed at clarifying your ideas on a subject unless you try to see *for yourself* what the theme or main point of a text is and unless you can make your interpretation of it as good as anybody else's by finding *within the work* evidence that supports your interpretation of the theme or main point.

If you learn to read affectively, paraphrastically, and dialectically, you come to *own* your own interpretation and analysis of a text. And by owning your own reading, you will be able to use it to clarify your thoughts and feelings.

READING AFFECTIVELY

One way to interact with any text is to read it affectively, letting your gut feelings come to the surface and then moving from these feelings to other kinds of responses.

When you read affectively, you may come to wonder, as I do occasionally, whether the word *feel* is overused. Consider the following scenarios:

- In a service club, you and your fellow members are debating how to spend the budget. One of the members says, "I feel we should give as much money as we can to the campus food pantry."
- In a political science class, you and your classmates are discussing the upcoming general election. One person says bluntly, "I feel that most people just haven't voted in recent elections because they're apathetic."
- Around the dinner table, you and your fellow diners are discussing the world news, and your friend says, "I feel a crisis is coming in Central Africa."
- In a group tutorial session, you and your study mates are preparing for a calculus exam by doing some sample problems. One of your study mates says confidently, "I feel that the answer to the first problem is 56."

Does *feel* mean the same thing in each scenario? Clearly not. In the first, your colleague might have been moved to feel compassion for the hungry people whom your campus food pantry helps, but clearly he is *proposing* that the club act on his feeling, one he hopes and the other members of the club share. In the second scenario, your classmate has probably seen statistics that in the last several general elections, fewer than half the eligible registered voters actually cast ballots. So your classmate really does not feel that most people don't vote because they are apathetic. She *thinks* that most people don't vote for that reason. In the third scenario, assuming that your friend has been keeping up with events in Central Africa, he probably does not feel a crisis is imminent. Instead, he *believes* that to be the case. In the fourth scenario, assuming that your study mate has been working the problems accurately, she probably does not feel the answer to the first problem is 56. Instead, she *knows* the answer is 56.

Pointing out the differences in these four verbs—*feel, think, believe,* and *know*—does not amount merely to nit-picking. As Chapter 4 explains, there are differences among what you know—that is, what you have relatively good evidence for; what you believe—that is, what you have some, but not all, confirming evidence for; what you think—that is, what you have a strong, informed hunch about; and what you feel—that is, what your emotions are saying to you about the text you are reading.

You may wonder whether it is a good idea to focus so strongly on your emotional reactions to your subject, considering that later on you may have to write about it in more detached, "intellectual" ways. After all, you may think, in college, shouldn't students be writing more about what they think, believe, and know than about what they feel? This is a good question and a legitimate concern. Most college writing should be thoughtful, confirming your beliefs and knowledge. But a major purpose of writing *affectively* is to clarify how you feel about your subject in order to prompt what you think, believe, and know. In other words, by writing about your feelings, you are allowing your thoughts, beliefs, and knowledge about your subject to emerge *in contrast* to your feelings.

For now, therefore, simply concede that an important first step in writing as inquiry is to allow yourself to *feel* as you read. As you reflect on a book, article, play, concert, conversation, interaction—whatever text you have read—ask yourself, "Does what this text says make me happy? Sad? Suspicious? Angry? Afraid? Apathetic? Bored? Enthusiastic? Lonely?" The list of emotions could go on and on. But no matter what you feel, ask yourself the most important question: *"Why do I feel the way I do?"* Don't just accept that your feelings need no explanation. To clarify your feelings on your subject, you need constantly to ask yourself, *"Why?"*

In the next several pages, you will encounter some reflective reading responses written by Jamie, a student in a college writing course. Jamie read "What We Expect: Preparing for College—A Statement by 12 Deans" and then wrote three reflective reading responses, each time using a different one of the three techniques.

Reread "What We Expect" and then read Jamie's reflective reading response based on reading affectively:

REFLECTIVE READING RESPONSE—READING AFFECTIVELY

1   I guess I feel a little bit nervous and embarrassed as I read this article. I am just in my first semester in college, and I have known all my life that I want to go to college, but there are some times that I wonder why I want to go. I know there are good jobs out there and you have to have a college diplomas to get one, but I know lots of people who had trouble finding a job after they graduated from college. I decided to major in architecture when I came here, but now I am thinking about changing my major to communications. But I'm kind of nervous about that. I wonder if changing your major slows you down and means that you have to go to college an extra year. These deans sound like they expect people to come to college with their minds completely made up and know why they came and what they want to do here. I am not so sure that I'm all that together. I'm pretty happy with how my high school prepared me for college,

though. All the subjects the deans talked about I'm pretty well prepared in, except for math. I really struggled through Algebra I and II, so I wonder whether I'm really ready for college calculus. I guess I'll find out next semester when I take it. I wonder why these deans wrote this. Do they get lots of people coming to their college who haven't had all these subjects? I read an article in U.S. Government last year about the high school as "cafeteria." The author said high school students have too much of a choice of what they take. I guess he would agree with these deans. It's a shame if some kid really wanted to go to a good college and didn't have someone to keep him from veering off into some crazy subject rather than taking the basics.

Jamie is honest about his feelings. He is nervous and embarrassed because he is sometimes uncertain about being in college. He is pleased with his high school preparation. He is sympathetic to students who do not get good guidance in preparing for college. But notice that Jamie generated some other things besides feelings by reading affectively. Jamie suggests that he *thinks* that changing majors might slow him down and cause him to spend an extra year in college. He even hints that he *believes* that many students who come to college are not well prepared because they have had too much choice in their high school courses. Even though Jamie wrote affectively for just twenty minutes, he generated two extremely challenging questions that he could pursue later, questions about things he might eventually like to *know:*

- In most people's college experience, does changing majors slow a person down considerably?
- How much choice in a course of study should students have in high school college preparatory programs?

Jamie's very successful affective reading was quite generative. It helped him consider not only what he feels but also what he thinks, believes, and *needs to know.*

If you choose to use *reading affectively* as the basis for your own reflective reading response, reread your composition carefully after you finish to see whether you can see similar questions, similar signposts pointing to what you might like to know about your subject, emerging in your own work.

READING PARAPHRASTICALLY

A second way to clarify your feelings, ideas, and beliefs about your subject is to read *paraphrastically*. This is a long, potentially frightening word. Don't be put off by it—it simply names a method you can use to put *yourself* into your reading of any text. The term *paraphrastically* comes from the verb *to paraphrase.* When you paraphrase a text, you rewrite its contents in your own words.

Some students may not feel comfortable paraphrasing a text because they think they are plagiarizing. They are not. You plagiarize in a critical paper or research report only when you paraphrase a text and fail to acknowledge, both in the body of the paper itself and in the Works Cited or References section, that you are doing so. So long as you properly acknowledge your work as a paraphrase of the original text, you are perfectly within the bounds of proper writing behavior. Indeed, writing concise paraphrases is one of the best things you can learn as you prepare to write critical papers and research reports.

Some instructors may not recommend paraphrasing, especially when a student writer casts part of a literary work—a novel, story, poem, or play—in his or her own words. Such instructors believe that the student writer is altering the artistry of the original text and, in essence, creating a new text in the process. These are both legitimate concerns. If any writer's output consisted solely of paraphrases of another writer's works, he could certainly be accused of being inartistic and unoriginal. But in this chapter, we are not concerned with paraphrasing a text in order to include the paraphrase in a larger work, such as a critical paper or research report. We are simply showing how paraphrasing can guide your writing of a reflective reading response that allows you to clarify your feelings and ideas as you read a text about your subject.

When you read paraphrastically to write a reflective reading response, operate in two stages. One stage produces a summary and the other a true paraphrase.

- First, when you have finished reading a text, select what you believe are its *most important* ideas and summarize them in about 100 words, or one substantial paragraph.
- Second, consider just a segment of the text that interests you and rewrite it, putting the ideas of the original text in your own words.

Here is Jamie's reflective reading response based on his paraphrastic reading of "What We Expect":

REFLECTIVE READING RESPONSE—READING PARAPHRASTICALLY, PART ONE

1   Summary: Twelve deans of college and universities recommend that students

who want to succeed in college should be curious, develop broad intellectual in-

terests, learn how to analyze and think critically, be value-oriented, and know how to work hard and manage their time. The deans recommend that high school students take a half or a whole year of arts courses, three or four years of a foreign language, two full years of history, enough math to prepare them to take college calculus, a full year each of biology, chemistry, and physics, and four full years of English, covering both literature and composition. They also say that participating in extra-curricular activities will help you succeed in college as well.

In Part Two, you might expect Jamie to paraphrase paragraph 9, the one in italics, since apparently the deans though this was their most important paragraph. Jamie, however, decided that paragraphs 6 and 7 seemed more important than 9, and he wrote this paraphrase:

REFLECTIVE READING RESPONSE—READING PARAPHRASTICALLY, PART TWO

1   Paraphrase of Paragraphs 6 and 7: Students who get the most out of college come with specific attitudes and skills. They are curious and good at analysis and critical thinking. They are willing to look at their values. They work hard and manage their time well. High school only does part of the job of developing these attitudes and skills, but high school courses could be designed to encourage them. Students should write papers in courses, because that allows them to think critically and analyze and interpret their reading. Students should do projects that require them to integrate and assess information, not just repeat back what they have memorized. Students should also be given deadlines that they have to meet so they can develop responsible work habits.

Jamie does a very good job of capturing the central ideas of "What We Expect" in his summary. For the purpose of clarifying his feelings, thoughts, and beliefs about the subject, however, the paraphrase is actually more helpful. Notice that in his paraphrase, Jamie raises two important questions about preparation for college:

- What exactly are "analysis and critical thinking skills," and how does your education improve them?
- How does your education help you consider your values?

Since it generated these questions, even Jamie's twenty-minute paraphrastic reading was a successful step in clarifying what he feels, thinks, believes, and needs to know about his subject. As Jamie did, if you decide to use the reading-paraphrastically technique to generate your own reflective reading response, look for ways to generate questions about your subject. You do not need to answer these questions now. Other papers in the Inquiry Contract will provide you the opportunity to do that.

READING DIALECTICALLY

A third method you can use to clarify your thoughts, beliefs, and ideas about your subject is to read *dialectically*. Again, this is a potentially frightening word, but don't let it turn you off. Though it has meant different things in various historical periods, in general the term *dialectic* refers to the ancient practice of coming to know a subject by asking a series of questions about it and by letting further questions develop in response to the earlier ones. Dialectic thus does not refer to repetitious questioning about the same point, like a young child who continually asks, "Why?" after each sentence he hears. Instead, dialectic refers to digging into a subject and clarifying one's way through it by asking a series of questions.

You need a careful method to read dialectically, and a good one was developed by Ann Berthoff, a wonderful person who taught for many years at the University of Massachusetts in Boston. In a book entitled *Forming/Thinking/Writing*, (Montclair, NJ; Boynton/Cook, 1982) she recommends that students keep a dialectical notebook when they read. In such a notebook, you simply draw a line down the middle of the page to form two columns. In the left column, you write notes about your reading: key points that you want to remember, central ideas, and so on. In the right column, you write notes to yourself in response to the "objective" notes in the left column. You write whether you agree or disagree, what else the note makes you think of, where this bit of information connects with another, and so on.

Though keeping a double-entry dialectical notebook is a rewarding way of clarifying your feelings, ideas, beliefs, and thoughts, I like to write reflective reading responses by extending Berthoff's concept by writing in a *triple-entry notebook*. In a triple-entry plan, you divide each page of your notebook into three columns. On the top of the left column, write QUESTION. On the top of the middle column, write TEXT'S ANSWER. On the top of the right column, write MY RESPONSE. As you read a text, then, stop as frequently as is sensible and ask yourself, "What *question* is the text posing to me right now?" Write this question in the left column. Then look back into the text and ask yourself, "How is the *text* answering this question?" Write that answer, in your own words, in the middle column. Now ask yourself the questions "How do *I* fit with this answer? How does this answer match up with *my own* experiences, my own personal ideas, attitudes, and beliefs?" Write your answers to these questions—perhaps in abbreviated note form—in the right column. This column, then, is the space for you really to make the reading your own, to claim its content in the realm of your own experiences and thoughts.

Here is Jamie's reflective reading response based on his dialectical reading of "What We Expect." He wrote eight entries for the reading. Obviously, he could have written more or fewer, but what he produced gives you a sense of what a student can accomplish by reading dialectically.

Question	Text's Answer	My Response
1. Paragraph 2: Why do some college students succeed and others don't?	The successful ones have better high school preparation.	Yeah, and someone had told them what to expect in college—longer, harder assignments.
2. Paragraph 3: What's wrong with the pluralism in American high schools?	It means that some students lack education in the basics.	It used to bug me that I had to take all hard college prep courses and my friends took gen ed courses and got off easier.
3. Paragraph 6: Which is more important—grades and scores or attitudes and skills?	Attitudes and skills—curiosity, critical thinking, value judgment, hard work, time management.	I agree—plus self-confidence and the ability to stick your neck out and take chances.
4. Paragraph 7: Can high schools do this alone?	No, but they can help instill the attitudes and skills.	Why don't these deans talk about the parents' responsibility?
5. Paragraph 9: What subjects are the basics?	Arts, foreign language, history, literature, math, and science.	What? No phys ed, sociology, or psychology? Why not?
6. Paragraph 10: Should colleges offer remedial courses?	No.	Hmm. I wonder what my pre-calculus refresher course really is?
7. Paragraph 13: What are English language skills?	Grammar and compositional skills.	Argh! I hate grammar drills, but I write okay.
8. Paragraph 15: What kinds of history should we know?	American and "Western."	Okay, but that ignores lots of Asian, African, Caribbean, etc.

FIGURE 5.1 Reflective reading response—Reading dialectically

Once again, Jamie's work is extremely valuable for clarifying not only what he already feels, thinks, believes, and knows about this domain but also what he *needs* to know about it. Notice a handful of questions that Jamie poses that he could take up later:

- Why are courses such as psychology and sociology not among the "basics" in these deans' views?
- What exactly are "remedial" classes? What would be the effect if colleges did not offer them?
- Are American and "Western" history the only kinds of history that students should know, or are they just the most important?

Any of these questions, or any of the questions generated by Jamie's reflective reading responses that emerged from his reading affectively or reading paraphrastically, represent queries that he could take up, points for further investigation in an Inquiry Contract about the aspect of the sample domain about the nature and purposes of higher education. Do the same thing yourself with your Clarification Project. Clarify what you already feel, think, believe, and know, but also generate questions to keep your inquiry going.

 ## In-Progress Task

You need to do this task three times, for about twenty minutes each, but I think you will find it an hour well spent. First, think about one course you are taking besides your writing course. Focus on a course that is really challenging you. Second, select the one technique from this chapter—reading affectively, reading paraphrastically, or reading dialectically—that you think works best for you. For one calendar week during the school year, use your preferred technique to write for twenty minutes a time for three times. Finally, read over what you write and ask yourself whether you feel better, worse, or the same about how you're doing in this challenging class.

6 Inquiry for Information

When you write about a challenging subject, you owe it to yourself to begin your inquiry by clarifying what you feel, think, believe, and know about it. But you soon discover that what *other people* feel, think, believe, and know about your subject is equally important. In fact, since the ultimate goal of your Inquiry Contract is to get some other reader or readers to think about your subject in a new way, you may find it finally more important to learn what other people feel, think, believe, and know about your subject than simply to state your own views on it. You will only be able to get people to accept your ideas, the fruits of your inquiry, if you can cast these ideas *in relation* to the feelings, thoughts, beliefs, and knowledge of the people with whom you want your writing to interact.

This chapter lays the groundwork for the Information Project, the third project in the Inquiry Contract. In the Information Project, which Chapter 7 sets out, you will do two things: You will find out what other people feel, think, believe, and know about your subject; and you will describe what you learn in an informative report that is accurate, exact, innovative, and comprehensive in its coverage.

Note an important distinction here: There is a difference between learning something about your subject and developing what you have learned into an informative report about it. The world is a blooming, buzzing arena of ideas and experiences, and writers must toss themselves into it to learn new facts, theories, and ideas. As they operate within this world of ideas and experiences, writers are not necessarily developing informative reports. They are acquiring ideas and experiences—they are *learning*—but the process of developing an informative report involves an active, conscious effort to *shape* these ideas and experiences into a package that readers can understand. In a sense, then, writers *create* the information they convey by manipulating it or trimming it to fit the package they create. Raw data—ideas and experiences unaltered by a strong, guiding writer—are difficult for readers to process. Writers must create a package of information that will lead the readers through the world of ideas and experiences.

Chapter 7 will explain in detail how to write an informative report, the main genre used in this part of the Inquiry Contract. But before moving to the genre, let's consider what is involved when writers must learn something about their subject and develop what they learn into a package of information for readers. In this chapter, let's consider three criteria you can use to help structure your gathering of information, and let's think about what options you have for finding out what other people feel, think, believe, and know about your subject.

THREE CRITERIA FOR ACQUIRING NEW KNOWLEDGE

Why should you want to learn something new about your subject? Why shouldn't you simply write all your compositions about what you already know? Because writing is hard work, writers often want to write only about subjects they already know lots about, thinking that choosing a familiar subject will make their task easier. It might. But when writers say they want to write about something they know lots about, they might also ask themselves, "Am I sure that easy writing is likely to be both good writing and writing that is good for me?"

I believe that writing is finally *better for the reader*—more lively and engaging—and *better for the writer*—more committed—when the writer writes about *new* knowledge acquired in the course of a writing-as-inquiry project. As you work to learn new knowledge that strikes you as lively, something you can feel committed to writing about, you can use three criteria to guide your search:

- "Factness," or the degree to which the material you learn can stand up to the scrutiny of careful questioning
- Comprehensiveness, or the degree to which the material you learn addresses most of the questions that educated, curious people would have about your subject
- "Surprise" value, or the degree to which the material you learn is genuinely new and engaging to inquisitive readers

Let's examine each of the criteria separately.

"FACTNESS"

We need to make up a new term, *factness,* to describe the first criterion. When you acquire new knowledge, you do not need to be certain that every bit of it is a "fact," something that can be completely verified by observation or experimentation. Of course, nothing is wrong with learning facts, and for some subjects you might write about, the more of them you have the better. But for many subjects, the most lively material you can learn consists of people's *ideas* about the subject, ideas that come from these people's experiences, observations, reading, writing, and conversations on the subject.

For instance, if you are inquiring into the aspect of the sample domain about the nature and purposes of a college education, you might want to learn some facts about, say, the different kinds of graduation requirements in addition to one's major courses at a small, private liberal arts college versus those at a large state university. Or, to take another example, you could learn some facts about the percentage of graduates of liberal arts programs who get accepted to medical schools versus the percentage of graduates of premed programs who get accepted. You could learn the first kind of facts simply by reading the college's and the university's catalogues, and you could learn the second by writing to the American Medical Association.

Such facts, data that you can verify empirically, often play an important role in an inquiry. By learning them, you would be finding out what other people *know* that you didn't know previously. But you could also try to learn what other people feel, think, and believe about issues concerning your subject. You could talk to faculty and students at a liberal arts college and a large university and ask them how they feel and what they think about the graduation requirements in addition to major courses. You could interview two successful doctors, one who earned a bachelor's degree in a liberal arts field before going to med school and another who went through a specific premed curriculum prior to med school. You could ask them to tell you how they feel and what they think about their undergraduate preparation. What they tell you may not consist of empirically verifiable facts, but it will have an air of *factness* about it: it will be information that they are deeply committed to, because it is grounded in their own experiences and observations.

As you inquire into your subject, allow yourself the luxury of learning both facts and information laden with factness. Don't neglect opportunities to learn facts, but rather than pledging that everything you learn about your subject must be a fact, work instead to apply the scrutiny of *factness* to the knowledge you acquire. Constantly ask yourself these questions about new knowledge:

- What is the source of the knowledge? Is the source reliable? How so?
- Is the source qualified to make informed observations? How so?
- Is the knowledge I acquire from this source consistent with that from other sources? To what degree?

Whether you learn new information about your subject by reading, talking to people, or engaging in some experience, ask yourself these questions about what you learn. If you are satisfied that what you learn is plausible and comes from a reliable source that is qualified to provide it, what you have learned has the quality of *factness*.

 In-Progress Task

Reread your Contract Proposal, noting any changes you want to make in its three sections: why the subject is important to you, what you know about it already, and what questions you need to ask about it. Choose *one* of these questions, and write brief responses in your learning journal to the following:

- Whom could I talk to who could provide me with information that has *factness* about this question?
- What could I read that would provide me with information that has *factness* about this question?
- What else could I do besides talk to people and read to acquire information that has *factness* about this question?

COMPREHENSIVENESS

The second criterion to use when learning what other people feel, think, believe, and know about your subject requires you to take a *comprehensive* view of it. If you have chosen to write about an aspect of this book's sample domain, you are beginning to realize that its aspects are immense in scope, so multifaceted that one could write dozens of books about them. The same thing is probably true of your domain, if you have chosen your own subject to inquire into.

Don't be put off by the potential scope of your subject. As you gather information, you should not expect that you will be able to learn everything there is to know about the subject or to inform your readers about every single aspect of it. But you should try to be comprehensive in searching for new information. What this means is that you must regularly ask yourself these questions:

- When curious, educated people consider my subject—when they hear about it in conversations, read about it, or encounter it in the media—what *questions* naturally come to their minds about it? What exactly do "inquiring minds" want to know about it?
- What are the most important *issues*, both for me personally and for the public at large, concerning this subject?

■ How can I learn *at least something* about one or more of these questions that is worth sharing with interested readers?

Taking a comprehensive view of your subject, in short, requires you to balance public and private curiosity, to ask both "What does the educated public want to know?" and "What do I want to know?"

Consider, for example, the aspect of the sample domain that deals with the ways education and work are related. In the past, when the general public considered this relationship, most people probably thought that if you got a good education—a bachelor's degree from a decent college or university—you would be certain to get a good job right out of college, a job that you could keep for the remainder of your working life until you retire. Within the past decade or so, however, the nature of the economy has changed in ways that make this assumption questionable. Therefore, most thoughtful people would probably be curious about a question like this:

> What is the average amount of time it takes college graduates in their early twenties who have finished their bachelor's degree in four years to find a job that they are satisfied with?

In addition, most intelligent people who think about this subject are probably interested in this question:

> Often students experience a tension between majoring in a field that seems to hold good job prospects versus majoring in a field that genuinely interests them and challenges them intellectually. What is the best way to deal with this conflict-laden situation?

These are only two questions, of course, and using them to guide an inquiry for new information about this subject would by no means amount to an exhaustive strategy. But they do represent the *kinds* of questions that are generally on the minds of curious, educated people who think about this subject. Thus, they are the kinds of questions that you should consider asking in your own inquiry. They are, moreover, questions that you can learn something about—their answers have a potential for *factness*. Answers to the first question are probably available in the government documents section of your institution's library. Responses to the second question could be generated by interviewing students near the end of their undergraduate years at your college or university.

Concerning comprehensiveness, here is the bottom line: When you inquire into a subject, you can certainly pose questions that are particularly interesting to you, but you need to balance your own personal curiosity with what other people are inquisitive about as well.

In-Progress Task

In your learning journal, write two challenging (relatively difficult-to-answer) questions about the subject you are inquiring into. For one of these, write what you believe is the most important question that comes to *other people's* minds when they think about your subject. For the other, write the most important question that comes to *your* mind when you think about your subject. If your own personal question is the same as the one you attribute to other people, think of a new question for yourself. Show your questions to someone else—your instructor, a member of your writing-as-inquiry group, a classmate or friend—and discuss how you might go about getting answers to these questions that demonstrate *factness*.

SURPRISE VALUE

The third criterion to use when looking for new knowledge about your subject is, I think, the most important. The knowledge you acquire should have some *surprise value*, for both you and your readers. It should tell your readers something they do not already know.

Some writers seem to find comfort in a kind of learning that amounts to cataloguing what they already know. They come across familiar facts, ideas, and concepts about their subject, and they believe that this information is all they, or their readers, really need to know. Such a cautious approach is not productive for writers who really want to inquire deeply into their subject. As you acquire new knowledge, you need to be continuously on the lookout for information—facts or laden with *factness*—that surprises you. You need to search for stuff about which you can honestly say, "Wow, I didn't know that!" Chances are if you didn't know it, your readers don't either. Readers generally do not need to be told things they already know. Like you, they relish new information, new insights, new perspectives.

For example, consider again the aspect of the sample domain about the relationship between education and work. When I first started looking into this subject several years ago, I came across some research about the number of jobs a person who earns a bachelor's degree now can expect to hold before he or she retires at age seventy. Most of these studies predict that the average college graduate in the early twenty-first century will change jobs four or five times during his or her working life. I can remember being surprised by that prediction, being moved to utter, "Wow, I didn't know that!" If, as I did, you think about your college education as preparing you for a job, you might be surprised to find out that you really need to be prepared not to do just one job but instead to know how to switch jobs and learn about new ones effectively and efficiently.

The liveliness, the intellectual excitement you feel when you learn something genuinely interesting, new, and surprising is infectious. Your reader will feel it too when you write about it. Keep your eyes open for it as you gather information about your subject.

 In-Progress Task

Reread your revised Contract Proposal, and pay particular attention to the second part of it, where you explain two things you already know about your subject. Show those two things to someone—your instructor, a member of your writing-as-inquiry group, a classmate, or a friend. Ask the person to answer this question honestly: "Is either of these statements new and surprising to me?" If either is, ask the person to explain to you *why* he or she finds it so. If neither is, ask the person to suggest to you the types of information about your subject that he or she might find new and surprising.

METHODS OF ACQUIRING KNOWLEDGE: A REVIEW AND A CRITIQUE

Now that you know about three criteria to guide your search for information about your subject, you might be asking the sensible question "I know what kinds of things to look for; now how do I find them?"

At the risk of oversimplifying, let me suggest that there are finally only three ways of acquiring new knowledge, of learning something in order to shape it into an informative report:

- You can have an *experience*—or perhaps a set of experiences— involving your subject. Some experiences are planned, and some simply happen. Some, such as experiments, take place in college classrooms or laboratories, and some, such as field trips, take you away from your college or university. Experience is a grand teacher.
- You can *read* some texts—and, again, remember the broad definitions of *read* and *text* from Chapter 4. Books, articles, and chapters

are texts, but so are questionnaires, concerts, lectures, public forums, and so on.

■ You can *converse* with someone who has had significant experiences with your subject or read significant texts about it or both.

Let's consider each of these methods.

Having direct, engaging experiences with a subject is undoubtedly one of the best ways to acquire knowledge about it. When you have the opportunity to go someplace, do something, engage in an activity involving your subject, you can develop an informative report by writing about your observations, your activities, your direct conclusions about the experience.

If you are inquiring into any of the aspects of the sample domain, there are abundant experiences you could have that would help you acquire new information. The very act of going to college is, of course, an experience that teaches you about the nature and purposes of higher education. But you can supplement that experience by attending lectures, discussions, or public forums where the goals and missions of your institution are discussed. Such events are almost always announced in the campus newspaper. You can also gain valuable, informative experiences with this subject by taking advantage of any tutorial services your institution offers and, if you are so inclined, working as a peer tutor in one of them.

If you are inquiring into the aspect of the sample domain that looks at the relationship between education and work, you can also have useful, instructional experiences. You can visit your school's career placement center. You can attend job fairs and mock interviews, even if you are not planning to graduate soon. If it is feasible, you can work in an internship or cooperative education program, which gives you some on-the-job experience for course credit. Ask your instructor whether your institution has such programs.

Unfortunately, it is not always possible for writers to experience their subjects directly. When I was in college, for example, a classmate wrote a long, critical paper about scientific expeditions to the South Pole. I am sure he would have liked actually to go the South Pole, but that trip was impossible. His paper was quite good, though, because he learned about his subject by reading extensively about the expeditions and talking to people who had been on one.

As Chapters 4 and 5 make clear, it is extremely important for writers to read the world around them actively—to *own* their readings by asking incisive questions and to broaden their notions of relevant texts not only by reading books and articles but also by "reading" lectures, concerts, public forums, and exhibitions that illuminate some aspect of their subject. Careful reading plays an important role in your Inquiry Contract and, indeed, in almost all of your important intellectual projects in school and beyond. When you read to gain new information about your subject, read widely and interactively, using the techniques of writing about your reading described in Chapter 5.

In addition to reading widely and interactively, you should read critically, taking special care not to believe something simply because someone put it in writing and published it. A wonderful teacher at Texas A & M University in Commerce, Richard Fulkerson, offers a convenient system for evaluating information you garner through reading. Fulkerson labels his system with the acronym STAR—for *substantiality, typicality, accuracy,* and *relevance.* Here are four questions that Fulkerson's system leads you to ask about any information you learn from reading:

- Is the material substantial—that is, is there enough of it for you to consider it a significant contribution to your inquiry?
- Is the material typical—that is, is it generally similar to the kinds of information you expect to find as you proceed through your writing-as-inquiry project?
- Is the material accurate—that is, does the author present the material in a way so that the facts seem correct and the conclusions supportable?
- Is the material relevant—that is, how closely does it pertain to the subject you are inquiring into?

As you work on your Inquiry Contract, you may have ample opportunities to find material to read on a feature of the Internet called the World Wide Web, a vast array of information sites on thousands of subjects. If so, you may find the Web to be an extremely useful resource, but you should be aware of two potential drawbacks to using it. First, the search engines that you may use to find information on the Web—such as Yahoo!, Infoseek, Lycos, Alta Vista, and others—are completely indiscriminant. Searching for information using them may turn up hundreds of sites that seem relevant to your inquiry but actually are not. Second, unlike books and articles that one usually finds in an academic library, the information on the Web is generally not screened or refereed by any organization or scholarly body. In other words, while the information in most books and articles has had to pass somebody's scrutiny before it was published, any information can be posted on a World Wide Web site, so what you find there may not be trustworthy. In general, when you find information on the Web, ask about it the same questions you would ask about any other—questions about its *factness,* comprehensiveness, and surprise value, as well as about it substantiality, typicality, accuracy, and relevance. Look for evidence that some smart, careful people have screened the information before it gets "posted" on the Web.

Though reading carefully is, no doubt, at the center of most college and university inquiry projects, I occasionally wonder whether some writers think that reading is the *only* way they can learn about a subject they are inquiring into. Too often, I fear, writers faced with challenging subjects to learn about head directly for the library catalogue or periodical indexes, find books or articles that may be relevant, and randomly dive into them. Perhaps reading books and articles, especially if they are not selected carefully, is not the best way to *begin* acquiring new information about a subject. An excellent learning technique to use—*before* you begin looking for texts to read, *while* you are actively reading, or *after* you have done so—is to have an actual conversation with someone who has had significant experiences, or has read widely, about your subject.

Academic life relies so heavily on the knowledge one finds in books and articles that the art of careful conversation is often overlooked as a method for acquiring knowledge. But careful conversation, in its own right, is extremely valuable for inquiring writers, and it is also a useful guide and partner to active, questioning reading. That is, having a careful, planned conversation with someone not only can teach you valuable information but also help you discover what you ought to read or do to acquire new information about your subject.

Here, then, is an overview of the three methods of acquiring information:

- When you can *do* something to learn about your subject, why not give it a try?
- When you choose to *read* something about your subject, do so critically and interactively, making your reading your own by writing about it as you read.
- Don't overlook the opportunity to *converse* and *discuss* your subject in a planned, careful manner with people whose ideas and experiences give them insights on your subject that might hold surprise value for you and your readers.

 ## In-Progress Task

Conducting a careful conversation brings you into contact with an exciting kind of knowledge gathering known as *oral history*. When we hear the word *history*, we tend to think of written documents, such as treaties and declarations, and books and articles that tell stories of wars, governments, and important social and political events. But for something to qualify as history does not mean that it must be found only in books and articles or that it be about grand, earth-shaking events. History consists of people's *lived experiences,* and even "ordinary" people have lived their lives in such a way as to accumulate significant insights on a wide variety of subjects. When writers get these people to talk about their ideas, observations, and experiences, the writers tap into the oral history that these people offer.

Two excellent examples demonstrate what a rich resource oral history is for writers. First, in the late 1960s, Eliot Wigginton, a high school English teacher, and his pupils in Rabun Gap, Georgia, began the *Foxfire* project. In *Foxfire,* the students as part of their writing course interview family members, friends, and well-known people in that part of rural Appalachia where they live. The students inquire into local history, getting people to describe what "ordinary" life in the region was like in past generations. The students investigate folk culture, asking people to explain how they do such things as make apple butter, cure a snake bite, and dig a well. Tapping into this abundant vein of oral history, Wigginton's students have written several books and issues of magazines on the region's history and culture. Second, Studs Terkel, a Chicago lawyer, social activist, and radio commentator, has gained fame by getting people to talk to him and then writing books about the conversations. In his book *Working,* for example, Terkel's interviewees describe what they do for a living and how they feel about their work. In *The Good War,* he entices people to talk about what they did in World War II and how they responded to the changes the war wrought on their lives. In *Hard Times,* he gets a wide range of people to talk about what they did during the Great Depression that plagued the United States (and the rest of the world) from 1929 through the early 1940s.

Here are two excerpts from the work of Wigginton's pupils and Terkel. To produce the first, the students in the Foxfire class interviewed men who lived near Rabun Gap about how to cure wood and what kinds of wood were best for various uses. To generate the second, Terkel interviewed Justin McCarthy about working in a Ford Motor Company plant near Chicago in 1933 while he was attending night school at nearby Northwestern University.

To "prime the pump" for the Information Project, introduced in the next chapter, read these two excerpts. Then, focusing on whichever one you like better, write a substantial paragraph in response to each of the following questions in your learning journal:

- To what extent is the information in this excerpt illustrative of *factness?* Explain.
- To what extent is the coverage in this excerpt comprehensive? Explain.
- To what extent does this information hold surprise value for you? Explain.

Show your answers to someone else who has read the same excerpt and discuss them.

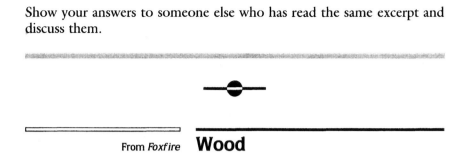

From *Foxfire* **Wood**

The fact that an area's natural resources are the most vital factor in determining the way of life of a self-sufficient people may seem too obvious to need mention. However, the role that wood played in the settling of the Southern Appalachians cannot be overemphasized. Whereas wood is now often a luxury, it was an absolute necessity here for centuries. It provided shelter for people and animals, fire for warmth and cooking, materials for wagons, tools, furniture, household utensils, toys, decorative objects, and a thousand other things. The trees themselves provided fruit, nuts, syrup, and the ingredients for many home remedies, and even gave clues as to what the weather would be in the coming months. The lives of the mountain people would necessarily have been drastically altered without this versatile, readily available resource.

The wood itself was used either green or seasoned, depending not so much on what kind of wood it was as on what it was to be used for. Pieces that had to fit tight and stay tight—the handles of tools, for example—had to be seasoned or else the wood would shrink and pull away as it dried. Items such as pegs, wheel spokes, fine furniture, buckets, and barrels had to be made of seasoned wood or they'd fall apart. For rafters, fence posts and rails, · shingles, rough furniture, and so on, the parts did not have to fit so tightly together to remain serviceable, so they could be constructed of green stock.

There are several ways to cure wood. The method chosen depended on the size of the pieces, and how quickly they were needed. Very small pieces which would fit into a pot were boiled. "Sometimes we boiled them all day and overnight, and they was cured good," says Harry Brown. The water would draw the sap out, and when the water itself evaporated, the wood would be ready to use. People also dried smaller pieces by the fire overnight, being careful that they didn't get too hot and warp or burn. They would often use this method to season tool handles, drying only the end that fit into the head of the tool.

Another way to cure lumber is to use a dry kiln. A large rack would be built three to four feet off the ground and covered with a roof—and sometimes walls—to keep out the rain. The lumber would be stacked cross-wise on the rack for maximum air circulation, and under the lumber several small fires would be built. A similar way, according to Harry Brown, was to "make a little rack and stack your lumber around it just like a teepee. Y'leave a space at th'bottom so's y'can get in, and build little fires under that. Sometimes people'd dry'em that way a week." In both methods the fires had to be tended constantly to make sure they didn't go out or get so large they'd warp or set the lumber on fire.

The simplest method of all was to stack the lumber crosswise and just leave it alone until it was needed. Small straight pieces such as tool handles and parts for furniture could be bundled together so they wouldn't warp, and set in a dry place. The problem was that it could take months for the wood to be properly cured, but for many, that made little difference.

"Back whenever they was puttin' up buildings," says Millard Buchanan, "they didn't cure nothin' only just what they could. See, they got t'cuttin' and fixin' t'put up a buildin', and it'd maybe take'em six or eight months t'get it hewed out, and sometimes they'd just pile it up. And then they'd go t'work on th'buildin' and cut it and lay it down. By th'time they got it done, th'wood had either cured a'layin' about or while they was buildin' with it. Why, it'd have all th'sun and air on it and it'd be dry. They didn't pay no 'tention to th'cracks bein' there nohow." ∎

Studs Terkel **Preface to the Battle of Detroit**

Justin McCarthy quit college in 1933. He was working at a Ford assembly plant in an industrial suburb, near Chicago.

"I sandpapered all the right hand fenders. I was paid about $5 a day. The parts were brought in from the River Rouge plant in Detroit. When I went to work in January, we were turning out 232 cars a day. When I was fired, four months later, we were turning out 535. Without any extra help and no increase in pay. It was the famous Ford Speed-up.

"The gates were locked when you came in at eight o'clock in the morning. They weren't opened again until five o'clock in the evening. People brought their own lunch. No commissary wagons were permitted on the grounds. Nobody bothered to tell me. So I didn't eat that first day. You were supposed to buy your own gloves. Nobody bothered to tell me that, either. Imagine my hands at five o'clock that first day.

"I was aware of men in plain clothes being around the plant, and the constant surveillance. I didn't learn till later that these were the men of Ford's service department. Many of them, ex-cons.

"If you wanted to go to the toilet, you had to have the permission of the foreman. He had to find a substitute for you on the assembly line, who could sandpaper those two right fenders as they went by. If he couldn't right away, you held it. (Laughs)

"If you didn't punch that clock at 8:00, if you came in at 8:02, you were docked one hour's pay. There wasn't any excuse. If you did this two or three times, you got fired.

"I made the mistake of telling the foreman I had enrolled at North-western University night school. He said, 'Mr. Ford isn't paying people to go to college. You're through.' "   ∎

7 The Information Project, the Informative Report, and the Art of Careful Conversation

In the Clarification Project, you devoted a good bit of time and energy to writing to yourself. The primary purpose of that project was for you to clarify for yourself what you feel, think, believe, and know about your subject as you begin a serious inquiry into it.

Now that you have done some clarifying for yourself, it's time to learn something new about your subject, something that will be interesting both to you and to other people. As Chapter 6 made clear, there are many ways to learn something new about a subject. You can read books or articles, see films or television programs, or have experiences involving it. In this chapter, let's concentrate on learning something new by having *careful conversations* with other people about our subjects. Understanding the art of careful conversation will help you see that the liveliest, most engaging information about a subject often emerges when you have the chance to interact with other people.

In the Information Project, which this chapter introduces, the focus of your inquiry shifts from yourself as the primary reader to *other people* as your readers, the people with whom you want your writing to interact. Look back over the three criteria for new knowledge explained in Chapter 6. Clearly, *factness,* comprehensiveness, and surprise value are "other people oriented." That is, when you acquire new knowledge and develop it into an informative report, you generate facts, ideas, and perspectives that seem reasonable and well documented to other people. You try to address most of the important issues that come to other people's minds when they think about your subject. You work to find material about which other people can say, "Wow, I didn't know that!"

Your aim in this chapter will be to accomplish all three of these goals. In your work with the Information Project, the third major stage in the Inquiry Contract, you will learn about a genre called the informative report. You will examine a student writer's informative report and learn about the processes she followed to generate her paper.

Before proceeding, however, we need to consider two ideas that will help you understand more about writing to convey information, both in your Inquiry Contract and in other classes. First, you may have noticed in the Clarification Project that the process of writing a reflective journal entry was a bit messy—you might have had lots of material scratched out and lots of notes to yourself in the margins as you drafted your work. As you move to the Information Project, don't think that just because you are trying to shape a piece of writing that has *factness,* comprehensiveness, and surprise value for other people that the messiness will disappear in your drafts. In the Clarification Project, you might have deleted and altered material, and you may have written (or at least thought), "Do I really feel [or think or believe or know] that?" In the Information Project, you will probably feel compelled to delete and alter material, and you may write (or think) to yourself, "Do *other people* really consider this material filled with *factness,* comprehensive, and surprising?" No matter whether you are writing primarily to yourself or to other people, you will probably talk to yourself a good bit while you are writing, and this talk is more productive if you *write it down* on paper or diskette.

Second, I think you will be astonished by how much you actually learn about your subject as you generate and develop information about it for other readers. By shaping and delivering information to others, you are motivated to justify for yourself that your data, ideas, and perspectives qualify as having *factness,* comprehensiveness, and surprise value—that is, that your material seems well documented and reasonable, that it addresses the most pressing questions about your subject, and that it is "news." Writing to inform others is one of the best methods of writing to learn for yourself.

Now, on to the project at hand:

The Information Project

First, reread your Contract Proposal and make any changes that you think are necessary, now that you have finished the Clarification Project. Pay particular attention to the part of the proposal where you describe what you would still like to learn about your subject. The Information Project represents an opportunity to learn at least part of it.

For the Information Project, you will plan and conduct an interview, a careful conversation, with someone who has unique experience, insights, or perspectives involving your subject. You need not interview a person who is an expert on your subject, although if you can find such a person, that would be good. But an expert may be hard to find. Identify a person who has thought seriously about the central issues concerning your subject, those issues that come to mind when you consider the criterion of comprehensiveness explained in Chapter 6.

After conducting the interview, write a report informing a group of curious, concerned, interested readers of what you learned in it.

The rest of this chapter will explain how to envision those readers and their importance to you, how to plan and conduct the interview, and how to organize your informative report.

CREATING A READER FOR THE INFORMATIVE REPORT

Do you remember the old "philosophical" question "If a tree falls in the forest and there's no one there to hear it, is there any noise?" Well, here's a writer's version of a similar question: If you put some words on a page or a screen, and there's no one there to read it, have you really written anything? The answer is clearly yes, you have written something, because *you* read the words you have written *yourself*. But there is another way to look at this question. You could answer, "No, if no one besides me really *reads* my words, then I haven't *really* written." Most of the writing you do in college and beyond is, of course, *really* writing because someone does actually read it. One of the most valuable things you can learn to do as a writer is to envision, to *create* mentally, the person (or persons) who ideally read your work.

Think for a minute about five different writing situations:

- In the first, you write a list of items that you need to buy at the bookstore.
- In the second, you write a reflective reading response, such as the one you wrote for the Clarification Project.
- In the third, you write a letter and send it, either by e-mail or snail mail, to a friend you know well.
- In the fourth, you write an opinion column and submit it to your local newspaper, to run on the page opposite the editorial page.
- In the fifth, you write a research paper for your history class.

In each of these situations, who is the reader and what role does the reader play?

- In the first, you are the sole reader. You jot down a list of items as you think of them and then check them off as you find each item at the bookstore.
- In the second, you are the primary reader. You write what you feel, think, believe, and know about a subject, and then you read your

entry carefully, asking yourself, "Do I really feel, think, believe, and know that?" It is possible, however, that someone else might read your reflective reading response, usually not to evaluate the writing but more often simply to learn what you feel, think, believe, and know about a subject so that this person can have good, intelligent conversations with you.

- In the third, your friend, the recipient of the letter, is the reader. As you write the letter, you can envision him or her reading it and processing the material it contains. You can probably even predict your reader's reactions to the letter's contents, and you may write things in the letter—exclamation points, emoticons, question marks, symbols, and drawings—showing that you know how he or she is responding.

- In the fourth, depending on which newspaper you submit your opinion column to, you may know a little or a lot about the readers. You may know approximately how many people subscribe to the paper. You may see people reading it in public places—in restaurants, parks, or on buses or trains. But you cannot know for sure who your readers are and how they will respond to what you write. You must try to imagine real people reading your column and, if you want to be effective, attempt to write it in a way that they will respond enthusiastically and positively.

- In the fifth, you know that your history instructor is your primary reader. He or she will probably write some comments in the margins or at the end of the paper and give you a grade on it. But your history instructor does not read your paper as an isolated individual, a "loner" or an outcast in his or her field. Instead, he or she reads your paper as a historian, as a representative reader for all the people who study and teach history as a profession. Thus, when you write the paper, you need to envision not only your instructor as reader but also a *forum* of history scholars as readers, and you must try to write in a way they would find effective and appropriate.

Notice that most of the writing you have to do in college and beyond is more like the fourth and fifth scenarios than the first three. That is, some writing situations—a shopping list, a journal entry, a person-to-person letter—have a definite reader specified within them. But other writing situations do not hold such a reader. Most writing situations in college and in jobs require you to *create* a reader—to cast someone mentally in this role—and then to envision, as specifically as you can, how he or she is responding to your writing as he or she reads each sentence, each paragraph, the whole composition. The writing you will do for the Information Project (and the two projects that follow it in later chapters) are like this. In these situations, your writing is stimulated, motivated by the *imagined presence* of *created* readers—you envision them *while you are writing*. Thus, you can answer the writer's version of the old philosophical question in this way: You really are writing, because you know someone else besides you will read your words—this someone, this *created reader*—even if you are not exactly sure who this person is.

As you mentally create a reader who will respond to your writing, think about the characteristics you envision this person to have, and then try to put them into a real person. Do with your created reader what you did with the friend who read your letter in the third situation earlier. That is, try to anticipate how he or she will react to the contents of your composition.

It is very important to begin now creating a reader whose imagined presence will guide your work on the Information Project. Think concretely. Try to envision a specific person who has these characteristics:

- He or she is curious, in the very best sense of that word, about many things. He or she reads widely and carefully.
- He or she is modest. That is, he or she does not try to show off how much he or she knows. In fact, this created reader does not really think he or she knows all that much. This reader simply wants to know more.
- He or she is encouraging to you. If you could imagine talking to this person, he or she would make you feel intelligent, make you feel as though you had acquired some information, ideas, and perspectives that would really be valuable to share with others.
- He or she writes a lot, especially in the margins of magazines or books and probably in a learning journal.

 ## In-Progress Task

In your learning journal or some other location, write to yourself about *specific, real people* you know who have these characteristics. You may not be able to locate these traits in one person. That's okay. It's rare to fine a person who is curious, well read, modest, encouraging, and who writes regularly. But try to call up from your memory at least one real person for each of the characteristics. Write the person's name and what *exactly* he or she does that illustrates the characteristic. Then, imagine constructing one person by combining the several people about whom you have written. Consider this imaginary one person to be your created reader. Try to make him or her come alive for you mentally.

PLANNING AND CONDUCTING YOUR INTERVIEW

In the Information Project, your primary goal in conducting an interview is to generate information—that is, facts, ideas, and perspectives that seem full of *factness*, comprehensive, and surprising to your created reader. As you work on this project, bear in mind one vital fact about interviews: they are *not* passive events for you, the interviewer. An engaging piece of informative writing rarely emerges from an interview in which all the interviewer does is ask questions and let the interviewee spout off. Instead, good informative writing emerges from interviews in which the interviewer does some background study about the interviewee, plans questions carefully, and, most important, *interacts* with the interviewee with follow-up questions during the interview. In other words, think of an interview as a careful conversation between you and the interviewee, rather than just as a chance for the interviewee to perform for you.

For such events to be generative—if you hope they produce lots of information that is laden with *factness* and surprising to your reader— you have to plan them carefully. Here is advice on planning and conducting an interview in three stages: what to do before, during, and after the interview.

BEFORE THE INTERVIEW

The most important thing to do beforehand, of course, is to find someone appropriate to interview. This task is not as difficult as it may sound. You need not find the world's most eminent expert on your subject. You simply need to identify someone who has had some interesting experience with your subject or who has some keen insights about it.

For example, if you are inquiring into the aspect of the sample domain about the nature and purposes of higher education, you could interview a dean at your institution, or one of your instructors, or your academic adviser. Alternatively, you could interview someone who has been a student at your college or university for a year or more and who seems to have a clear idea about why he or she went to college, chose your particular institution to attend, and continues to study there. You could even interview members of your own class or writing group about their perceptions of what college is all about and what a college education is good for.

If you are inquiring into the aspect of the sample domain about the relationship between education and work, you could interview someone who is currently working in a field you would like to work in someday. You could interview a career counselor. You could interview someone who has changed jobs frequently or regularly.

After identifying someone to interview, get in touch with the person, secure his or her permission to talk with you, and set up the day, time, and place you will meet. Then do as much homework as you can about your interviewee. If the person has a résumé or a *curriculum vitae* available, ask for a copy. If the person has written something, even if it is not directly about the subject of your inquiry, read it. This advice holds even if you are interviewing another student. Ask to see a copy of a successful paper he or she has written recently. If anything has been written about your interviewee, read it. Doing this homework will help you prepare your questions for the interview, and your interviewee will be more willing to talk with you seriously and in detail if you convince him or her that you have some effort invested in the conversation.

In-Progress Task

If you know whom you intend to interview, write that person's name in your learning journal or some other location. Then write a substantial paragraph to yourself about why this person is a good person to interview for your inquiry project. If you don't know for sure whom you intend to interview, write the names of three potential interviewees, and then, for each, write one sentence about why he or she would be good to interview and one sentence about any problems you think you might encounter interviewing this person. Discuss your potential interviewees with your instructor or member of your writing-as-inquiry group, and try to decide which one you will interview.

After selecting the person to interview and doing as much homework as you can, now start to write the questions you intend to ask at the interview. Here is where two important concepts that you have learned about recently come into play: the idea of the *created reader* and the principle of *comprehensiveness*. Envision your created reader as a real person. Imagine that you tell this person about the subject you are inquiring into. What are the most important issues, questions, or concerns about your subject that you think would occur to your created reader? You need to write questions that will get your interviewee to talk about these issues, questions, and concerns.

You should plan on your interview lasting about one hour. Therefore, you should write a list of five to eight substantial, relatively open-ended questions. Write questions that fall somewhere in the middle of a continuum raging from *yes/no* questions at one end to vague, completely open-ended questions at the other. Avoid both of these extremes. A *yes/no* question generally stops a conversation, and a vague question is difficult to answer. Most important, write questions that allow your interviewee to talk about specific experiences he or she has had or specific ideas or observations he or she has encountered. Questions that encourage the interviewee to spout nothing but lofty generalizations seldom help you write a good, solid informative report.

 ## In-Progress Task

Jamie, my former student whose work you read in Chapter 5, conducted an inquiry into the aspect of the sample domain about the nature and purposes of higher education. He was particularly interested in the role that "general education" or "liberal studies" courses play in higher education. These are the courses that you have to take that are not for your major but are instead designed to help you become a well-rounded, liberally educated person. Jamie decided to interview the dean of the College of Liberal Arts and Sciences at a large, state university. The dean is ultimately in charge of all academic matters in the college, which at this university consists of twenty-three departments in the humanities, social sciences, and natural and life sciences. The dean is also responsible for helping design and implement the general education curriculum at the university. It is a huge, important job. Look carefully at the six main questions that Jamie initially planned to ask the dean:

1. What do you think is the relationship between a student's general education courses and the courses the student takes to prepare for a specific career?
2. How would you describe the overall mission of the general education curriculum at our university?
3. How do you know whether the general education curriculum is succeeding—that is, accomplishing this mission?
4. Do you think courses that emphasize a student's basic abilities to read, write, and calculate should be part of the general education curriculum?
5. What, if anything, is about to be changed in the general education curriculum? In other words, what's new?
6. What sort of support services for students in general education courses are available at the university?

In your writing-as-inquiry group or with someone else, discuss whether these questions seem comprehensive. Discuss whether you think the questions would generate specific responses from the dean or whether you think they would encourage her to be very general and abstract in her responses. Discuss what you think Jamie should do to revise these questions.

In addition to planning five to eight main questions, you should allow yourself the leeway during the interview to ask no more than two follow-up, clarification questions for each main question. It is a good idea to write out *one* of these follow-ups, then remember that you can ask one *additional* follow-up that you generate on the spot. It is these follow-up questions that turn the interview from a one-sided affair in which the interviewee does all the talking to a careful conversation where both parties talk.

With your main and follow-up questions written out, put them in the order you intend to ask them. It is best not to begin with your most complicated or difficult question. Give your interviewee a chance to warm up and get the conversation going with a good, substantial question, but perhaps not your most crucial one. Then put your most challenging question second or third in your list. Put at the end of the list those questions that you would like to discuss but that, if you run out of time and have to omit them, you would still get good information.

 ## In-Progress Task

Look back over the list of questions that Jamie planned to ask the dean and consider again any revisions you would make in them. Then, using either Jamie's list or your revised one, put the questions in the best order and discuss the order with your writing-as-inquiry group. What kinds of follow-up questions could you envision asking if you were using this list of questions? Do you need to add a question that you could use to get the interview started successfully?

Finally, before the actual interview, ask someone to role-play the interviewee with you so you can practice taking notes. This person does not necessarily need to be an appropriate person for you to interview about your subject. He or she must simply agree to give some kind of extended answers to a couple of your questions (usually just the first two will suffice) so you can get a sense of how quickly people talk in interviews and how much you will be able to write down. As you will see, I recommend that you take notes during an interview rather than tape-record it and that you write up your interview notes immediately after the interview. You will need, therefore, to develop a note-taking system that will serve you during the interview and make sense to you afterward.

DURING THE INTERVIEW

You need to take two kinds of materials to the interview: a secure pad, the kind that your paper won't fall out of, and several sharp pencils. There is nothing more maddening during an interview than having your papers go flying all over the room, your pen run out of ink (which is why pencils are better), or your last pencil break.

You may wonder why, during this age of high-tech recording equipment, you should even think about taking notes manually during the interview. Why not just tape-record it? Writing is better for two reasons. First, tape recorders are potentially frightening, cannot always be trusted to "hear" a conversation accurately, and require a good bit of mechanical fumbling. It is amazing how many people are afraid, often for no good reason, of committing themselves on tape. They will look suspiciously at the tape recorder and mutter quietly, "Is that thing on?" And sometimes it is hard even for the interviewer to know that the recorder is on. There is always the temptation to switch it off, rewind, and listen to part of the conversation, just to see whether the recorder is picking it up. And that, of course, breaks the flow of the interview. What's more, the tape inevitably runs out at a vital moment in the conversation. Then you have to turn the tape over and try to re-create the conversation that the tape missed. Such an interruption also spoils the spontaneous, generative nature of the interview.

Potential mechanical problems aside, there is a better, more substantial reason for taking written notes during an interview. The very act of writing up your interviewee's responses to your questions forces you to concentrate on the material in ways that simply talking into a tape recorder does not. As you write, you often think of good follow-up questions, see connections among ideas that you had not seen before, and begin to draw some preliminary generalizations and conclusions about your subject even in advance of writing more formally about it.

Conduct the interview in a location where you and your interviewee can talk without interruption and where you can comfortably write. It is ideal if you and your interviewee can sit at a table.

During the course of the interview, keep one eye on the clock. Don't rush through your questions, but be sure you have time to ask the most important ones. You will be surprised how quickly the time passes and how much an interviewee has to say about a good subject.

Once you pose a question, you should keep the interviewee talking about it and talking slowly. Don't sit there silently writing away while your interviewee is answering the question. Make eye contact, moving your eyes between the interviewee and your pad. Talk back to the interviewee, but don't simply grunt phrases such as "Uh huh" and "Yeah." Tell your interviewee that you appreciate his or her responses by using such phrases as "Great," "How interesting," and so on. Some interviewees will tend to give very short responses to your questions. In these cases, feel free to say such things as "Tell me more about that" and "Can you go into a little more detail about that?" But don't consider these as your follow-up questions. They are simply nudges you can use for any question, main or follow-up. Often such "tell me more" questions will really open up a reluctant interviewee.

Finally, feel free to ask your interviewee to pause a minute while you write a note or to slow down a bit because you need to write notes. This is not annoying to the interviewee. On the contrary, it demonstrates that you are paying close attention and taking his or her responses very seriously.

At the close of the interview, be sure to thank the interviewee and ask whether he or she would like to see any composition you may write using material gathered in the interview. Some interviewees will ask that they be permitted to approve anything you write using the material. Do not feel insulted or defensive about such requests. Indeed, granting them is a courtesy you owe to the interviewee.

AFTER THE INTERVIEW

The most important thing you should do after the interview is this: *As soon as possible,* write out the notes you took, fleshing out the interviewee's responses in complete phrases and sentences. It is vital that you do this while the interview is still fresh in your mind. Keep your expectations realistic during this process. No matter how thorough your notes from the interview are, it is inevitable that your reconstruction of the conversation may not be precise, word for word. That's okay. Write out the interviewee's responses to your questions as fully as you can, doing your best to capture the flavor of the interview, if not every single word of it. In this process, you may feel free to delete such "thinking utterances" as "um," "well," "you know," and so on, that the interviewee might have said. As soon as you have finished transcribing the responses, write a separate paragraph or two in which you reconstruct the details of the interview, describing precisely where and when it took place.

Both during this processes of writing out the interviewee's responses and after you have finished, you should engage in what I call the *filter-and-conclude* process. Just as happened while you were taking notes during the interview, while you are transcribing the responses into complete phrases and sentences, you will begin to see meaningful ideas emerging—generalizations about your subject, perhaps central ideas you think are important—that you may want to write about in the future. Now is the time to make note of these ideas in your learning journal or someplace else. These ideas represent what *you* make of the data you gathered and the *conclude* part of the filter-and-conclude process. The *filter* part refers to the activity you engage in as you look over the interviewee's responses and decide which parts are not useful—in other words, which parts you believe will not figure in any composition you write using the interview data. One hint, however: Even if you determine during this filter-and-conclude process that something you learned during the interview will not be useful in your writing, never throw away anything pertaining to the interview. When you are writing later, you may realize that you need to include some data, ideas, or perspectives from the interview that you did not think initially would be pertinent. Keep your questions, notes, outlines, and drafts from the Information Project until you are absolutely certain you won't need them.

A PRELIMINARY STEP TOWARD THE INFORMATIVE REPORT: "WHAT DID I LEARN?"

Once you have identified your interviewee, done your homework, planned and conducted the interview, written up your notes, and put them through a conscientious filter-and-conclude process, you are ready to begin shaping what you have learned into a package of information that will engage your readers' attention and teach them something they didn't know before. This package is the informative report, and the rest of this chapter is devoted to explaining how to produce this kind of writing, describing one writer's work on the Information Project, and analyzing her informative report.

First, however, you need to take one additional step as a transition between conducting your interview and writing your informative report. This step is writing a "What Did I Learn?" document and is described in the following task:

 ## In-Progress Task

Write a one- to two-page document that will supplement your written-out and expanded interview notes. This document, called simply "What Did I Learn?" can serve both to summarize your experience of learning something new about your subject and to prepare you to write your informative report.

To write a "What Did I Learn?" document, write just one fully developed paragraph in response to each of the following questions:

■ What is the *one newest and most surprising* thing I learned about my subject by conducting the interview and writing up my notes and conclusions?

■ What is *one additional* new and surprising thing I learned?

■ What are *two* important issues or questions about my subject that I have *not* learned anything about by conducting the interview and writing up my notes and conclusions?

■ If someone were to call into question the *factness* of what I learned about my subject by conducting the interview and writing up my notes and conclusions, how would I respond?

WRITING ABOUT YOUR CAREFUL CONVERSATION: THE INFORMATIVE REPORT

When some writers write up the results of interviews, they revert to a simple question-and-answer format that looks something like this:

> *Interviewer:* I need to ask you some questions. May I ask you one?
>
> *Interviewee:* Of course, you may. And I would be happy to answer your questions.

Nothing is actually terribly wrong with such a format, but it has features that make it the wrong one to use for the Information Project. First, it is often a difficult chore for readers to read writing like this. What the reader is getting is raw, unprocessed data, often complete with unfocused questions from the interviewer and irrelevant, "filler" responses from the interviewee. Second, when you write about an interview using such a format, you don't learn as much about your subject as you do when you convert the question-and-answer format into sentences, paragraphs, and passages that introduce important ideas and develop them with paraphrased or quoted material from the interview.

The informative report at the end of the chapter, written by one of my former students, illustrates the genre in detail, but let's consider some general guidelines about it in advance. To write an informative report about your interview, first envision a group of readers. When you planned the interview, you created an ideal reader who is curious, modest, encouraging, and (to use an odd term) "writerly." Now, when you write your informative report, imagine that you are writing to an entire group of such created readers, and imagine that you are their teacher, their leader, their guide. Your primary purpose is to inform these readers of what you learned during the interview that will be surprising, new, and interesting to them.

Look back over your notes from the interview, both those that you took during it and the expanded version that you wrote afterward. Read carefully the "What Did I Learn?" document that you wrote. Just as you used the idea of *comprehensiveness* to plan the questions for the interview, now use the principles of *surprise value* and *factness* to organize and write the informative report. Choose items to include in the report according to their surprise value and newsworthiness, and explain them by demonstrating their *factness.*

To plan the introduction to the report, think about the thing you learned that you believe will be most surprising and newsworthy to your readers. Begin your report by *indirectly* introducing the *question* you asked during the interview that uncovered whatever fact, perspective, or idea you think your readers will find most surprising. It is better, I think, not to come right out and state the question. Instead, suggest to your readers that this question represents an important area that they should be concerned and curious about.

After indirectly introducing this major question, the remainder of the first one-quarter to one-third of the informative report should be devoted to doing two things:

- You should answer this implicit question. Explain to your reader exactly what you learned that you think is most newsworthy and surprising to them.
- You should offer illustrations, examples, stories, and details you learned during the interview that give this newsworthy fact, idea, or perspective an air of *factness.*

In doing these two things, look for opportunities to work with the exact words, phrases, and sentences that your interviewee used, putting such exact wordings in quotation marks. Using the exact words will make your report come alive and seem more realistic to your readers.

When you quote your interviewee directly, you may use either entire sentences he or she said, or you may select important words or phrases from a quotation and embed them in your own sentences. Here are examples of each technique, drawn from the sample informative report at the end of this chapter:

Full-sentence quotation introduced by complete sentence: As a result of his experience, Brian has developed a philosophy for recent college graduates to go by: "Sometimes you have to take what you can get and hope you like the job."

or

Full-sentence quotation introduced by attributor: As a result of his experience, Brian has developed a philosophy for recent college graduates to go by. He said, "Sometimes you have to take what you can get and hope you like the job."

Part of a longer quotation embedded in your own sentence: Brian had only one thing to say about companies who only hire people with practice-oriented degrees; these employers are "short-sighted, narrow-minded, and sometimes just stupid."

Notice three things about these techniques of using direct quotations. First, when you choose an attributor phrase such as "He said" to introduce a complete sentence, put a comma after the phrase, not a colon. However, if you put the complete sentence after an introductory sentence and you do not use an attributor phrase, put a colon after the complete sentence. Second, use attributor phrases that show your interviewee was talking to you. Use such phrases as "She said," "She explained," "He pointed out," "He remarked," and so on. Avoid such attributor phrases as "She smiled," or "She grimaced," and so on. Third, when you are quoting only part of a longer quotation, be sure to write your own sentence so that the quoted material fits within the wording of your sentence.

The rest of the informative report should follow the same pattern you established in your introduction. Look back over your sets of notes from the interview. List, *in descending order of importance,* what else you learned. In other words, ask yourself, "After this one fact, idea, or perspective that I began the report by explaining, what is the *next* most surprising and newsworthy thing I learned, and then what's *next* most surprising and newsworthy after that, and so on?" If your interview is like most students', you can probably list three, four, or five facts, ideas, or perspectives that you learned, in addition to the one you started with. For each one, indirectly introduce the question that you posed and then "unpack" the answer to it, offering the data, testimony, and opinions from your interviews to provide the answer with a sense of *factness.*

A SAMPLE INFORMATIVE REPORT

In an undergraduate class I recently taught, one of the students, Katie, inquired into the aspect of the sample domain that looks at the relationship between higher education and work. In her Contract Proposal, she noted one question she was really curious about: Does a college education really prepare you for a job? In her Information Project, Katie refined this large question, found a good interviewee, and developed an excellent set of interview questions to guide her careful conversation with him. Katie's major question for the Information Project was this: Why is it that so many people end up working in jobs that are not directly related to their majors? To learn some facts, ideas, and perspectives about this question, Katie interviewed Brian Kirby, her boss in the university's Office of Sponsored Programs, where she was a work-study employee at the time.

Here are the questions that Katie asked Brian during the interview:

- What was your major in college? Why did you choose to major in that field?
- How well do you think your undergraduate major prepared you to get a job?
- What kinds of jobs did you look for after you graduated?
- What kind of job did you get?
- Have you changed jobs since your first one? Why?
- Do you think colleges and universities should do anything different to help students prepare for jobs?

Here is the final draft of the paper Katie wrote, based on the careful conversation she conducted in the interview. In the margins are some comments I have added, to show you how the genre of the informative report works. As you read the paper, see whether you can tell what kinds of follow-up questions Katie asked.

WHERE AM I GOING?

1 Recently, I have noticed that many college graduates whom I have spoken with do not work at jobs relating to their undergraduate majors. With the exception of people majoring in fields such as commerce, education, and pre-medicine, most students either find that they need further education in order to become part of a profession or they end up taking a job that has little or nothing to do with their undergraduate studies. Brian Kirby, the grants administrator in the Office of Sponsored Programs at DePaul University, was able to help me understand why many graduates find themselves in such a position.

Implied question: How well does your major prepare you for a job?

Most Surprising conclusion Katie reached

2   While speaking with Brian, I learned that he and many of his friends graduated from college earning liberal arts degrees which did not necessarily prepare them for a particular job, but rather many different types of jobs.

Story of Brian's shifting view provides "factness"   When Brian started his undergraduate education at the University of Notre Dame, he was a pre-engineering major. Later, he realized that declaring a major in engineering would be "too specific," so he decided to study a more general area, the "Great Books." Since he did not have any future jobs in mind, he believed that a liberal arts major would open many doors for him; he would learn organizational, writing, and critical thinking skills. Soon after graduation, Brian realized that his preconception was not quite correct.

3   Once Brian graduated from Notre Dame, he was unable to find a job "equal to [his] abilities." His plans were to work at Prudential Insurance Company as a underwriter, but when that didn't come through, because he did not have the business experience or some previous job experience that the em-

Second conclusion: It's job experience, more than training, that counts.   ployers required, he started applying for technical writing and editing jobs. What he learned as a result of the rejections was that most of the jobs required some business experience or previous job experience. Although he thought that his undergraduate education had prepared him for the work force, the employers did not. Soon, Brian had no other choice than to accept any job he was offered.

4   He found himself doing data-entry. He enjoyed working at this job because there were other recent graduates who couldn't find employment either. They all called data-entry their "transitional" job and enjoyed working together because they were all in the same predicament. After nine months, Brian realized that he was the only recent graduate still working there and, as a result, he grew increasingly bored. Therefore, he quit.

5   Brian spent the next three months looking for work while living with his fiance and his sister. During this time, he took up many new hobbies; his favorite was cook-

ing. Although he wanted to go to graduate school, he couldn't because he was running low on money. His hope was to work at a nearby institution, the University of Minnesota. With this plan, he could work, save the money he made and take free classes simultaneously, but after sending many resumes, he still did not have a job. That is when he decided to join a temporary service.

6   His first job with the company was a disaster. Brian was assigned for two weeks at Target's internal travel office. After three days he quit because he didn't like the people and was given the job of stapling airline tickets. He was not using his undergraduate knowledge. He decided to give the temporary job service one more chance. He was lucky; Brian took a job with the University of Minnesota.

3rd conclusion: You get job experience often by accident and luck.

7   The new job required typing and was to last two days, but since Brian was typing seventy words per minute and his boss liked him, she decided to keep him on for two and a half more weeks. This time, she had him alphabetize a box full of papers that were in desperate need of being filed.

8   Unfortunately, the job was temporary. But his boss, the administrator of internal grant programs at the University of Minnesota, had more work for Brian since they were understaffed. As a result, the temporary job was extended for six more months. Since Brian knew that he would remain at the university for an extended amount of time, he decided to enroll for classes. Although Brian's responsibilities as office assistant initially included letter writing, data-entry, and other miscellaneous tasks, after some time, Brian helped revise the database so keeping track of grants would be easier, revised the grant application, and helped organize meetings. Ultimately, Brian remained a full-time employee at the University of Minnesota for a total of two and one-half years and earned a master's degree in religion.

9   After receiving his graduate degree, Brian was planning to enroll in a Ph.D. program in religious literature, but since he and his wife had made the decision to move to Chicago after graduation, he started to look for a job. Brian started his search

Fourth conclusion: A part-time job can grow into something bigger and better.

in the *Chicago Tribune* where he eventually saw an interesting advertisement. The position for grant administrator at DePaul University's Office of Sponsored Programs interested Brian because they sought a person with a graduate degree in the social sciences and the job entailed the same type of work he had done at the University of Minnesota; so he applied.

10 *Katie gets Brian to return to the main question: Does your undergraduate study prepare you for a job?*

Although he had no intention of taking a job similar to the one he has now, one that does not relate to either of his degrees, he still believes that, "Yes, undergraduate school was great preparation." Since his undergraduate university developed his organizational analysis, writing skills, and the ability to give effective presentations, he can now use those skills in his present job. Although undergraduate school didn't have a direct effect or give him the knowledge for the actual content of his job, it helped strengthen his thinking process.

11   Although college enhanced many of Brian's skills, he still believes that universities need to be changed. If it were up to him, college would last for five to six years. The first three years would consist of general liberal arts studies that have no "practical consequences," so that students can experience all types of classes without having to worry about a concentration. He says, for instance, that accounting is too limited and becomes specialized too early. Brian's view is that students should be allowed to be free to try new courses without the feeling of being tied down.

12   Brian had only one thing to say about companies who only hire people with practice-oriented degrees; these employers are "short-sighted, narrow-minded, and some just stupid." Brian believes that some employers think people can only do jobs they learned in class. Although he understands that it is easier to judge experience than quality, employers are not taking enough time to research prospective job candidates. As a result of his experience, Brian has developed a philosophy for recent college graduates to go by: "Sometimes you have to take what you can get and hope that you like the job."

In-Progress Task

After you have read Katie's informative report carefully, meet with your writing-as-inquiry group or with one or two other people who have read the composition. Concentrating only on the quality, organization, and development of Katie's ideas—not on her sentence structure, style, mechanics, punctuation, or grammar—make a list of two things Katie did well in her report. Then list at least two specific things Katie might have done differently as she planned and wrote this paper that would have improved it as an informative report.

8 Exploration: Raising Questions and Resisting Closure

One of the greatest understatements in the history of archaeology was uttered by Professor Howard Carter in 1922. Carter and his colleague, Lord Caernarfon, were leading a team of explorers who were excavating the tomb of Tutankhamen, the now-famous boy pharaoh of ancient Egypt. As they finally made their way into the tomb, Carter went first, carrying a candle. He stopped short, amazed, and Caernarfon asked him what he had found. "Wonderful things," replied Carter.

It's time for you to find wonderful things. By this point in your writing-as-inquiry project, you have identified a subject; begun to clarify for yourself what you feel, think, believe, and know about it; and learned something new about it. You may be thinking, "Oh, I'm getting to be something of an expert on this subject," and you may feel prepared to begin drawing some conclusions about it—taking positions and changing people's minds.

At the risk of sounding impertinent, let me suggest that now may *not* be the moment for you to begin drawing conclusions or thinking about points you want to demonstrate, argue for, or prove about your subject. Now is the point in your project where you want to start asking *hard* questions about your subject. Now is the moment when you need to *examine* the depths, the nooks and crannies, of your subject, trying to find the rich veins it contains for future parts of your inquiry, when you will develop, demonstrate, argue for, and "prove" central ideas and points about your subject. Now is the moment when you need to raise *many* questions about what you have learned so far without feeling compelled to answer these new questions with any certainty. In short, now is the moment for you to *explore* your subject further.

Exploration is an activity that writers too frequently neglect. Often they push themselves to find a thesis, a central idea on which to base a long composition, too quickly. Mind you, nothing is wrong with having a thesis. It is a problem, however, to feel that you must arrive at a thesis quickly when you are writing about a complicated subject. When this happens, writers usually come up with theses that are too shallow, too broad, or too simple. A shallow thesis offers too little direction and too few possibilities for development in the composition. An excessively broad thesis offers too wide a perspective on the subject and does not sufficiently focus the composition so that readers follow and accept the writer's ideas. An overly simple thesis commits the reader to develop, argue for, or "prove" a position that readers either already accept or find dull and unchallenging.

Chapter 9 will have more to say about theses. Indeed, the entire chapter is about the Exploration Project and the exploratory essay, a genre built around a complex, multifaceted thesis that emerges from your writing-as-inquiry project. But for now, let's resist the temptation to close the inquiry prematurely by stating a thesis. Let's see what exploring the subject can do to enrich the inquiry.

As you read this chapter, notice that there are three *In-Progress Tasks* for you to complete. Each task explains a strategy for exploring some specific aspect of your subject. You may use one or more of them as part of your writing-as-inquiry project. Completing each strategy requires about an hour's work and prepares you to work on an exploratory essay, explained in Chapter 9, about your subject.

Before we examine these strategies, we need to address two pressing questions about exploration:

- Why and how do explorers work?
- How does exploration operate in a writing-as-inquiry project?

ON EXPLORING: WHY AND HOW?

Explorers come from many professions. Archaeologists dig into the past by looking for physical evidence of previous civilizations. Historians examine the past's documents, both spoken and written texts. Anthropologists and sociologists probe the ways of life in different cultures. Psychologists unpack the life of the mind. Botanists, geologists, and zoologists look for new forms of life on Earth. Astronomers and physicists scan the galaxies looking for new forms of life beyond. Critics of art, literature, and music try to find what works of culture mean and how such meaning is created.

In some cases, explorers have been motivated by a financial interest. For example, most of the European explorers in the fifteenth and sixteenth centuries who "discovered" the new world were seeking to find new sources and routes for trade. But even when explorers are moved to their enterprises by desires for power or wealth, they are also probably inspired by a genuine sense of curiosity. "I wonder what life is like there?" they must ask. "I wonder what I will find out?"

This curiosity, though, does not usually lead an explorer to venture blindly into the exploration, simply encountering whatever is out there randomly. On the contrary, an explorer almost always has a framework on which to base his or her work, a hunch or hypothesis that will guide the search. In 1492, Columbus hypothesized that he could find a trading route to India by sailing west from Europe, even though his purported destination lay to the east. In 1953, British scientists James Watson and Francis Crick hypothesized that the structure of DNA, one of the chemical substances that transmits the genetic code from parents to offspring, is a double helix, a pair of twisting coils that intersect. Just as Columbus's hypothesis was confirmed by his experience, so was Watson and Crick's validated by experimentation. In general, then, explorers think they know a bit about their subject, so they plan an expedition, an experience, an experiment that lets them capitalize on this bit they know. They then expect that this expedition will enable them to learn a great deal more that builds on this bit they know.

This is precisely the path that your writing-as-inquiry project has been following. You have identified a subject and clarified it. You have learned something about it. Now it's time to explore some other aspect of it. The remainder of this chapter sets out three strategies, each of which leads you to build on what you already know about your subject. Use these strategies to *raise questions* about your subject so that you can see possibilities for further, more incisive writing about it.

Notice the *limited* nature of each exploratory strategy. By this point in your writing-as-inquiry project, your subject may have gotten quite big, perhaps too big to explore the whole thing at once. As you explore, therefore, pick one aspect of the subject at a time and raise critical questions about it.

But first, one more idea to get us in the exploratory frame of mind. . . .

THE ESSENCE OF EXPLORATION: "WHAT IF . . . ?"

For any one of the three exploration strategies to work, you need to agree to play a little mind game with yourself. That game is called simply "What if . . . ?" Perhaps an analogy will help describe this game. Imagine that you own a crystal prism, a beautiful piece of glass with many facets cut into it. Next, imagine that you cannot move and the crystal prism is locked in place, static, right in front of your eyes. You have only one view of the surrounding world available to you, the one before your eyes, through the prism. Now, however, imagine that you are released from this locked-in-place position, that you are free to pick up the crystal prism, to hold it at various angles before your eyes, to look at the world around you through it from the many perspectives that its cut facets provide.

Playing the "What if . . . ?" game is like living in the second scenario. To play the game successfully, you cannot believe that there is only one way to think and behave about your subject. To play "What if . . . ?" you need to try to see your subject from many angles, to come up with multiple ways of thinking and acting about your subject, and each of the exploration strategies explained and demonstrated in this chapter are illustrations of the game. Eventually, in Chapters 10 and 11, we will reach the end of your writing-as-inquiry project and you will focus on one specific way of seeing your subject. For now, however, keep an open mind. Resist closure.

EXPLORATION STRATEGY 1: SCRUTINIZING THE STATUS QUO

The first strategy for raising questions about your subject represents an adaptation of ideas originally developed by James L. Kinneavy, a scholar who teaches at the University of Texas, and published in his book *A Theory of Discourse* in 1971. Kinneavy describes a five-step process for exploring a subject. (The language of Kinneavy's explanation has been altered and expanded a bit to allow you to use it to explore your subject.)

- First, review the *status quo* about your subject. That is, write a full paragraph that explains at least *two* things that most people feel, think, believe, or know about it.
- Second, explain the problems inherent in this *status quo* view of the subject. For *each* thing that you propose people feel, think, believe, or know about the subject, explain at least one *problem* or *drawback* in the fact that people feel, think, believe, or know that.
- Third, identify and explain a *crisis* in the *status quo*. Write a full paragraph that explains what in particular makes a change in people's feelings, thoughts, beliefs, and knowledge about the subject necessary or desirable right now.
- Fourth, consider alternatives to the *status quo*. In a full paragraph, explain at least *two* ways that people could think or behave differently than they currently do in regard to the subject.
- Fifth, test the outcomes of each of these ways of thinking and behaving. Write a full paragraph about how the world would be different if people thought or behaved in each of the alternative ways you propose. In this paragraph, explain both a *benefit* of this new way of thinking or acting and a *drawback* to it.

Here is a demonstration of this exploration strategy, one that explores one part of *status quo* thinking about the aspect of the sample domain that concerns the relation between education and the changing nature of work. Unlike our work with this domain in earlier chapters, which examined the relationship between the education one gets in school and the type of job one gets, this demonstration is concerned with the on-the-job education that people receive after they get hired and go to work.

A bit of background information on the aspect of the domain that this demonstration will explore is in order: With the changing nature of both work and the American workforce, many businesses and industries have instituted on-the-job education programs to help workers learn to read and write more effectively. Workers can take reading and writing "refresher" courses, at the business or industry location or at local schools. Here, then, is the part of the domain we intend to explore in the form of a question:

> When businesses and industries decide to train production- and service-level workers to read and write effectively on the job, what kind of education do these workers receive?

Now let's explore this aspect using the Kinneavy strategy:

- **What is *status quo* thinking about this subject?** Most experts on worker education and leaders of industry in the United States want to train production-level workers to be "functionally literate" in their specific jobs. That is, when workers are taught to read and write on the job, they should be taught to read and write *only* the kinds of things they have to read and write on the job. So, for example, if workers have to read safety manuals and write productivity reports to other workers, they should only receive instruction in how to read a safety manual and how to write a productivity report.
- **What are the problems with this *status quo* thinking?** Two problems are apparent here. First, this line of thinking assumes that educational planners and instructors can completely separate the kinds of reading and writing one must do on one's job from the kinds of reading and writing one does away from one's job. Second, and perhaps more troubling, the impetus to teach "functional literacy" on the job suggests that the primary function workers accomplish in their lives is to do their jobs well. In other words, this *status quo* thinking fails to admit that a person's job can be seen in a broader perspective, as a satisfying part of a person's more unified view of his or her life.
- **Why is now the time to try to change this *status quo* thinking?** Experts from several fields agree that the workplace in industry, business, and service is changing rapidly, creating new kinds of products and relying heavily on computer technology, so workers are going to need increasingly more critical reading and writing abilities to get and keep their jobs. Since the economy needs more

literate workers, now is the time when people concerned about the economy—leaders of business, industry, education, and labor—must work together to find the *best* ways to prepare such workers.

- **What are some alternatives to the *status quo* thinking?** Here are two different ways of thinking about teaching functional literacy skills to workers on the job. First, those planning worker education programs could assume that reading and writing already play some important roles in the lives of the workers they want to train, and these planners could consciously try to *connect* the job-oriented reading and writing abilities they want workers to master to the kinds of reading and writing the workers do outside their jobs. Second, these educational planners could ask the workers what kinds of reading and writing abilities *they* would like to have to make their whole lives—not just their lives at work—richer and fuller, and the educational planners could try to offer some of these worker-oriented (in contrast to work-oriented) abilities in their programs.

- **What are the benefits and drawbacks of each of these alternatives?** The principal benefit of the first alternative—connecting the workers' reading and writing on the job to their reading and writing off the job—is that it will help them learn something new (the job-related reading and writing skills) by building on something old and familiar (their everyday reading and writing abilities). This alternative has two drawbacks: The workers may do very little reading and writing away from their jobs, and they may not be able to see the connection between their off-the-job reading and writing and their on-the-job training. The principal benefit of the second alternative—asking the workers what kinds of reading and writing abilities they would like to develop—is that it will suggest to the workers that their ideas are important to the company, that the company wants them to be satisfied, fulfilled people, not just productive workers. The main drawback is that the abilities to read and write effectively on the job may get lost in the many reading and writing abilities that workers might want to develop for other settings—their homes, neighborhoods, churches, and children's schools, for example.

 In-Progress Task

Write the *one aspect* of your subject you would like to explore in the form of a question, and then write five full paragraphs, using the Kinneavy model to explore it.

EXPLORATION STRATEGY 2: A TREE OF POSSIBILITIES

A second strategy comes from John J. Ruszkiewicz, another professor at the University of Texas, whose 1982 book, *Well-Bound Words*, describes a very flexible approach for exploring a subject. Ruszkiewicz's strategy allows, even invites, writers to digress and welcome the unexpected insights into their subject that often come from such digressions.

The following adaptation of Ruszkiewicz's structure calls for an *annotated tree*. That is, the exploring writer sets out a tree of exploratory possibilities and then writes a sentence or two for each limb and branch of the tree created. Here is one flexible structure for the tree:

Main idea or issue or problem

Cause of this idea, issue, or problem

Related idea, issue, or problem A

Related idea, issue, or problem B

Related idea, issue, or problem X

Attitudes toward the main idea, issue, or problem

Pro	Con
Point A	Point A
Point B	Point B
Point C	Point C
Point X	Point X

Notice four important things about this exploratory tree. First, and most important, you do not have to fill in every branch. You can simply fill in whichever branch you can generate an idea for, but the more branches you can fill in, the richer and eventually more productive your exploration will be. Second, to create it, simply write a word or phrase for each branch you chose, then write one complete sentence fleshing out the word or phrase on the branch. It is important that you write out your complete sentence for each branch quickly. Single words and phrases are often too brief and obscure to guide a good exploration. Third, an important part of the tree is the area of related ideas, issues, and problems. Consider these points as containing possibilities for additional trees. In other words, you can use whatever you list as a "related idea, issue, or problem" as the "main idea, issue, or problem" in another tree and generate even more complicated (and, ideally, useful) explorations of your subject. Fourth, notice that both "related idea, issue, or problem" and the points under "Pro" and "Con" have *X* as their final number. What this means is that there is no set number of these ideas or points you have to raise. Simply write one sentence about as many of them as you can.

Here is a demonstration of this strategy, a demonstration that explores a different aspect of the sample domain about the nature and purposes of a college education. Once again, begin the demonstration by casting the point to be explored in the form of a question:

> Is the primary purpose of getting a college degree to prepare you for a specific career, or is it to prepare you for a variety of careers by providing you with a liberal education?

Now we fill in the branches of the exploratory tree with thought-provoking words and phrases.

Main idea or issue or problem
The idea of a college education as vocational preparation
Cause of this idea, issue, or problem
The economy
Related idea, issue, or problem A
Uncertain job market
Related idea, issue, or problem B
High cost of getting a college education
Related idea, issue, or problem X
Certain professions highly valued
Attitudes toward the main idea, issue, or problem
Required national service for all college students
between their second and third years

Pro	Con
Point A	**Point A**
A break from the routine	Interruption of studies
Point B	**Point B**
Exposure to new cultures	Loss of personal freedom
Point C	**Point C**
Time to reflect on goals	Ideological opposition
Point D	
Hands-on job experience	

Now we can flesh out the words and phrases by writing complete sentences:

- The main issue that this tree explores is this: Perhaps too many people see getting a college education as strictly a matter of vocational preparation, or training for a specific job.
- Certain pressures in the economy cause this kind of thinking.
- One related issue is the uncertain job market that college graduates often face.

- A second related issue is that many college graduates will be in debt when they finish school, and they want to prepare for a specific job that will help them pay off their debt.
- A third related issue is that students think college can prepare them for certain professions that hold the promise of great wealth—law, medicine, and business, for example.
- Here is a rather far-out suggestion, an attitude toward the main issue, that might address this potentially unhealthy thinking about college as strictly vocational preparation: What if all college students were required to do at least three or four months of national service, in the armed forces or in civilian organizations, between their sophomore and junior years?
- There would be at least four advantages to this plan. First, it would provide students with a break in their studies right at the point when many of them are feeling rather "stale" in school. Second, it would provide students with healthy exposure to people and places in different cultures. Third, it would give students time to reflect on their personal goals, thus making their later choices about career preparation better informed. Fourth, the national service could provide hands-on job experience to students while they are still in their traditional college years.
- The plan has three major drawbacks. First, it would interrupt students' college careers right when many of them are achieving momentum in their studies. Second, it would limit students' personal freedom to do as they please. Third, some students might be ideologically opposed to the whole idea of national service.

Before leaving this exploratory tree, let's take a look back at the related ideas, issues, and problems raised in it. Notice that any of these issues about how economic realities lead students to view college as vocational preparation are worthy of exploratory trees of their own, as are most of the points listed under *Pro* and *Con*. In sum, a good exploratory tree should be heavily hung with the fruits of potential further inquiry and exploration.

 ## In-Progress Task

State the aspect of your subject you would like to explore as a question. Then fill out as much of an exploratory tree as you can with suggestive words and phrases. Finally, go back and flesh out your words and phrases into complete sentences. Don't overlook individual branches as sites for further explorations.

EXPLORATION STRATEGY 3: A STRING OF DISSOCIATIONS

"Things aren't always what they seem" is an adage wise enough to have been preached by famous thinkers from Plato through Samuel Johnson to W. S. Gilbert and Arthur Sullivan. The saying lies at the heart of a third strategy you can use to explore your subject, raising questions about it but not necessarily coming to closure by answering them. This strategy is an adaptation of the work of the modern Belgian philosopher, Chaim Perelman, who calls it the *dissociation of ideas.*

Perelman explains that one effective way to persuade people to accept your ideas is to propose a distinction between *appearance* and *reality*—in other words, between the way things *seem to be* and the way you think they *really are.* You claim for your central ideas—the points you want your reader to accept—the status of *reality.* Ideas or points that oppose or otherwise conflict with yours, you argue, are merely *appearances,* not *realities.* Thereby, you *dissociate* your ideas, your points—the *reality*—from the others—the *appearances.* By playing with these distinctions and creating a *string of dissociations,* you can explore your subject.

As was true with the first two strategies, you must play the "What if . . . ?" game conscientiously to construct a string of dissociations. It may not be obvious what kinds of statements actually fit on both sides of the distinctions you must draw. The distinctions may feel as though they are fabricated. That's okay for now. It's only by taking a risk and trying to see these distinctions that you will open up unseen nooks and crannies in your subject.

As with the exploratory tree, do not view this list of dissociations as something you *must* fill out. You may skip the ones that don't bring anything to mind for you.

Here is how to use this strategy to explore your subject. For *any* of the following distinctions that seem possible to draw, write *one full sentence* in response to *each* question:

- What is one idea, issue, or problem about the subject that is *apparent* to most people? How does this apparent idea, issue, or problem differ from the *real* idea, issue, or problem?
- What is one *opinion* that many people hold about the subject? How does that opinion differ from the *truth* or from *informed knowledge* about the subject?
- What is one feature or aspect of the subject that people typically notice and comment on? How is that feature merely an *accident* and not really the *essence* of the subject?
- What is one *value judgment* that people frequently make about the subject? How is this value judgment simply a *relative* evaluation, not an *absolute truth?*

- What is one thing that many people believe about the subject *in theory*? How does this theoretical belief differ from *practical wisdom* about the subject?

To demonstrate this strategy, let's reexamine an idea that we worked with in Chapter 4, one that falls under the rubric of the sample domain. A few years ago, a group of college and university presidents and deans began to investigate ways to streamline their schools' curricula so that students who were willing to take overloads in most of their terms could graduate in three years rather than four. As a convenient shorthand in our demonstration, let's call this idea *the three-year plan*. Here are some dissociations involving it:

- **Concerning the three-year plan, what is one idea that is apparent to most people?** It is apparent to most people that getting a college education is expensive. If you can eliminate one year in which you would have to pay tuition and still get a degree, it might be a good idea to do so. **How does this apparent idea differ from the real idea, issue, or problem?** The real issue may not be whether you can actually save money by finishing a college degree in three years but whether, if you are constantly taking an overload and trying to hurry through your curriculum, you can learn the material in your classes effectively.
- **What is one opinion that many people hold about the three-year plan?** Many people think that getting an education is simply a matter of sitting through a number of classes. If you can persist through a series of classes for three years rather than four, why not do so? **How does this opinion differ from the truth or informed knowledge about this idea?** The truth is that getting an education is obviously more than just sitting through and surviving classes. You need to focus, to concentrate, to engage yourself in your classes to make the knowledge you acquire your own.
- **What is one feature of the three-year plan that people typically notice and comment on?** People usually comment on the great savings of time and money students can accrue by finishing their bachelor's degrees in three years rather than four. **How is this feature merely an *accident* and not the *essence* of the subject?** The savings of time and money are mere accidents of the three-year plan. In essence, the three-year plan represents a more hurried, less contemplative kind of higher education.
- **What is one *value judgment* that people usually make about the three-year plan?** People usually make value judgments about the economy of the three-year plan. Not only do students avoid an extra year of educational expenses, but they also get out into the job market and begin earning money a year earlier. **How is this**

value judgment simply a *relative* evaluation, not an *absolute* truth? This value judgment is relative only to the economy. It does not consider the absolute value of an education that prepares a student not simply to earn money in a single job for which he or she has been trained but instead to take his or her place in a flexible, creative professional world, one that may require him or her to hold four or five different jobs in a lifetime.

- **What is one thing that many people believe about the three-year plan** *in theory?* In theory, many people believe that it is best to get into the job market as quickly as you can and start earning money; therefore, they support the three-year plan. **How does this theoretical belief differ from** *practical wisdom* **on the subject?** This theoretical stance differs from people's practical wisdom in that many people, reflecting on their college careers years later, often think that the most valuable ideas and perspectives they acquired were not learned in courses that prepared them to take a specific job.

 ## In-Progress Task

State the aspect of your subject you would like to explore. Then explore this aspect by creating a string of dissociations, posing at least one full sentence in response to each of the dissociative questions you can answer.

9 The Exploration Project and the Exploratory Essay

Part of the adventure of getting a college education is learning how to call into question the meaning of a term that previously seemed clear and unproblematic to you. One such term may be *essay*. You have probably heard this word regularly from elementary school right up to the present. You have, no doubt, been directed to write essays for many of your classes, either on examinations or in formal papers. You may have been asked to compose essays about some incident you vividly recall from your past or about some person who was particularly meaningful to you. You may have been required to submit an essay to qualify for a scholarship or to be admitted to your college or university.

Part of our goal in this chapter is to cast an eye back over these writing experiences and ask whether the word *essay* is the most appropriate term to define them. Our major goal in the chapter, however, is to learn how to produce a genre called an *exploratory essay*, not simply to analyze essays we may have written in the past. The exploratory essay, you will find, is a genre strong and substantial enough to embody the complicated thinking you are generating in your writing-as-inquiry project.

Before turning our attention to the meaning of *essay*, however, let's examine the project that will guide our work in this chapter.

The Exploration Project

For this project, you will write an exploratory essay. Assume that your reader is part of the same group whom you envisioned as the readers of the informative report in the Information Project. Remember the characteristics of these "created" readers: They are curious and therefore read a great deal about many subjects. They are modest and want to know more. They are encouraging and make you feel comfortable explaining your subject. They write a great deal and consequently understand what you are going through as you develop your writing-as-inquiry project.

As you write your exploratory essay with these readers in mind, give them one additional characteristic. Assume that they *like* questions—that they enjoy raising challenging questions and pondering possible answers to them, but not necessarily coming up with hard-and-fast answers to them.

Your goal in this essay is to "unpack" for these readers a complicated, multifaceted, sophisticated idea about your subject, an idea that has grown from the Clarification and Information Projects and from the exploration strategies explained in Chapter 8. Your purpose in this essay is to raise *at least two* questions (but perhaps even more) about your subject. Ideally, these will be questions that you have not addressed yet in the previous projects in your Inquiry Contract. For each question you raise, moreover, you should pose *at least two* answers and explore the benefits and drawbacks of answering the questions in the manner you propose.

Writing an exploratory essay is a valuable activity in its own right. Doing so places you in the tradition of great essayists of European and American culture—writers such as Michel de Montaigne, Samuel Johnson, Virginia Woolf, Joan Didion, and James Baldwin, to name just a few. Writing an exploratory essay also plays an important role in your whole writing-as-inquiry project. The exploratory essay represents the "garden" in which you can grow potential persuasive goals—possible theses, one of which you might use to unify the final composition in the Inquiry Contract, the working document, described in Chapters 10 and 11.

As you begin to work on the exploratory essay, reread everything you have done so far in your Inquiry Contract—the Contract Proposal, the reflective reading response, the informative report, and all notes, drafts, and outlines that accompany these projects. In addition, reread the notes you made using the exploration strategies explained in Chapter 8. Ask yourself (and it might be a good idea to write for a while in response to this question), "How does my subject now seem more complicated than it did when I started working on the Inquiry Contract?"

To write an exploratory essay, you need to put your subject into an appropriate context for your created readers, propose a central question about your subject, craft an "explorer statement" that suggests additional questions you intend to address in the essay, and then "walk through" the potential answers to these questions, illustrating your ideas with specific descriptions and stories that show your reader how you are thinking. In the exploratory essay, questions prevail, but not necessarily definitive answers to these questions.

The remainder of this chapter will explain all these intellectual "moves" that go into writing your exploratory essay. At the end of the chapter, you will find an exploratory essay written by a student in a college writing class. You might find it helpful to read this essay now, as you prepare to work on your own.

WHAT IS AN ESSAY?

All people engaged in the business of education—teachers, administrators, and students alike—use the word *essay* frequently. But I wonder whether we use the term too loosely. We tend to call any piece of writing that is not a poem, a play, a short story, a letter, or a novel an *essay*. Thus, for example, when a history professor asks students on an examination to explain the causes of the Peloponnesian War, she probably includes the phrase "write an essay" in the question. When a student wants to know more about the operas of Puccini, his music teacher might suggest that he read "the essay about *La Bohème* in *Grove's Musical Dictionary.*" When several friends are discussing the contemporary political scene, someone might refer to "an essay by Clarence Page on the op-ed page of yesterday's *Tribune.*" And in English classes, both the instructor and the students might use the word *essay* to describe a composition that has an introductory paragraph with a thesis statement at the end of it, three paragraphs of development, each starting with a topic sentence, and a concluding paragraph that "restates" the thesis.

Are all of these pieces of writing really *essays*? What features do they share that would cause you to call all of them by the same name? What do they have in common in terms of form? Certainly, they are all written in prose. That is, they are not composed of metrical lines of verse, like poetry, nor do they use continuous, repeating dialogue like drama. But is that enough to say they are all the same thing? Certainly not. Short stories, novels, and letters are written in prose, but they are not essays.

What about their length? It is possible that all of these pieces might be the same length. If you were to word-process them, double-spaced with one-inch margins, they *might* all run between three and five pages. Some might be shorter than this, and some longer—much longer, in fact, since some essays run twenty to thirty pages, or even longer. In general, though, the things we call *essays* are longer than a single paragraph but shorter than, say, an encyclopedia article. But, of course, a relatively similar length is hardly a criterion for inclusion in any meaningful category, so length is hardly what defines an essay.

What about their subject matters? Even in just the four examples listed, we can see that what people call an *essay* can be about anything—historical facts, a nineteenth-century opera, contemporary politics, or whatever you chose to write your compositions about in your previous writing classes. In short, an essay can be about anything.

So if we cannot say what an essay is according to its form, length, or subject matter, what characteristics can we use to define the term? We should notice, first, that the word *essay* originated not in a noun, a word that names a *thing*, but instead in a verb, a word that describes an *action*. *Essay* comes from the French verb *essayer,* which means "to try." Given the term's origin in a verb, let's try to examine what an essay *does* rather than what it *is*. Specifically, let's try to describe an essay in terms of what you, the writer, can do with your subject matter and how you, the writer, interact with your readers when you write an essay.

In general, let's agree to call an *essay* a composition in prose in which you set out for your readers' inspection a complex idea (or more than one). In addition, let's say an essay is a composition in which you specifically try to lead your readers through a consideration of the many facets and corners of the idea(s) but in which you do not necessarily come to closure or have a final word on your central ideas. Think of an essay, then, not so much as a piece of writing in which you prove or demonstrate an idea but more as a piece of writing in which you ponder or even play with ideas.

Equipped with this definition of an *essay,* let's take one additional step just to clarify our work on the Exploration Project and the exploratory essay. Let's invent some additional terms to name the kinds of compositions that you, your teachers, and your classmates might have called *essays* in the past and may do so in the future as well.

Important note: Be very careful about using the terms we are about to discuss outside your writing class or writing-as-inquiry group. They are not universally used terms, and many teachers and writers may prefer to use the general term, essay, *for all nonfiction prose compositions.*

Here are three terms, names for different types of prose compositions, that can focus our work. For the purpose of discussion, let's put these three types of writing on a continuum:

Theme ——————— *Exploratory Essay* ——————— *Open Essay*

Notice that this is a *continuum,* not a *taxonomy* of types of compositions. That is, there is no hard and fast line that absolutely separates the three types. They do differ, however, in three dimensions of writing activity, three kinds of "moves" you can make in relation to your subject matter and your readers:

- Concentrating on a single, well-focused central idea and achieving closure, a sense of "the final word" on this idea;
- Developing this central idea in a "straight-line," sequential fashion;
- Explaining the nuances and implications of this central idea for your readers.

Let's agree to call a *theme* a composition that accomplishes these three activities exactly as they are stated here. That is, when you write a theme, you state a single, well-focused idea, commonly called a *thesis statement.* You work to achieve closure, a sense of "the final word," on this idea by developing it—providing examples, illustrations, and details about it—in a linear, sequential fashion. That is, you "line up" the parts of the composition so that one part leads logically to the next. You try hard to explain the intricacies and implications of the central idea so that they are clear to readers. You do not leave much, if any, room for readers to draw their own conclusions.

It is extremely important for college students to know how to write themes. Many, if not most, essay examinations given in college and university classes require you to write themes, whether the examination sheet uses that word or not. In addition, a great many papers you must write for your classes will be extended themes, in which you focus on a single, clear idea, develop it in a straight-line fashion, and make your ideas as clear and unambiguous as possible. If you have not done so before, you should work hard to understand and internalize the structure of the theme, but you should realize that it is not the *only* genre you will write in your classes and career.

Here is a relatively brief example of a theme about the sample domain, our inquiry into the nature and purposes of higher education. I wrote this theme myself, but in it I played the role of a student who chose to attend college and major in management so that he could eventually open his own business. A theme like this might be written in response to a typical first assignment in many college writing classes. This frequently given assignment asks students to explain, to an audience of their classmates, why they have decided to go to college. Notice how this sample theme accomplishes the three types of writing activity explained earlier:

- It focuses on the single idea called for by the assignment and puts this idea in a thesis statement.
- It develops this idea, its thesis, in a straightforward, direct-line fashion.
- It tries to "close the holes" for the reader, making sure no important idea remains ambiguous or unexplained.

SAMPLE THEME

WHY I CHOSE TO GO TO COLLEGE

1   Even if your family and friends pressure you, going to college represents a choice that you must finally make on your own. There are sensible, legitimate alternatives to college, after all, such as enlisting in the military or learning a skilled trade through an apprenticeship program. While these options are appropriate for some people, I chose to go to college for three reasons: I hope to learn the science of busi-

ness management, I want to take full advantage of the open-minded intellectual atmosphere, and I would like to develop a network of friends and potential colleagues for the future.

2   I intend someday to own and operate my own business. While I am certain that I could learn a great deal of "real-world" managerial skills simply by getting a job in someone else's business and learning the ropes that way, I think I will be a better manager if I take a full range of courses that teach me the theories of economics, finance, organizational structure, and communication that a successful manager needs to know. I suppose that one could learn these subjects by reading independently, but why not come to college where you have the chance the study them with experienced, trained experts and educators? If I can get a part-time job in a business while I'm taking these theoretical courses, I think I can really capitalize on my college training after I graduate.

3   Going to college, however, means more than simply taking courses in your major field. Getting a college education involves different kinds of learning experiences that help you become a more well-rounded, open-minded person intellectually. Some of these learning experiences take place in the courses that colleges and universities refer to as "distribution requirements" or "general education" or perhaps "liberal studies" courses. Taking these courses in the humanities, natural sciences and math, and social sciences will help me indirectly in my career as a business manager by giving me a broader knowledge and greater intellectual flexibility to solve problems. A good college education, however, offers you more opportunities to learn liberally than simply taking classes. Most college and universities provide a range of extramural activities—concerts, lectures, plays, colloquiums, art exhibits, and so on—that you should take advantage of. I want to live the intellectual life to it fullest at college, and taking advantage of these extramural events is part of that.

4   Finally, college is more than classes and educational activities. Going to college gives you the opportunity to meet people whose backgrounds and experiences

may differ from yours considerably. By getting to know these people, by exposing myself to the ways their lives and cultures affect their thoughts and actions, I hope to build friendships that I can take away from college and enjoy throughout my life and career.

5   I see going to college as a privilege, not a right or duty, and I would like to make as much of the opportunity as possible.

The single idea, the thesis, that this theme focuses on can be summarized, from the writer's perspective, as follows: "I went to college to learn the science of management, to get a liberal education, and to meet different kinds of people." The theme leaves little room for the reader to be confused about this central idea. Its development is direct and straightforward—first one reason, then the second, then the third. And in each paragraph, the writer provides explanations and examples that are designed to make the reasons he went to college clear and unambiguous for the reader.

As useful as the theme is in many classes, particularly in those for which you have to write examinations or research papers, it is not the genre that you should plan to use for the Exploration Project. In other words, a theme is not an exploratory essay. Before we examine that genre, though, we need to look at a type of composition that sits at the opposite end of the spectrum from the theme.

At the other end of the continuum, let's agree to call an *open essay* a composition that develops a series of related ideas, not a single, well-focused one, but does not attempt to reach closure, a sense of the "final word," on any of them. An open essay usually does not develop in a straight-line, sequential fashion. Instead, it might be said to build on the writer's almost-free associations on the subject matter of the composition. The open essay does not attempt to explain fully the nuances and implications of the ideas it takes up. Instead, its principal aim is to *complicate* the ideas it considers.

My former colleague and sometime coauthor, William Covino, is a major proponent of using the open essay in teaching writing. In his book *Forms of Wondering* (Portsmouth, NH: Heinemann, 1990), Covino describes the open essay as a genre in which "you exploit the ways your subject is connected to other subjects" and "practice deliberative associative thinking" (285). He outlines four steps for writing an open essay:

- Write a five-paragraph theme.
- In each paragraph, pick a concept—a general or abstract word—and write an "expansion" paragraph about that concept. Focus on the concept's past uses, its role in your personal experience, its conse-

quences, what others have said about it, another concept that is broader or more important than it, a particular instance of it in public life, how it is defined in other cultures, or some variation of these.

- In each paragraph, pick an action and write one "expansion" paragraph about it, focusing on the action's past uses, its role in your own personal experience, its consequences, what others have said about it, another action that is broader or more important than it, a particular instance of it in public life, how it is defined in other cultures, an analogy to another action, or some variation of the above.
- Mix the original paragraphs and the expansion paragraphs "in an order that *implies* (hints at) a 'train of thought' on your part." (285–90)

"From an open essay," Covino writes, "readers come away with an *experience* rather than a particular point" (290).

Following Covino's open-essay method, I converted my composition about going to college from a theme to an open essay. Here's how I did it:

- From the first paragraph of the theme, I selected the concept of "alternatives to college" and wrote an expansion paragraph about what other cultures think about that. From the first paragraph, I also selected the action of "learning a skilled trade" and wrote an expansion paragraph about the consequences of doing so.
- From the second paragraph of the theme, I focused on the concept of " 'real-world' managerial skills" and wrote an expansion paragraph on Junior Achievement companies, an example of real-world managerial skills in public life. From the second paragraph, I also selected the action of "reading independently" and wrote an expansion paragraph drawing an analogy between reading independently and wandering through the woods.
- From the third paragraph of the theme, I focused on the concept of "liberal education" and wrote an expansion paragraph about a quotation concerning this concept by the nineteenth-century poet and literary critic Matthew Arnold. Also from the third paragraph, I selected the action of "going to plays" and wrote an expansion paragraph about my own personal experience as a theatergoer.
- From the fourth paragraph of the theme, I focused on the concept of "friendship" and wrote an expansion paragraph about another concept that may be broader and more important for some college students, "simple acquaintance." From the fourth paragraph, I also selected the action of "making friends and acquaintances" and

wrote an expansion paragraph that contrasted the past uses of this action with its present uses.

- From the fifth paragraph of the theme, I selected the concept of the "privilege of going to college" and wrote an expansion paragraph about how other cultures view this concept, and I chose the action of "taking full advantage of going to college" and wrote an expansion paragraph drawing an analogy to "testing the waters" of a clear, refreshing river.

- After writing all these expansion paragraphs, I mixed them in with the original paragraphs of the theme and rearranged the entire composition to hint at my train of thought.

Here is the open essay that resulted:

SAMPLE OPEN ESSAY

WHY I CHOSE TO GO TO COLLEGE—AN OPEN ESSAY

1   Even if your family and friends pressure you, going to college represents a choice that you must finally make on your own. There are sensible, legitimate alternatives to college, after all, such as enlisting in the military or learning a skilled trade through an apprenticeship program. While these options are appropriate for some people, I chose to go to college for three reasons: I hope to learn the science of business management, I want to take full advantage of the open-minded intellectual atmosphere, and I would like to develop a network of friends and potential colleagues for the future.

2   Other cultures do not put such intense pressure on young people to go to college because their societies provide reasonable and profitable alternatives to it. In Germany, for example, teenagers are counseled into a variety of internships as part of their formal education. In these internships, which might last several years, students learn a skilled trade and are usually guaranteed a job after completion. A trained, skilled craft or trade worker is highly respected in German culture.

3   Learning a skilled trade certainly has financial consequences—you can get a good job, after all—but the psychological consequences of learning a trade should not be underestimated. When you are accepted into an internship, learn the skills

necessary to perform your craft, and succeed in securing a productive job in a trade, you feel better about yourself as a person. You achieve a well-deserved sense of accomplishment and fulfillment.

4   I intend someday to own and operate my own business. While I am certain that I could learn a great deal of "real-world" managerial skills simply by getting a job in someone else's business and learning the ropes that way, I think I will be a better manager if I take a full range of courses that teach me the theories of economics, finance, organizational structure, and communication that a successful manager needs to know. I suppose that one could learn these subjects by reading independently, but why not come to college where you have the chance the study them with experienced, trained experts and educators? If I can get a part-time job in a business while I'm taking these theoretical courses, I think I can really capitalize on my college training after I graduate.

5   Working with Junior Achievement provides high school students with the chance to experience an instance of "real-world" management skills in a very public setting. Junior Achievement companies organize themselves into management structures, decide how their product will be manufactured, marketed, and delivered, and then distribute the profits according to the preset plans. If a Junior Achievement company succeeds, it does so because its managers—the students themselves—have planned well. If it fails, it does do usually because of poor management.

6   I doubt that I could learn many managerial skills simply by reading independently about them. In many cases, reading independently is like trying to find your way through a heavily wooded forest with just a flashlight and no one to guide you. You can usually see a couple of feet in front of you, so you are not going to bump into a tree and hurt yourself. But you cannot see where the path ahead of you might lead, and you spend lots of time going up "blind alleys," paths that do not lead where you want to go and contain lots of distractions that impede your journey.

7   Going to college represents more than simply taking courses in your major field. Getting a college education involves different kinds of learning experiences

that help you become a more well-rounded, open-minded person intellectually. Some of these learning experiences take place in the courses that colleges and universities refer to as "distribution requirements" or "general education" or perhaps "liberal studies" courses. Taking these courses in the humanities, natural sciences and math, and social sciences will help me indirectly in my career as a business manager by giving me a broader knowledge and greater intellectual flexibility to solve problems. A good college education, however, offers you more opportunities to learn liberally than simply taking classes. Most colleges and universities provide a range of extramural activities—concerts, lectures, plays, colloquiums, art exhibits, and so on—that you should take advantage of. I want to live the intellectual life to its fullest at college, and taking advantage of these extramural events is part of that.

8   As the nineteenth-century British poet and critic Matthew Arnold wrote, "We experience, as we go on learning and knowing, . . . the need of relating what we have learned and known to the sense which we have in us for conduct, to the sense which we have in us for beauty." This quotation, it seems to me, captures the essence of the usefulness of a liberal education. We learn ideas, information, and perspectives from a wide variety of sources so that we can ask ourselves, "Now that I know all this, what am I going to do differently in my life? How is the world going to seem a richer and more beautiful (defined broadly) place to me?"

9   I believe my liberal education has been deeply enriched by the experience of going to plays. The art of drama seems to me so much richer and more fulfilling than other art forms—literature, film, music, dance, and visual arts. Certainly all these art forms bring vital, important, and engaging stories to life, but to my taste, no novel, painting, concert, or recital makes a narrative more alive and engaging than an excellent play well performed.

10   While I know I will learn a great deal from taking challenging courses and going to extracurricular events, I know that college is more than classes and educational activities. Going to college gives you the opportunity to meet people whose backgrounds and experiences may differ from yours considerably. By getting to know

these people, by exposing myself to the ways their lives and cultures affect their thoughts and actions, I hope to build friendships that I can take away from college and enjoy throughout my life and career.

11   Perhaps I should not expect too much of the friendships I make in college, though. Another concept that may be broader and, to a student, ultimately more important than friendship is simple acquaintance. There is a matter of definition at work here. You might say that people whom you casually meet—say, in a class or in your dormitory or apartment building—are your "friends." But are they really? Would you confide in them if you needed to talk about something serious? Would you trust them to help you out if you were in need? Perhaps it would be better to refer to the many people whom you might meet in college as "intellectual and social acquaintances"— people who know what kind of thinker you are from encountering you in classes, and people who know what kind of social creature you are from talking to you at parties, for example. You may make a few friends at college, but you will probably come into contact with a great many intellectual and social acquaintances.

12   In the past, students might have felt compelled to make friends and acquaintances in college simply for the fun of getting to know people like themselves. Now, however, as students leave college and go into the world of work, they may wish they had become acquainted with many more people from different backgrounds and cultures than their own. The world of work requires you to adapt to and get along with people who may be radically different from anyone you have met before.

13   I see going to college as a privilege, not a right or duty, and I would like to make as much of the opportunity as possible. You can really only understand what a privilege going to college is in the United States when you contrast the percentage of students who go on to some form of higher education here with another country. In the People's Republic of China, for example, only 3 percent of students graduating from secondary school go on to postsecondary education. In Great Britain, about 15 percent go on to a university. In the United States, over 60 percent of all students graduating from high school are able to go on to college.

14   Taking full advantage of everything a college education provides is like suddenly finding a cool, clean river flowing by your house on a hot, humid day. The river is there—it's clean, safe, inviting, challenging, and refreshing. Why not at least put your feet in and test the waters? Why not jump in for a swim?

Notice how the open essay differs from the theme. The theme focuses on a single, clear idea—its thesis. The open essay examines many ideas that are related, in varying degrees, to a single idea. The theme develops its thesis in a direct, straight-line fashion. The open essay invites the writer (and by extension the reader) to digress and diverge off the straight-line path of development. The theme tries to close any possible "holes" of interpretation for the reader. The open essay, by its very nature, says to the reader, "There are lots of gaps here—lots of opportunities with this subject matter for you to muse, to ponder, to contemplate connections. So let yourself do it!"

Many writers find writing an open essay a liberating, mind-expanding experience. Unfortunately, few opportunities arise in college and university classes to write an open essay, to associate freely on paper or diskette and, in the process of doing so, *build* a challenging train of thought. As with writing a theme, however, the ability to write an open essay is a valuable talent. If the occasion presents itself—if it would ever be appropriate for you to write a personal, open essay—give it a try.

The open essay, however, is just a bit *too* open to accomplish the work of the Exploration Project. The open essay does not so much *guide* and *lead* a reader to explore the complications that every challenging subject matter contains as it simply *presents* them for the readers' inspection. For our project, in which we hope to *suggest* or *point* to central ideas that we might develop more fully in working documents, we need to consider the genre that sits at the middle of our continuum, the *exploratory essay.*

The exploratory idea does concentrate on developing a central idea, a *thesis*, but the central idea must be rich and complex enough to embody the complicated thinking that has gone into exploring the subject. That is, the thesis of an exploratory essay must be *multifaceted*. An exploratory essay must invite the reader to see the subject matter from several perspectives, not just one. Thus, an exploratory essay does not necessarily try to achieve closure on its thesis, a sense of "the final word" about it. An exploratory essay develops in a sequential manner, but when you write an exploratory essay, you are permitted, even encouraged, to digress occasionally from this sequential development in order to add details that emerge from your mental associations. You are permitted, even encouraged, to show the reader how your mind is associating and connecting ideas and to suggest how the details you add are important for you personally and for your culture. Because an exploratory essay does not attempt to achieve complete closure on its central idea, it both explains intricacies and implications of its thesis and complicates the thesis by raising additional questions about it.

A SAMPLE EXPLORATORY ESSAY

Reprinted here is an exploratory essay written by Jeanette Doane, a student at DePaul University, as part of her Inquiry Contract about an aspect of the sample domain. You read Jeanette's Contract Proposal when you started to work on your Inquiry Contract, and you will get to know Jeanette's work much better in Part Two of this book, where her work is used to illustrate the Trim-and-Target Method of revising.

Jeanette wrote a series of compositions about the treatment of boys and girls in school. Pay careful attention to her exploratory essay here. You'll see it again in a radically different form in Part Two, where it appears in first-draft and final-draft form.

Notice five features of the form and organization of an exploratory essay that Jeanette's paper demonstrates:

- An exploratory essay nearly always begins by setting out the context of the issue it is exploring and by suggesting, without stating directly, why this is an important issue for readers to consider.
- An exploratory essay rarely contains a single sentence that one can say is a distinct thesis statement, but it does have a central idea, a thesis, that it offers to readers, often indirectly, in the first one or two paragraphs.
- An exploratory essay nearly always has what I call an "explorer statement," in which it suggests the directions that it will take and hints at the questions it will raise.
- An exploratory essay "walks through" the development of its central idea by openly showing the reader where the writer's thinking is going, by providing generalizations, by providing specific stories and descriptions, and by showing transitions from one idea to the next.
- An exploratory essay frequently ends by focusing on the question "So what?" It does not necessarily return to or reiterate its thesis; it does, instead, challenge the reader to think about what the implications of being convinced by this main idea would be.

Each of these features is annotated in the margins of Jeanette's essay.

GENDER BIAS: AVENUES FOR CHANGE

1   Although the treatment of women has improved dramatically over the years, one must admit that society does not yet value the sexes equally. This lack of equality is particularly evident in education; young women do not receive the attention,

funding, and praise that their male counterparts enjoy. Why is the dropout rate higher for women than it is for men? Why do male athletic programs

Establishes the im-portance of the issue and sets it in context

receive more money than those for women? Why do teachers ask males more questions and spend more one-on-one time with their male students than they do with their female students? Most gender bias is due to society's reluctance to change antiquated views. What can be done by teachers, parents, and administrators to alleviate the problem?

2   While many people recognize the need for gender reform at all educational levels, most do not know how to go about changing the system. In addition, many do not even want the educational system to change. It has been

Writer uses own experience as a starting point

my experience that many feminist attempts are written off as being "femiNazi extremist measures." I cannot tell you how many times both men and women have agreed that change is necessary, only to dismiss every suggestion for reform as being completely unrealistic and not worth the effort. This attitude is precisely the prob-

"Explorer" state-ment: suggests the main idea the essay will develop

lem in so many areas of concern today. People and society are unwilling to change the traditional roles of men and women. Young women will only cease to be docile, dependent, pretty puppets once society convinces them that their ideas and insights are valued as much as those of their outspoken, independent, confident male counterparts. This will only occur once people realize that change is imperative now.

3 *Status quo think-ing reviewed*

Current thinking on gender issues in schools is split between those who believe that change is necessary now and those who feel that feminists are spending too much time and energy trying to reform a system that doesn't need to be changed. After all, what was good enough in the past

Shows the writer's thinking at work

is good enough for today's students, right? Conversations with many family members and classmates have convinced me that despite their politically correct appearances, a lot of people are still caught up in the archaic thinking of the past. Unfortunately, the past is not good enough any more; if

women on a whole are ever to achieve complete equality, the   *Change the* status
quo *now*
proper preparation of young girls must start now.

4   In an age where more women are entering the workplace than ever before, it
makes sense to teach young girls the characteristics necessary to succeed in the
professional world. However, young women are torn between two worlds. Academia
says that females are as intelligent and capable as men, while the media portrays
ideal women as pretty, thin, dependent, quiet, well-behaved individuals with the self-
esteem of ants. Consequently, *Reviving Ophelia* author Mary Pipher says, society is
turning out more troubled girls than ever before. What will happen when these young
women, riddled by eating disorders, sexual promiscuity, and lost identities enter the
workplace? Unfortunately, many of these girls will never finish   *Another thought-*
ful question sug-
high school, let alone earn their post-secondary degrees.   *gests the writer's*
train of thought
Those who do manage to become successful still lack self-confidence and feel enormous pressure to be perfect. These problems are not limited to
race or class, but they are exclusively female. As the real world becomes harsher, it
will be even more difficult for adult women to sort out the problems of their adolescence. This will most likely cause problems in their relationships with others, especially those of the family. In order to ensure that healthy, well adjusted women enter
the workplace and become productive members of society, society needs to start
preparing them at an early age.

5   One method of preparation, and perhaps the most ex-   *One alternative;*
notice the concrete
treme, is to completely segregate boys and girls in terms of   *detail with which*
it is developed
education. In addition, the school itself would not hold traditional gender roles; administrators and teachers of advanced subjects could be female instead of almost exclusively male. Cafeteria workers, cleaning staff,
groundskeepers, and secretarial staff would be equally divided in terms of gender.
Students would wear some sort of uniform, (preferably pants) in order to take the
focus off of designer labels and physical appearance. Family members would be encouraged to take an active part in the educational process.

6   At an early age, girls would be the ones to run the VCR or slide projector; they would carry the sports equipment as well as set out the milk for lunch and mix the paints for art class. Both traditionally male and female toys would be available to them; textbooks and library books would portray women in a positive light. Elementary school teachers would encourage girls to develop their rambunctious, outspoken personalities rather than chiding them for not being quiet and lady-like.

7   Such development in personality would continue throughout the traditionally difficult middle school and high school years. Special classes would focus on sexuality, self-confidence, and positive body image. Students and teachers would discuss the portrayal of women by the media; they would also explore their families' expectations of them and traditional gender roles. Class selection would be determined on the basis of interest and ability rather than on stereotypical gender roles. Both concentrations in humanities and those in sciences will be considered perfectly acceptable. Most importantly, students would be encouraged to determine what type of person they want to be; they would learn the importance of forming strong, healthy relationships with both the men and women in their lives.

8   The curriculum of such a school would concentrate on forming a strong base of knowledge in all areas, with the opportunity for students to take elective courses in the fine arts, industrial arts, mass media, and home economics. Discussion based seminars in which the students are active participants and make decisions regarding the structure of the class are wonderful for culturing self-esteem and confidence; they also prepare young women for their high school and post-secondary education. Health classes would educate young women about eating disorders, alcohol and drug abuse, and the dangers of early sexual activity, but the real focus would be on maintaining a positive body image and a healthy lifestyle. Young women would be encouraged to retain their active, imaginative, energetic personalities rather than succumbing to the personality of the traditional, well-behaved, respectful, docile lady. Of course, they would still be taught to be respectful and polite, but they would be encouraged to develop their personalities rather than stifle

them. This would eliminate many problems, because most psychologists agree that typical problems of adolescence stem from the child's struggle to become their own person while realizing that they need to please others in order to be accepted and loved. Often, they feel that accep-   *Ironic tone shows writers mind at work*
tance will be offered only if they conform to traditional roles. After all, everyone loves a well-behaved, quiet, polite girl who doesn't cause trouble.

9   Segregated education has many benefits, the most im-   *Writer outlines benefits of the proposed alternative*
portant being that young women are encouraged to develop and maintain distinct personalities and huge levels of self con-fidence. Class participation and input into course development will prepare girls for education at the university level, as will increased levels of self-esteem. Young women will generally be a lot happier; they will pursue education and careers in subjects they are interested in rather than those they feel pressures to like. In addi-tion, rates of teen pregnancy, dropout, suicide, and eating disorders should drasti-cally decrease; it is no secret that these problems are directly related to low confidence and self-esteem levels.

10   One major drawback of segregated education is that men   *Writer analyzes potential draw-backs to plan*
and women are not segregated in the real world. How can women claim to be equal to men when they cannot be edu-cated with them? In addition, one might claim that girls taught in segregated envi-ronments might get the impression that men are bad, which could lead to negative relationships with the men in their lives. However, I don't think that this would be a substantial issue; girls will only learn that they are equal by experiencing the same things that their male counterparts do. Unfortunately, this simply cannot happen in today's boy/girl schools. I have numerous friends who attended all-girls Catholic schools, and they had nothing but praise for them. However, I have heard some of them say that they wished they had at-   *Writer thinking through the issue*
tended single sex elementary schools as well, for this is when

traditional sex roles begin to become firmly implanted. Girls' and boys' schools could have mixers, joint field trips, and dances in order to facilitate interaction between the sexes; teachers would emphasize that men are in no way bad, and would encourage healthy relationships between males and females.

11 *A second alternative, again described with concrete details*

Another method for instituting gender reform in today's schools would be to completely wipe out everyone's mind and start fresh. Elementary school classrooms would be completely integrated; boys and girls would never be ridiculed by being forced to sit together or pitted against each other in singing contests. In addition, schools would attempt to be more gender sensitive. Textbooks and library books would portray women positively; students would discuss traditional gender roles and why they are not always accurate. Both bays and girls would have equal opportunities to use equipment and have one on one time with the teacher. Health classes stressing healthy lifestyles and positive body image would be required for all students.

12 *Benefits and drawbacks to the second alternative handled in the same paragraph*

A benefit of simply revising the existing system is that it would teach boys and girls to actively socialize and get along at an early age. On the other hand, antisexist schools and classrooms that attempt to make everything equal for men and women have not worked thus far. The main reason for the failure of these systems and the reason why I don't believe it will ever work is that society is not going to change easily, and in a system that is not radically different from one that is in place now it won't be forced to. I concede that schools do not exist in a vacuum, and that students of an all-girls' system would still be affected by media influences. However, I do think that it is the best alternative and most effective system feasible at this time.

13

Ends with consideration of "so what?"

In short, a lot of changes that I would institute in an all-girls' school would be in place in traditional boy/girl schools. However, the fundamental problem with this system is that most people are reluctant to change their views on certain issues; unfortunately, gender is one such issue. In order for such change to work, the media, government, and most importantly, families must make a commitment to educating our young women and preparing them to be healthy, happy adults. How can a little boy realize that women are not inferior to men when he sees his father beat up his mother or refuse to let him play with dolls? How can a small girl learn that she is as capable and intelligent as boys are when she watches her older sister starve herself in order to be more attractive to teenage boys and sees her mother meekly obey her father's unreasonable whims? The answer is simple: they can't. It is only with efforts from all sides that we can save the young women of the future from falling into the same trap that so many girls before them have.

In-Progress Task

After you have read Jeanette's exploratory essay carefully, meet with your writing-as-inquiry group or with one or two other people who have read the composition. Concentrating only on the quality, organization, and development of Jeanette's ideas—not on her sentence structure, style, mechanics, punctuation, or grammar—make a list of two things Jeanette did well in her essay. Then list at least two specific things Jeanette might have done differently as she planned and wrote this paper that would have improved it as an exploratory essay.

10 Writing to Make a Difference: Changing Minds and Influencing Action

As you have discovered through working on your Inquiry Contract, writing provides lots of educational benefits for you. When you propose a subject to inquire into, clarify for yourself what you feel, believe, think, and know about it, then learn something about it and report what you have learned, you have done *yourself* a great service. You have probably learned more about your subject than if you had simply read or heard lectures about it. You may feel as though you have changed your mind about the subject you have been inquiring into. You may also feel that you now want to act differently in regard to your subject. That's good!

But while your own learning is important, writing has more than a self-serving value. Ultimately, writing is a tool, an instrument to effect change. It is important to use writing to change your own mind and influence your own actions; it is equally important, if not more so, to use writing to change other people's minds and influence their actions.

This chapter introduces some principles of thinking and writing that come into play when you try to do just that—change other people's minds and influence their actions. The chapter sets the stage for the final project in the Inquiry Contract, the Working Documents Project, described in Chapter 11, for which you will produce a document designed to address a specific group of readers whose minds or actions you hope to influence. The Working Documents Project will allow you to draw on insights and use material that you have generated in all the previous projects in the Inquiry Contract. In preparation for the final project, we need to examine the nature of the transaction involved when you write to change people's minds or actions, focus on some important definitions you should know about this kind of writing, and examine three important strategies you can use in writing projects of this kind.

WHAT DO YOU WANT TO ACCOMPLISH, AND WITH WHOM?

The first step in writing to change people's minds or actions is obvious. You need to decide, at least tentatively and provisionally, (A) *how* you would like people to think or act differently and (B) *who* you would like to think or act in this way. As you will see, these two decisions are closely related. As simple as it might sound to make these decisions, both of them require considerable thought, and your thinking about them might undergo considerable revision as you work on your writing-as-inquiry project. You need to be flexible and let your thinking change as necessary. For simplicity of reference, let's call Decision A your *persuasive goal* and Decision B your *audience.*

As you think about both of these decisions, consider two terms from an important piece of scholarship about effective communication, an article written in 1968 by Lloyd Bitzer called "The Rhetorical Situation." Bitzer explains that in any situation in which you want to use language to get people to think or act differently—that is, in any *rhetorical situation*—you will find three elements. The first two are related to Decisions A and B.

First, Bitzer explains, in any rhetorical situation there is an *exigence*—a gap, a lack, something missing, something that needs to be done—that *can be* addressed by your writing. Suppose, for example, that you are working on an Inquiry Contract related to an aspect of the sample domain about the nature of a college education. Specifically, you are inquiring into the role that extracurricular activities play in a liberal education. You determine that students at your college or university are missing out on important educational opportunities because they don't know about the many student organizations they can join. You have discovered an exigence, a problematic situation that you *can* address with a piece of writing—perhaps an open letter to students or a brochure about student organizations. In response to this exigence, you establish for yourself a *persuasive goal:* you would like your fellow students at least to know about student organizations and ideally to join one, and you can work toward accomplishing that goal by writing something.

Second, Bitzer points out, a rhetorical situation contains an *audience,* a group of readers (or listeners) *capable of acting on this exigence.* The last phrase is particularly important. When you are writing to change people's minds and actions, you need to think carefully about who is a likely candidate for such a change, about who is really in a position to think or act in the way that you are proposing. If your persuasive goal is to get students to know about the range of student organizations and ideally to get them to join one, then your audience is not all students but a subset of that group—those students who *don't* know about student organizations and don't belong to one. There is no sense in writing to students who already belong to an organization. That approach, to use an old expression, would be "preaching to the choir"—trying to convince those who already believe. The audience in a rhetorical situation consists of *those people whose minds or actions you need to change.*

Notice how decisions about your persuasive goal and your audience are closely related. For the persuasive goal described in the previous paragraph, your audience could not be the college or university administrators. They are not capable of acting on the exigence and the persuasive goal you have set out. They don't join student organizations. If, however, you determine that the college or university administration does not do enough to promote student organizations and therefore students don't know about them or join them, then you have determined a different exigence and a different persuasive goal, one that would involve a different audience. In response to this new exigence and persuasive goal, you could write a letter to a dean or director of student services, with the goal of getting him or her to work toward promoting student organizations.

 ## In-Progress Task

In your learning journal, write a brief paragraph explaining a possible persuasive goal for a final project in your Inquiry Contract, the exigence that motivates that goal, the audience to whom such a project would be directed, and the genre you would produce. Then write another paragraph briefly setting out the same items for a *different* persuasive goal.

SHAPING THE WRITING FOR THE AUDIENCE

As you think about what your persuasive goal is and what audience might be in the position to act on it, you also have to consider carefully *what* you want to write or say to this audience to get them to think or act in the way you want. This consideration brings up a third element that Bitzer says one always finds in a rhetorical situation. He calls this element the *constraints* of the situation. I prefer to use a term from classical rhetoric to label this element—*appeals.* In a rhetorical situation, the appeals include those ideas, attitudes, and beliefs that the audience holds that you, the writer or speaker, must bring up and capitalize on if you hope to influence the audience's thinking or behavior in the way you want. For example, in your open letter to students who need to know about organizations, you might stress both the professional and the social benefits of joining an organization. You could capitalize on your audience's belief that part of the reason for getting a college education is to develop interpersonal skills that will serve you in whatever field you choose after college and to build a circle of new friends and acquaintances.

We will look later at three distinct yet interrelated ways to appeal to your audience: by appealing to their emotions and "self-interests," by appealing to your own credibility as a person and a writer, and by appealing to your readers' patterns of reasoning. Before examining these three kinds of appeals, however, we need to devote a little more attention to defining an audience in a rhetorical situation. After all, appeals are only appealing when they speak to readers who can respond to them.

THE WRITER-READER TRANSACTION: READERS (ONE TO MANY) WITH ATTITUDES (LOTS OF THEM)

When you think about how to appeal to an audience to get them to think or act in a new way about your subject, you are taking part of the work you have already done on the Inquiry Contract one step farther. By this point in the contract, you no doubt understand a good deal about envisioning readers for your writing. You wrote primarily to yourself in the Clarification Project, but you worked up a profile for an envisioned reader for the Information and Exploration Projects. In doing so, you thought about how to appeal to this reader, though we did not use the term *appeals* in our discussions. You envisioned a reader who would be interested in learning about your subject and probing its complicated corners; thus, you thought about appealing to your hypothetical reader's innate admiration for intelligent treatments of complicated topics. You conceived this person as a cooperative reader, one who would help you learn about and explore your subject; thus, you thought about appealing to your reader's inherent kindness and intellectual curiosity.

Determining who your audience is and how to appeal to them is considerably more complicated when you are trying to change their minds or actions. First, for many writing projects, even those for which your purpose is informative or exploratory, as in the previous two projects in the contract, you do not write to one hypothetical person whose identifying characteristics you get to create by using your imagination. In most writing situations, your audience will vary according to number and identity—how many readers you are writing to and how precisely you can identify their characteristics, their traits that your writing should appeal to.

In some situations, you might write to one person whose ideas, attitudes, and beliefs you can identify. For example, if you were to write a letter about student organizations to the dean of student affairs at your college or university, you could make some inquiries about the dean; speculate in advance of writing your letter how he or she might react to whatever it is you are proposing; and then, as the second half of this chapter demonstrates, work to appeal directly to the dean's ideas, attitudes, or beliefs. In other situations, you might write to one reader—perhaps your instructor—who can be thought of as representing many other readers. The next section of this chapter explains this idea in more detail. In still other situations, you might write to many people, all of whose characteristics you can identify and appeal to with some certainty. For example, if you attend a college or university where many students live off campus and commute to school and you choose to write an open letter (a possibility for the Working Documents Project described in Chapter 11, by the way) to these students about joining student organizations, you might be able to predict what their attitudes toward joining one might be. In yet other situations, you might write to a large group of readers whose characteristics you cannot identify; thus, deciding how to appeal to their ideas, attitudes, and beliefs might require some speculation on your part. For example, if you were to write an opinion-piece editorial column (another possibility for the Working Documents Project in Chapter 11) about the usefulness of student organizations and try to publish it in the local town, city, or regional newspaper that covers your college or university, you would know that the column might be read by thousands of people, but you might not be certain how they feel about your institution, its students, and the possible interactions they might have with your school's student organizations.

In addition to differing according to how many readers you are writing to and how fully you can identify and appeal to them, writing situations vary according to the degree to which your readers are willing to accept your persuasive goal, the new way of thinking and acting you are proposing. Think about a spectrum of readers, with attitudes toward your persuasive goal ranging from positive to neutral to antagonistic. At one of this spectrum, you might be writing to readers about whom you can safely say, "Hey, these people are on my side. They are already leaning toward what I want them to think or do. I simply need to help them make the decision they already want to make." At the middle of this spectrum, you might be writing to readers who in effect say to you, "Okay, just let me have the information, or let me read your ideas, or let me consider your main point, and I'll tell you whether I can accept it. I'm not leaning one way or another—I'm neutral." At the other end of the spectrum, you might be writing to readers who in effect tell you, "You should probably know in advance that you and I differ on the important issues about your topic, so your information, your explorations, your ideas had better be really good if you want me to accept what you have to say. You're going to have to change my mind."

 ## In-Progress Task

For each of the possible persuasive goal-exigence-audience-genre combinations you developed for the last In-Progress Task, write a paragraph in which you assess the degree to which you can identify the audience specifically and the degree to which the audience is predisposed to accept your persuasive goal.

ONE READER (YOUR INSTRUCTOR, PERHAPS) AS AN EXEMPLAR OF MANY

All this discussion of determining who your readers are might seem to mask a simple truth for you. "Get real," you might be saying. "My instructor is the reader. She will be the final judge of my writing and will give me a grade on it." True enough for most writing situations in college—your instructor is the reader. Faced with this inescapable fact, then, you might first ask the following questions about your reader when you are planning any writing project:

- What is my instructor's attitude toward writing in general? Is she or he a stickler for correctness? Does he or she like long papers or short? Elaborate writing or simple?
- What is my instructor's attitude toward me, my subject, my inquiry? Where does he or she fall along the spectrum of cooperative and encouraging to neutral to antagonistic?
- What does my instructor already feel, think, believe, and know about me, my subject, my inquiry? How do I know she or he feels, thinks, believes, or knows these things?

But before you spend too much time trying to psych out your instructor and figure out what exactly he or she wants, consider this potentially oddball question: Are you sure that your instructor is, in a manner of speaking, just *one* reader, just *one* person?

Let's keep going with this oddball reasoning. I propose that your instructor is not *simply* your instructor. That is, the attitudes, feelings, and ideas she or he has about your writing, your subject, and your inquiry are ones that many people in his or her field share. Oh, your instructor may have a few individual quirks and pet peeves about writing. In general, however, it's wise to think about your instructor not as an isolated, quirky, different reader but as an *exemplar*—a *model reader* in his or her field, a person who is *similar* to other readers and, therefore, *representative* of readers in the field. If you can think about your instructor as being *one of many* rather than just *one*, you will have more information to work with when you try to determine what feelings, beliefs, ideas, and attitudes you need to appeal to, and potentially change, with your writing.

This term *exemplar* might be new to you. An *exemplar* is an ideal model of a certain type of person. For example, many people think Mother Theresa was an exemplar of the type of person devoted to charity and service, that Martin Luther King Jr. was an exemplar of the type of person dedicated to nonviolent political activism, and that General George Patton was an exemplar of the type of person who believes in the essential nobility of military service.

So how is your instructor an exemplar? Most instructors are exemplars of three types of readers. First, a college or university instructor is almost always an exemplar of genuinely curious, well-educated people who read widely and enjoy studying clearly focused, well-developed books and articles on a variety of subjects. Therefore, think of your instructor as an exemplar of *educated generalists*. Second, an instructor is usually an exemplar of people who believe that whatever they read and take seriously must be clearly and correctly written, following the rules of standard written English. Therefore, think of your instructor as an exemplar of *correctness-oriented readers*. Third, an instructor is nearly always an exemplar of some group of people who have a deep, sometimes intense, interest and special knowledge in some particular domain of inquiry. Often this subject is one that the instructor has studied in his or her undergraduate or graduate education, but it might also be a field the instructor has been led to investigate by her or his own innate curiosity. Therefore, think of your instructor as an example of *committed specialists* in some subject.

The reason you should think about your instructor not as an isolated, individual, quirky reader but instead as an exemplar of these three types of people has lots to do with your success in writing to change people's minds and actions. When you write to change minds and actions, you say to your reader, in essence, "I don't necessarily want to *become* you, but I want to become *like* you, at least long enough for you to consider my ideas and see whether you can accept them." To get this message across to your reader(s), you should think not only about the actual people he, she, or they are but also about the *type* of people he, she, or they are *like*. Considering your reader, especially your instructor, as an exemplar, as one among many, can help you determine what you need to use your writing to change—what feelings, beliefs, and ideas you want to influence and what actions you want to promote.

APPEALING TO THE INTERESTS OF YOUR READERS: WHAT'S IN IT FOR THEM?

Once you have gotten a good start toward marking hard decisions about exigence, audience, and persuasive goals, you can start planning how exactly you want to *appeal* to your readers so they will be convinced that your exigence is one they can respond to and your persuasive goal is one they want to act upon. The next three sections of this chapter will explain three distinct, yet related, strategies for appealing to readers whose minds and actions you want to influence.

One way to get your readers to think or act in a new, different way about your subject is to appeal to their interests and emotions and those of the people they care about as well. For thousands of years, teachers have referred to this "move" in writing as an appeal to the audience's *pathos*.

A question that comes naturally when someone is trying to get us to think or act in a different way is this: "What's in it for me?" Put yourself inside the perspective of the readers whose minds or actions you are trying to influence and ask the same question: "What's in it for them?"

As you begin to generate answers to this question, think first about all of the different concerns and emotions that people have and respond to: love, loyalty, a sense of justice and fairness, ambition, a hope for wealth and prosperity, a desire for physical pleasure, and so on. (The list could go on and on, of course.) Then think about what there is within your persuasive goal, the new way of thinking and acting that you are proposing, that might appeal to these general interests and feelings. As you consider these things, bear in mind that any appeals to your readers' interests and emotions should be genuine and appropriate to the rhetorical situation. You should not stir up your readers' ambition, for example, or stimulate their desire for physical gratification simply because doing so will get their attention. You must look for something *within the rhetorical situation* that will call forth these interests and feelings.

In addition to considering what general interests and feelings in your readers you can appeal to, you should also think about your readers as either individuals or a group of people with special interests. Indeed, the image of a "special interest group," as that term is used in politics, academic disciplines, and the professions, provides a helpful perspective here. A special interest group is a collective of people who choose to bond together because they want to gain insights and information about similar topics or because they want to achieve common goals. As the prior section pointed out, when you decide on an audience who is capable of carrying out your plan, of thinking or acting in the way you hope they will, then you can consider what *particular* interests, feelings, and emotions you might appeal to in your writing.

Suppose, for example, that you are writing an open letter to the administrators of your college or university, asking them to provide more support for student organizations. In your letter, you might appeal to their general feelings of commitment to offering a sound, quality education for all students, and you might appeal to the administrators' particular interests. You might stress, in this regard, how developing an effective system of student organizations will bring great credit to them among their peers and help establish them as national leaders in their field.

 ## In-Progress Task

For each of the potential audiences you have identified in your tasks in this chapter, write a brief paragraph explaining how your project might appeal to their feelings in general and their special interests in particular.

APPEALING TO YOURSELF AS A CREDIBLE PERSON: GOOD SENSE, GOODWILL, AND A "WILD CARD"

In addition to appealing to the feelings and interests of your audience, you can also influence their minds and actions by appealing to yourself as a credible person. Teachers call this an appeal to the writer's *ethos*. There are three major strategies that you can use to establish your credibility with your readers.

The first is perhaps the most obvious. Let's call it the "good sense" strategy. You should do everything you can to show your readers that you have a solid, well-informed perspective on your subject matter—that you have done both some homework and some legwork on your topic, that you have both read and talked widely about your domain and have accumulated a considerable repertoire of interesting and relevant facts, stories, and points of view about it. Suppose, for example, in your letter to the administrators about their support for student organizations, you included an array of facts and details about how other colleges and universities similar to yours support organizations. You might tell the story of a specific person whose life was influenced positively by participating in a student organization. You would come across as a trustworthy person of good sense.

The second strategy you can use to establish your credibility is directly related to the "what's in it for me" appeal described in the previous section. Let's call this second "ethical" tactic the "goodwill" strategy. You should do everything you can to suggest to your readers that you have their best interests in mind when you propose your persuasive goal, when you try to get them to think and act in a different way about your topic. When you show your goodwill to your readers, you appeal to their attitudes and emotions of trust and care—your *ethos* appeals to their *pathos.*

In some cases, you should be able actually to show the readers that you are on *their* side, that not only are you not adversaries but you are, instead, cooperative allies. In your letter to administrators about student organizations, for example, you could emphasize that you and they *share* a concern for offering excellent, liberal education to students. In other cases, however, your persuasive goal may seem far removed from what your readers currently think and do in relation to your topic. In these instances, you need to make a special effort to show the readers that even though you are asking them to change, you sincerely believe that the change would be good for *them,* not simply what *you* want.

Think of the third strategy you can use to establish your credibility with your readers as your "wild card" ethical tactic. Unlike the good sense and goodwill strategies, which you can employ in all situations when you are writing to change minds and actions, this wild card tactic is tied to the particular features of your actual writing situation: your persuasive goal, in all its complexity, and your audience, however fully you can identify them. You should do whatever you can, *related to the specific writing situation at hand,* to demonstrate to your readers that you possess the *particular* personality characteristics and attitudes that would influence them to accept your persuasive goal—to think and act the way you would like them to in relation to your subject. In your letter about student organizations, for example, you might mention that you have special experience in setting up student organization information fairs, and this experience could be a valuable resource for the administrators. Playing a wild card like this enables you to show yourself as a particularly appropriate person for your readers to pay attention to in the specific situation at hand.

 ## In-Progress Task

Read over the work you produced for the Clarity, Information, and Exploration Projects. Determine what material you have generated so far that would help establish you as a writer of good sense and goodwill for the final project in your Inquiry Contract.

APPEALING TO YOUR READERS' SENSE OF REASON: TOP-DOWN AND BOTTOM-UP

A third way to appeal to your readers is to reason with them and, perhaps more important, to *show* them what a reasonable person you are. Since antiquity, teachers have called this appeal *logos*. Let's simply call it the logical appeal. Reasoning clearly and explicitly about your topic is appealing to readers in its own right. It also helps establish your credibility as a person of good sense, and it appeals to the desire for even-handedness and fair treatment of topics that most readers appreciate. The three major appeals you can make in writing designed to change minds and actions, therefore, are closely related: *pathos, ethos,* and *logos* intricately reinforce one another.

Reasoning with your readers means more than simply providing them with whatever array of facts, stories, and perspectives about your topic you may have acquired. Reasoning about your topic entails putting these bits of evidence into *patterns* that lead readers to conclude something about your topic, to generate an innovative, interesting idea about your subject.

You can use two basic reasoning patterns to lead your readers to a conclusion about your topic. Let's call the first the top-down pattern. Here's essentially how it works: As explained earlier in this chapter, when you determine who your audience is, you consider what they already feel, think, believe, and know about your topic. Thus, you can say (or suggest strongly) to your readers, "In general, you believe X about my topic. Here is a specific fact, story, or perspective that fits within this general belief about X. Therefore, you can conclude that X is true." For example, in your letter to administrators, you might reason with them as follows:

- The mission statement of this college argues that learning to interact with others and develop useful networks with other people is a vital part of a liberal education.
- Participating in organizations provides students with these interactive, networking experiences.
- Therefore, student organizations are central to the liberal education mission of the school and deserve your support.

The second reasoning pattern works in a different direction than the first. Let's call it the bottom-up pattern. Let's say you want your audience to believe a certain, specific proposition about your topic. To appeal to their sense of logic and reason, what you need to show them is not a *single example* that illustrates your proposition but instead a *repeated pattern* of examples that shows a *general tendency* for the proposition to be true that you want the audience to believe. Again, in your letter to administrators about organizations, you can relate a series of stories about specific people who have really rounded out their liberal educations, formed solid friendships, and built the basis for their lives and careers by working in student organizations. A single example usually does not move a reader to accept your position, but a pattern of examples can be quite persuasive.

 In-Progress Task

For each of the persuasive goal-exigence-audience-genre combinations you have developed for the tasks in this chapter, write a brief paragraph explaining one piece of top-down reasoning *and* one piece of bottom-up reasoning that you could use in a final project for your Inquiry Contract.

CALLING IN YOUR CARDS: USING YOUR PROJECT TO PLAN EXIGENCE, AUDIENCE, GOAL, AND APPEALS

The ideas covered so far in this chapter can be assembled into a checklist you can use to plan the final composition in your Inquiry Contract, one of the working documents described in Chapter 11 or an alternative "working" genre that you choose in consultation with your instructor. Here is the checklist:

■ What is the exigence for writing your final composition? That is, what is missing, what needs to be done that you can accomplish in a final document in your project?

■ What is your persuasive goal? How would you like people to think or act differently in regard to your subject?

■ Who is your audience? That is, what specific person or group of people are capable of understanding your exigence and acting in response to your persuasive goal? Who *can* think or act in the way you are proposing?

- How can you appeal to the emotions and interests of these readers so they will act in response to your persuasive goal?
- How can you appeal to your own good sense, wisdom, and connection to the writing situation so that your readers will act in response to your persuasive goal?
- How can you appeal to your readers' reasoning and patterns of thinking so that they will act in response to your persuasive goal?

In addition to working with this checklist to plan your final composition, now is the time to "call in your cards" from all the previous projects in the Inquiry Contract and to determine how you can use the ideas, perspectives, and information you have developed in your culminating composition.

The most productive place to look for an exigence, something that needs to be done, and a possible persuasive goal, the particular way you would like your audience to think and act in regard to your subject, is in the Exploration Project and the exploratory essay. All three of the exploration strategies direct you to focus on an exigence. All three say to you, "Here is what most people currently feel, think, believe, and know about your subject, and here's a problem with the fact that they feel, think, believe, or know that." In addition, your exploratory essay, ideally, proposes at least two ways that people could think or act differently about your subject and explains the benefits and drawbacks of thinking or acting in this way. If it is appropriate, you could now use *one* of these as your persuasive goal for a working document.

A likely site for you to find ideas, information, and perspectives to plan your appeals to readers' *pathos* and *logos* and to your own *ethos* is the Information Project and the informative report. Remember the principle of *comprehensiveness* introduced in Chapters 6 and 7—that is, what readers typically feel, think, believe, and know about your subject. You can return to this principle as you plan appeals to *pathos,* the emotions and interests of your readers, and *logos,* particularly top-down appeals. Notice how a top-down appeal begins with either an open statement or a suggestion about what your audience feels, thinks, believes, and knows.

Finally, look back to the Clarification Project, the reflective reading response, the Information Project, and the informative essay as sources for facts, data, information, and perspectives that are laden with *factness* and surprise value. Effective appeals to *logos* rely on such material. You can arrange it into patterns of repeated examples for bottom-up logical appeals. You can use it to make claims about your subject in the middle part of top-down logical appeals. In addition, material that is full of *factness* and surprise value shows that you are an ethical, credible person with the good sense to do lots of reading and talking about your subject, and it appeals to your readers' sense of curiosity about your subject.

You have worked very hard on your Inquiry Contract. Use what you have generated.

 ## In-Progress Task

Nearly everything you have written in your Contract Proposal, reflective reading response, informative report, and exploratory essay has at least some potential use as you plan the final composition in your Inquiry Contract. In your learning journal or elsewhere, write a paragraph in response to each of the following questions:

- In the Exploration Project and the exploratory essay, do you suggest an exigence, something that needs to be done that you can accomplish by writing? What is it? Is there an important idea that you can use as the basis for a persuasive goal? That is, do you see in this project and essay a specific way that you would like people to think or act differently in regard to your subject? If so, what is it?
- In the Information Project and the informative report, what did you learn about how to appeal to readers that you can use to plan your final project? How can the principle of *comprehensiveness* as explained in Chapters 6 and 7 help you plan the appeals you might use to get readers to act on your persuasive goal? How in particular is the principle of comprehensiveness helpful in planning a top-down logical appeal?
- In the Clarification Project, the reflective reading response, the Information Project, and the informative essay, what did you read and learn that you can use to plan your appeals for the final paper? What material did you read, what conclusions did you come up with, that you can use to show readers that you are a sensible, intelligent, credible person? What facts, information, and perspectives did you generate that have enough *factness* and surprise value for you to use to use as you reason with readers and appeal to either their top-down or bottom-up reasoning?

11 Working Documents

Russell Baker,
Growing Up

At this time, I had decided the only thing I was fit for was to be a writer, and this notion rested solely on my suspicion that I would never be fit for real work, and that writing didn't require any.

Thomas Edison,
The Golden Book

There is no excuse for hard work.

When the humorist and prolific writer Russell Baker looked back on his teenage years in his memoir *Growing Up*, he realized the irony of his idea that writing does not require any hard work. In retrospect, Baker would probably have acknowledged that Thomas Edison's terse line about hard work more faithfully captures the essence of effort that must go into all worthwhile projects—including writing. It is true: writing is hard work. But it is hard work that pays great dividends. If you hope to have an impact on others, if you hope to be able to capture people's minds and influence their actions, you can develop no more useful talent than the ability to write clearly, simply, directly, and persuasively. Other abilities serve you well, of course—the ability to read critically and carefully, to speak forcefully and compassionately, to listen sympathetically, to remember facts, dates, and names diligently, to name a few. However, the ability to write in order to create change is the crowning ability. When you learn to write in ways that affect people's minds and actions, you draw together the ability to read, speak, listen, and remember in a dynamic package.

Our goal in this chapter is to introduce the final project in the Inquiry Contract, the Working Documents Project, a composition designed to influence people's thinking and perhaps affect their actions as well. The chapter will explain how to organize and give structure to three genres that are specifically designed to achieve those goals: the opinion-piece editorial column, the open letter, and the brochure. Along the way, we will examine why it is important for college students to think of themselves as writers who can and do change people's minds and actions, and we will discuss how some other genres besides the opinion-piece editorial column, the open letter, and the brochure—specifically more "academic" types of writing—do so.

Before proceeding to the project, however, let's review four important features of documents that can influence people's thoughts and actions:

- These documents respond to an *exigence*—a sense that there is something missing, something that needs doing that *can be* done by writing.
- They target a specific audience, real readers who are concerned, or can be convinced that they are, about this exigence, this something that needs doing.
- They focus on achieving a *persuasive goal*, getting this audience to think and/or act in ways they are not doing already. They work toward achieving this goal by appealing to the credibility, wisdom, and goodwill of the writer and to the feelings, personal interests, intelligence, and thinking of the audience.
- They make use of a *genre*, a type of written composition, that is uniquely suited to getting people to think or act in new ways in regard to the subject matter at hand.

Remember that these four features—exigence, audience, goal, and genre—interact and are all unified under the general goal of changing minds and actions. But it's worth your while as a writer to pose to yourself separate questions about the four features:

- What needs to be done that's motivating me to write?
- To whom can I write who would share my motivation—or, in some cases, whom I can convince to share my motivation?
- What exactly do I want them to think or do?
- What kind of document am I going to write?

The Working Documents Project

Reread everything you have done so far for your writing-as-inquiry project—the Contract Proposal, the self-reflective journal entry, your interview questions and notes and informative report, your notes from the exploration strategies and your exploratory essay, and your notes from the final In-Progress Task in Chapter 10.

Define an exigence, something that is currently *missing* or *needs changing* in the way most people feel, think, believe, and/or act in relation to the subject of your inquiry. Determine an audience, a set of readers who are already concerned about this exigence or whom you could convince to be concerned about it. Focus on a persuasive goal—how you would like these readers to think about your subject or what you would like them to do in regard to it. Think carefully about how you hope to appeal to the readers to get them to think or act in ways consistent with your persuasive goal.

Then write one of three kinds of documents—an opinion-piece editorial column, an open letter, or a brochure—that aims to achieve this persuasive goal, to address this exigence, with these specific readers. Alternatively, with your instructor's guidance, write another kind of working document that similarly achieves a persuasive goal with a specific set of readers.

The remainder of this chapter is devoted to unpacking the organizational structure of the three working documents genres and to examining a model of each. Before doing so, however, we need to consider briefly how college and university student writers are likely candidates to change people's minds and influence their behaviors.

COLLEGE WRITING, PUBLIC DISCOURSE, AND "NEW" KNOWLEDGE

One major difference between writing in high school and writing in college, a difference you may have discovered already, is that writing in college frequently has a *communal* function. In other words, when you write a composition in college, you are often expected to put an idea into play for inspection and possibly even debate in your class, and perhaps beyond your class in seminars and colloquiums that are part of your major. As Chapter 10 explained, even if the only person who actually reads your composition is your instructor, you must learn to think of him or her as an *exemplar* of other audiences, a representative of different forums in which you want your central idea to circulate, be considered, and, ideally, be accepted. In most papers you write, this idea you put into play is supposed to be something "new" and original that you have crafted, a perspective that emerges from your own thinking, not something that you simply parrot back from the class readings or the instructor's lectures.

This expectation that college students should, at least in theory, put their ideas into play for general inspection is as old as universities themselves. The tradition is particularly rooted in American institutions. During the eighteenth and nineteenth centuries, in the early, formative years of American higher education, students attended colleges and universities not so much to train for specific careers as to prepare themselves to assume roles in public life, particularly in government, the church, and education. Enrollment in colleges and universities was much smaller and more restricted then, and people who attended and graduated were expected truly to be leaders in their communities and society. Given this expectation, a great deal of college students' writing instruction was geared toward preparing them for these public roles. They composed long essays about current political affairs and ethical issues, and they were expected to write and deliver speeches, often to the assembled faculty and student body, about current events. Only gradually, in the second half of the nineteenth century, did a college education come to be seen as training for a specific job. With this gradual shift, the public nature of college students' speaking and writing experiences also began to change, and instruction was adapted to help students learn to write and speak well in their college classes and their specific careers, rather than in generally public settings.

In colleges and universities today, some, but certainly not all, students are taught to write essays that might be read by audiences outside the university. Some, but not all, students learn how to deliver speeches about current affairs in public forums. Instead of mingling with the *general* public, college students' compositions now usually interact with the *academic* public composed of their classmates, their professors, and readers with varying levels of expertise in their major fields. In a great many of their classes, moreover, college students today are taught to write in genres that are *working documents* in those specific fields. A person studying early childhood education, for example, is taught to write a genre called a *case study,* a composition that responds to an exigence (usually, the need to know more about a certain personality or behavioral type of infant or young child), addresses an audience (other students, professionals, teachers, and perhaps even parents concerned with early childhood education), has a persuasive goal (to provide concrete observations of a child and to argue what those observations mean in general, theoretical terms), and assumes a specific form (usually a theoretical introduction, followed by a description of the child's observed behaviors and a discussion of what the observed behaviors imply for theory and practice in the field) mandated by the rules of the genre. The case study is thus very much a working document in early childhood education.

Nearly every academic field has a genre that has a working document within it. In some fields in the humanities, a genre called the *critical paper* that lies someplace on the spectrum between the theme and the exploratory essay, as described in Chapter 9, is the principal working document. A *critical paper* has a complicated, often multifaceted thesis such as an exploratory essay. It usually provides evidence, examples, and support for this thesis in a sequential, straight-line fashion like a theme, but it also usually discusses objections and alternatives to the thesis, as an exploratory essay does. If you are asked to write a critical paper (sometimes your instructor may simply call it a *paper*), you should ask lots of questions about whether it should have a distinct thesis, what kind of support you are expected to provide for it, and whether the genre your instructor has in mind permits you to consider alternatives as you develop the thesis.

The genres that the Inquiry Contract leads you to write, particularly the informative report and the exploratory essay, are very useful for producing compositions for college and university classes—compositions, in other words, that are directed toward an academic audience. Similarly, documents such as the critical paper and the case study are important for many of your classes. But college and university students need to see themselves not only as students but also as citizens of their communities, nations, and worlds, and they need to participate in this citizenship by writing. In this chapter, therefore, our focus is on three working document genres that are usually read by the *general* public rather than by an *academic* audience. As you plan and produce your composition, you need to think carefully about what the general public feels, thinks, knows, and believes about your subject, not simply what the *status quo* thinking about it is within your college and university classes.

We have two good, closely related reasons for focusing on these public, working document genres. First, these genres are important in their own right for college students, who should be leaders in their communities and societies, to learn to write—no more or less important than, say, the theme, the exploratory essay, and the critical paper. Second, it is not unreasonable to think that you, the student writer, can be a public figure with your writing, that you can use writing to address actual problems that you, your families, and your communities must confront. You can use writing to change people's minds and actions in public spheres.

WORKING DOCUMENT 1: AN OP-ED COLUMN

One important kind of working document can be found in nearly every newspaper, from major dailies published in large cities around the world to small weeklies and most college and university papers. This is the opinion-piece editorial column, also known as an "op-ed" column. Each newspaper issue usually prints more than one of them; they can usually be found on the page facing the editorial page (the page that carries a reduced version of the paper's masthead, under which are printed two or three editorials, anonymous pieces stating the newspaper's position on issues of interest to its readers). They are called op-ed columns because they are located on the page opposite from the editorial page, though some people claim that nickname comes from abbreviating the two terms *opinion* and *editorial.*

A typical op-ed column is designed to convince readers to think or act in some new way about a particular subject. An op-ed column has three parts:

- A statement of the subject, issue, or problem at hand;
- A series of comments, explanations, illustrations, and examples about the subject, issue, or problem;
- A conclusion, direction, or solution concerning the subject, issue, or problem.

While every op-ed column has these three parts, not every one includes them in this order. Some actually begin with the conclusion, then move to the statement of the subject, issue, or problem, and then provide comments, explanations, illustrations, and examples. Some begin with a bit of description—a scene that illustrates the subject, issue, or problem at hand—then provide comments, explanations, illustrations, and examples of the subject, issue, or problem, and conclude by stating the problem and giving the solution.

Reprinted here is an op-ed column, "The Sorcery of Apprenticeship," that relates to the aspect of the sample domain about the role education plays in preparing students for the world of work. Written by Wilfried Prewo, the director of the Chamber of Commerce and Industry in Hanover, Germany, the column originally appeared in the *Wall Street Journal* in February 1993. Prewo's column makes a useful contribution to our thinking about the relation between schooling and work. More important, for our purposes in this chapter, it provides a clear model of the structure and organization of an op-ed column.

Wilfried Prewo # The Sorcery of Apprenticeship

President Bill Clinton has talked about youth training, or apprenticeship programs, as part of his larger U.S. investment program. In this thought Mr. Clinton is right on target. But building an apprenticeship program need not mean an extensive widening of federal or state bureaucracy. To see how this is so, it is worth taking a moment to review the German apprentice-ship model.

The German economy today is productive largely because of one out-standing factor: a highly skilled labor force. That labor force is the product of systematic youth training: Some 66% of our labor force is represented by certified graduates of the nation's youth training system. The strength of this asset is reflected in the fact that the economy is productive despite some major disadvantages—such as world-class income-tax rates and labor costs that per hour are 60% higher than those of the U.S.

Government Not Involved

The German youth apprenticeship system may be large, but it is based in the private sector. Training takes place on the job. The typical apprentice spends four days a week at his training company and one day in public vo-cational school. Apart from states funding schools and federal law setting broad guidelines, government is not involved.

In 1992, some 595,000 German teenagers between the ages of 15 and 19 left school and entered an apprenticeship program. Some 1.6 million young people, or 6.5% of the labor force, are enrolled in apprenticeship programs.

Typically, teenagers leaving school sign a contract with an employer who will train them for two to three years in any one of some 380 occupa-tions: 36% become craftsmen, 22% industrial blue-collar workers (for ex-ample, machinists or chemical lab assistants), 32% are in office, trade, and other service-sector occupations (salespersons, secretaries, bankers), 8% in the public sector, and 1% in agriculture. Apprentices receive a salary of $500 to $800 a month, or 20% to 25% the salary of a certified employee who has "graduated' from an apprenticeship program.

Together city and regional chambers of industry and commerce orga-nize the system. They register the apprenticeship contracts, certify train-ing companies, regulate and supervise the program, settle disputes, establish examination boards staffed by volunteers, organize midterm and final exams (88% pass), and issue certificates recognized all over Germany and, increasingly, across Europe.

In the Hanover Chamber of Industry and Commerce, where I work, we administer 29,000 apprentices in 166 occupations (18,700 white-collar; 10,300 blue-collar); 7,400 supervisors train the trainees in 5,300 partici-pating companies. In 1992, we administered 12,750 final exams with 6,000 volunteer examiners, and enrolled 13,000 new apprentices. Of our total chamber staff of 215, 40 work in the training department.

For Mr. Clinton, who focuses on the underemployment of young peo-ple, the German system has big attractions. One is the seamless transition from school to training to work. Some 70% of young Germans sign up for apprenticeships—and, if they perform well, guaranteed jobs. Contrast this with the aimless wandering from minimum-wage job to minimum-wage job of many American high-school graduates. At age 25, Americans who have not attended college often find themselves no higher up the job ladder than they were at age 18. Their German counterparts, by contrast, usually hold well-paying skilled jobs.

Americans traditionally have wanted a college education for their children. An important factor in the German success, though, is recognizing that college is not always the answer. Many jobs, in fact, do not call for a costly college education. The America pro-college bent often yields overqualified and directionless people: An otherwise unemployed biologist works as a chemistry lab assistant. In Germany, a lab assistant is a person trained as such. There's no wasteful academic detour.

The German system, however, does not close the door on education. In their late 20s, about 10% of ex-apprentices enroll in further training to become supervisors. In 1991, 17,000 such Germans received such higher certification in industrial jobs; 16,000 in office jobs. The cream of the alumni crop then trains the apprentices in the workplace.

The system strengthens the tradition of internal advancement. Hilmar Kopper, the chief executive of Deutsche Bank, the largest in Germany, does not have a university degree. He joined his bank after high school as an apprentice. Werner Niefer, retiring president of Mercedes, started there 50 years ago as a mechanics apprentice.

For the jobs-oriented Mr. Clinton, it might be worth noting that youth training is the best unemployment insurance. In May 1992, German unemployment was at 6.2%, but for those with occupational training only 4%. Here, youth unemployment is below the general jobless rate, a relationship that is the reverse in most other countries. In the U.S., youth joblessness is double the average.

What works and what doesn't? Germany's centuries-long experience in apprenticeships has shown youth training works best when it is based in the workplace. Teenagers, particularly less-gifted teenagers, have strong doubts about the relevance of high-school classroom work. In the workplace, young apprentices are among adult workers, so they have models to emulate. The reward for their successful work is a clear one—after certification, a quadrupling of their paychecks.

For employers, the system has many advantages. Curricula change in a bottom-up process with technology, not top-down when school boards think so.

Worthwhile Investment

Training does cost dearly. In 1991, German industry spent $27 billion for equipment, company supervisors, and salaries for training the 1.6 million apprentices. Subtracting their contribution to an output of $10 billion, the net cost was $17 billion or $10,500 per apprentice. But for industry, this is a worthwhile investment promising lower turnover. The evidence: Of their own accord, businesses offer 22% more apprenticeship slots than there are applicants.

Germany, of course, is not the only mass model; Denmark, Austria and Switzerland also have good systems. Not every detail can be transposed to America, a country whose companies would probably require a substantive tax credit to be enticed into undertaking training in significant numbers. Concentrate, though, on the salient features: The administration should set a national framework, offer tax credits and, on the state or local level, provide vocational schools. Otherwise, it can—and should—keep its hands off.   ∎

Notice how Prewo's column combines the four general features of working documents. He assumes that an area of concern for his initial audience, the readers of the *Wall Street Journal*, people generally concerned with keeping the U.S. economy strong, is how to produce a qualified, effective workforce for American business and industry. Thus, in his column he creates an exigence—the readers' need to know about the German apprenticeship system—that he expects this audience respond to. Considering both exigence and audience, we might say that Prewo assumes that many readers of the *Wall Street Journal* are interested in promoting such a work-oriented educational system in the United States. Yet he also assumes that members of his audience are wary of excessive governmental intrusion and regulation in matters concerning education and the economy, so he specifies his particular persuasive goal: to convince the readers that a successful apprenticeship system, one that could take the place of college for many students, could be supported by the private sector and would not entail governmental bureaucracy and red tape. The op-ed column, as a piece of reasoned writing designed to state and support a central idea, the persuasive goal, is the ideal genre to address Prewo's exigence with this particular audience.

Prewo's column begins by setting out the issue at hand: the role of youth training, or apprenticeship, programs in the overall U.S. investment strategy. He offers a statement of his persuasive goal in the first paragraph: "building an apprenticeship program need not mean an extensive widening of federal or state bureaucracy." In paragraphs 2–6, Prewo provides general background information about the success and logistics of the German apprenticeship program. He then moves in paragraph 7 to explain how his own organization, the Hanover Chamber of Commerce and Industry, participates in the program. Paragraphs 8–13 provide Prewo's assessment of the benefits of the apprenticeship system: it provides job stability and mobility for German youths; it offers an alternative for students for whom a college education is not the right option; it leads to further on-the-job education for workers; it fosters internal advancement of workers within companies; it keeps unemployment in Germany low; and it provides young workers with good, adult role models. Paragraph 14 hints at what Prewo sees as the only drawback to the system, its expense. In the final paragraph, after mentioning other successful apprenticeship programs in Denmark, Austria, and Switzerland, Prewo returns to, and reinforces, his persuasive goal by stating that federal, state, and local governments should offer tax credits for companies who hire apprentices and should encourage local schools to cooperate with the program, but essentially government should "keep its hands off" any apprenticeship program.

Notice how Prewo appeals to his readers, how he encourages them to accept his persuasive goal—in short, how he gets his readers to think in new ways about youth training and perhaps even to take action in regard to the subject. His appeals to the emotions and self-interests of his readers are strong. He clearly senses that one "red flag" issue for his readership in the *Wall Street Journal* would be excessive governmental control of any training program, so he points out early (paragraph 4) that the German government is only minimally involved in this program. He seems to appeal to an American businessperson's sense of shame about inadequate job training: in paragraph 8, he refers to "the aimless wandering from minimum-wage job to minimum-wage job of many American high-school graduates." Similarly, he knows how to demonstrate to his readers that he is an ethical person and writer. Throughout the column, he shows his good sense and intelligence by providing an array of statistics and *factness*-laden information about how the apprenticeship program works in Germany. He argues for the *practical* wisdom of the German apprenticeship program by showing, in paragraph 10, how it emphasizes hands-on, on-the-job training, with instructors coming from "the cream of the alumni crop." He employs the "wild card" ethical appeal by explaining, in paragraph 7, how he is personally involved in the apprenticeship system. In addition, Prewo's reasoning is distinctively top-down. At the level of the whole composition, notice how the pattern of his thinking works:

- President Clinton says he is concerned about the underemployability of American youth and wants a better youth job-training program.
- Germany has an excellent youth job-training program that leads to high employability.
- Therefore, America should consider implementing an apprenticeship program similar to Germany's.

You can also see Prewo's top-down reasoning working within individual sections and paragraphs of the column. Notice, for example, the pattern of his thinking in paragraph 9:

- Americans traditionally want a college education for their children, but college is not always the best route for all students.
- Germany has developed a sensible alternative to college with its apprenticeship system.
- Therefore, Americans should support an apprenticeship system as an alternative to college.

In a relatively short composition, Prewo covers all the major appeals carefully. He speaks to his readers' emotions and self-interests; he shows himself to be an involved, intelligent, and credible person; and he takes his reader through a sensible pattern of reasoning about his subject.

Prewo's structure is a fairly traditional and straightforward one for an op-ed column: he introduces the issue at hand and offers a statement of his persuasive goal. He provides both general and specific support for his goal and returns to reinforce it at the end. His model is a good one for you to follow in writing your own op-ed column.

 In-Progress Task

Consider two alternative methods for beginning Prewo's op-ed column. First, write a paragraph of description—of a specific place, with real people doing real things—that would serve to introduce the issue at hand to readers. Second, write a paragraph of narration—a brief story—that would make a point about job training for young people and would, similarly, serve to introduce the issue at hand.

WORKING DOCUMENT 2: AN OPEN LETTER

A second kind of working document, the open letter, also has roots in journalism, but you can find open letters in other places besides newspapers and magazines. Occasionally they are published in bulletins and notices to students, and in recent years, not-for-profit social service organizations have begun publishing open letters on their sites on the Internet.

An open letter looks like a formal letter that you might write to another person, but its looks are deceptive. When you write an open letter, you direct it to a specific person or group of people whose minds or actions you want to influence (this being your general persuasive goal, after all), but you try to publish it in some medium where other people, whose minds and actions you would also like to influence, can read it. The open letter is thus a genre built on a kind of ruse: you write to a specific person or group of people, but you open up your letter to public view.

An open letter has the same three parts as an op-ed column:

- A statement of the subject, issue, or problem at hand;
- A series of comments, explanations, illustrations, and examples about the subject, issue, or problem;
- A conclusion, direction, or solution concerning the subject, issue, or problem.

As with an op-ed column, not every open letter places these three parts in this order. Again, some begin with descriptive details to introduce the subject, issue, or problem; others begin with a brief narrative or story.

In structure, organization, and format, an open letter looks like a regular, formal letter. Sometimes it begins with a formal salutation, and it refers throughout to the targeted readers—the specific people to whom it is addressed—as *you*. It usually concludes by reiterating the persuasive goal, letting both the ostensible targeted readers and the "eavesdropping" other readers know how the writer wants them to think or act.

Here is an example of an open letter, one that was published in the *Detroit News* on August 7, 1997. The author, Inez Allison Lewis, is not a professional writer. As you can see from the note at the end of the letter, she is a retired dress designer who lives in Detroit. But, clearly, she was so engaged by a controversy discussed in public circles in the summer of 1997 that she felt compelled to write this open letter. A little background on the controversy is in order: Tiger Woods, a young man who had been the national collegiate golf champion as a student at Stanford University in California, decided to forego his academic athletic eligibility and join the Professional Golf Association. In his first year as a pro, Woods won the very prestigious Master's of Golf championship. In the publicity that followed Woods's meteoric rise to success, newspaper, magazine, and television stories showed his close, warm, supportive relationship with his father, an African American, and his mother, an Asian American. A great deal was made of Woods's being the most successful African American professional golfer ever, and people from all cultural backgrounds hailed him as a role model for young African American athletes. Yet Woods refused to refer to himself as an African American, claiming that to do so would deny his mother's Asian heritage. The open letter picks up the rest of the story.

Inez Allison Lewis # Open Letter to Tiger Woods: Be True to Your Diverse Heritage

Inez Lewis is a retired Detroit dress designer.

News Flash: Tiger Woods, you have a dilemma. I do not believe you have one, but the July issue of *Ebony* magazine claims you do.

"Black America and Tiger's Dilemma," reads the title splashed above the warm portrait of you and your father on the cover. It should have read, "Black America's Dilemma Over Tiger Woods."

Several "major African Americans," as *Ebony* describes them, debate the ongoing controversy surrounding the cornucopia of your ethnic heritages. The vast majority in the article praised your history-making accomplishments on the golf course, but attacked you for acknowledging both of your parents.

The maelstrom began following your appearance on *Oprah,* when you said it bothered you to only be called African American because you did not want to deny your mother's Asian heritage. You also said that while growing up, you referred to yourself as "Cablinasian"—Caucasian, black, Indian and Asian.

"You don't know who you are," sneered some in the audience. But Oprah's shining moment occurred when she rose to the occasion and declared, "Tiger Woods knows exactly who he is."

Your mixed heritage is an undeniable fact. It is your bloodline, and it cannot be debated away.

You never denied your black heritage on *Oprah,* so I cannot grasp the problem. It appears that the *Ebony* cover story was a thinly disguised act of revenge to punish you for telling the truth.

The fact is, this dilemma happened because some black Americans do not have the courage to publicly claim their other heritages, as you did, because they fear the reprisal from fellow blacks. However, these same people often proudly yet privately volunteer the truth of their own white, Native American and other heritages among themselves. What hypocrites!

Dominic Pangborn, 45, of Grosse Pointe Shores is also of mixed race ancestry. This president of a Detroit graphic design firm said, "Everybody is multiracial, basically. Forget this nonsense of who's what race."

There are no "pure" African Americans among those whose ancestors were brought here in chains. Africans who immigrated to this country, and later became citizens, are the only African Americans.

As soon as the first black slave woman was forced to bear the biracial children of her white master on these shores, those children became our ancestors.

Later, Native Americans began to intermarry and have children with blacks.

So, unless someone in the Northern Hemisphere can trace their roots back to a single African slave who bore children to another African, and whose offspring bore children to other Africans for the next 400-plus years, we are all multiracial.

More recently, the number of interracial marriages quadrupled between 1970 and 1994, and many of those marriages produced children.

On the other end of the spectrum, some geneticists have said 95 percent of "white" Americans have widely varying degrees of black heritage. An example of this is illustrated in the book, *Life on the Color Line* by Gregory Howard Williams, dean of the Ohio State University College of Law. Williams appears to be 100 percent white, was raised white, and did not learn until later in his life that he is, in fact, part black.

University of Michigan professor of anthropology Ann Laura Staler has said there is no such thing as biological race.

Some black critics clamor for you to claim only your African heritage so they can point to you with pride and say, "He's one of us." But you also are "theirs," "theirs" and "theirs."

If the jealous and disgruntled cannot claim you exclusively, they want to kill your spirit. Unfortunately, they apparently are still entrenched in the outdated and absurd "one drop" law of the segregated "Jim Crow" era. The rule is that if you have one traceable ancestor who is black, and 20 who are white, you are black.

But law still cannot define race. Yes, we do look black, and Fuzzy Zoeller has already demonstrated how you will always be treated, despite your millions of dollars in earnings.

The issue is not how people perceive you. Everything is about truth. The truth is, you are black, white, Native American and Asian. You do not owe the public anything. You and your extraordinary parents will always be my heroes.

Thank you for not dignifying the magazine's cleverly disguised comments with a response, as they requested.

Continue to be true to yourself and continue to soar from glory to glory.   ∎

Exigence, audience, and persuasive goals are evident in Lewis's open letter. First, she clearly believes the controversy over Tiger Woods's ethnic heritage has created an exigence, a lack of understanding about ethnic heritage, that she feels compelled to address in this letter. As the genre of the open letter allows, Lewis is able to present this exigence to several audiences, all of whom are capable of responding to it. First, and most obviously, she is writing to Tiger Woods. Since Woods has been, from the very moment of his becoming a professional golfer, an extremely public celebrity, we might guess that his staff of public relations specialists showed him this letter. Second, using the "ruse" of the open letter, she is writing indirectly, yet very forcefully, to the "major African Americans" who, she says, criticized Woods for refusing to refer to himself solely in that ethnic category. More broadly, she is writing to all readers of the *Detroit News,* many of whom had probably been keeping up with the Woods controversy in the summer of 1997.

The genre of the open letter not only allows Lewis the leeway to write to several audiences but also provides her the opportunity to accomplish a slightly different persuasive goal with each one. Her persuasive goal with Tiger Woods, the way she hopes he will think and act, is evident in the title of the open letter and the final sentence: she wants him to be true to his complex ethnic heritage and thus to "[c]ontinue to be true to yourself." Her goal with the "major African Americans" who criticized Woods is a bit more hidden: she wants them to recognize what she sees as their hypocrisy for failing to admit that they may be of mixed ethnic heritage themselves. Her goal with the general readership of the *Detroit News* is even broader: she wants them to think in a new way about the whole concept of racial background and ethnic heritage, seeing it as more complicated than people usually acknowledge.

Lewis's open letter operates with a straightforward, three-part structure. In the first part, she sets the context for a "dilemma" that she will eventually dismiss, and she suggests that the dilemma might not rest with Tiger Woods but instead with another segment of her readers. An article in the July 1997 issue of *Ebony* magazine had suggested Woods had a dilemma involving his ethnicity and had quoted several prominent African Americans who were concerned that Woods would not ally himself solely with that heritage. In the seventh paragraph, Lewis discounts this dilemma. Woods never denied his African American heritage, she claims; instead, he simply refused to claim it as his only heritage. What's the problem, Lewis asks? Is Tiger Woods the problem because he would not deny his mother's ethnic background, or are the "major African Americans" the problem because they would not admit publicly that they, too, might have a "mixed" background?

In the middle part, paragraphs 8–16, Lewis works to complicate the whole issue of ethnic heritage that lies at the heart of this alleged dilemma. Sharing anecdotes about some black Americans' cultural backgrounds, alluding to published statements by a president of a Detroit graphics design firm, the dean of the Ohio State University law school, and a University of Michigan professor, and hinting at the history of ethnic intermarriage in the United States, Lewis concludes that ethnic heritage cannot be seen in a simple, this-or-that perspective.

In the final section, paragraphs 17–22, she returns to the ostensible audience of the open letter, Tiger Woods, and addresses him directly, acknowledging that part of his ethnic heritage is, of course, African American (fellow golfer Fuzzy Zoeller, incidentally, committed a major gaffe by subtly disparaging Woods's ethnicity in an interview not long after the Master's tournament) but urging him to continue to hold onto to his principles—as the title puts it, to "be true to your diverse heritage."

Though not a professional writer, Lewis clearly knows how to appeal to her readers' emotions and reasoning and how to establish her own credibility. Notice how she appeals to *pathos:* In the very first paragraph, she gives her open letter an air of danger and distress, by claiming "News flash," just as old-time television programs used to do when important news was breaking. She refers to the controversy as a *maelstrom,* a complicated word meaning "a violent storm, usually producing whirlpools that sink ships." By stirring up her readers' emotions over the alleged dilemma, Lewis's dismissal of it is made all the stronger. Later in the letter, she confronts directly her readers' sense of cultural pride, by suggesting, in paragraph 18, that anyone who still believes in "pure," uncomplicated ethnic heritage is still living in the horrid past of "Jim Crow" laws, which denied civil rights to anyone with even some African American background. She ends her letter with a flurry of warm emotions, embracing Tiger Woods and his multiethnic parents as her "heroes."

Lewis appeals to her own credibility largely by citing support from authorities who lend her open letter an air of factness. We may not know who exactly Dominic Pangborn is, and we may not completely understand why a University of Michigan anthropology professor is in the position to testify in Lewis's behalf, but we accept their perspectives because they seem to be committed representatives of Lewis's position. We are certainly moved to believe Lewis by the story she cites from Gregory Howard Williams, who discovered his ethnic background late in his life.

Finally, Lewis's appeal to *logos* is built on a combination of top-down reasoning and *dissociation,* the exploration strategy explained in Chapter 8. Notice how her reasoning is structured:

- Several prominent African Americans criticized Tiger Woods for not solely claiming his African American ethnic heritage.
- Ethnic heritage is only superficial—an appearance, not reality. In reality, many, if not most, people come from mixed ethnic heritage, and the whole concept is not as simple as people think.

■ Therefore, Tiger Woods should be embraced, loved, and praised for acknowledging the reality of complicated ethnic heritages, not criticized for adhering to the oversimplified view of the masses.

The open letter is one of the most versatile, flexible genres you can use to influence people's minds and actions. It allows you to address many audiences, and achieve several persuasive goals, in a single document. Think about its possibilities for your final composition.

 ## In-Progress Task

If you intend to write an open letter, write a full paragraph in response to the following questions in your learning journal to help you plan it: Who will be the ostensible audience for the letter? That is, to whom will it be addressed in the title and opening? What other readers do you hope to address besides the ostensible audience? What persuasive goals do you hope to accomplish with the ostensible audience and with other potential readers?

WORKING DOCUMENT 3: THE BROCHURE

A third kind of working document, the brochure, is designed to focus your readers' attention quickly and in a concentrated fashion on how they might think or act in regard to your subject. A brochure is usually brief. A typical printed brochure contains text, graphics, and pictures printed on the front and part of the back of an 8 ½- by 11-inch piece of paper. The contents of the brochure are placed on the page so that the piece of paper can be folded to form three 3 ¾- by 8 ½-inch panels on each side of the sheet of paper. An alternative to the printed brochure, a computerized Web page/electronic brochure, is becoming a very popular genre for writers who want to change minds and actions. A Web page is usually no longer that two or three screens in a windowed environment. Though it is an electronic genre, the Web page has the same kind of contents—text, pictures, and graphics—as a printed brochure. If your college or university has a computer laboratory, or if its Writing Center uses network computers, you can probably learn how to create a Web page, an electronic brochure, and post it on a network, either locally within your institution or on the Internet.

Both printed brochures and Web pages typically try to achieve their persuasive goals using one of two organizational structures:

question-and-answer or problem-then-solution. The nature of these two structures is self-evident from their names. The first poses a question and then answers it, and the second describes a problem and offers a solution.

Some question-and-answer brochures actually raise and address several questions, but they do so one at a time. For example, the Chicago Community Trust, an organization partly devoted to secure better funding for public schools in Chicago, publishes a magazine called *Education Reform in '97: Opportunity for Action,* which is essentially a collection of eight one-page, question-and-answer brochures about the issue of unequal school funding. Look at the titles:

- Why Should Homeowners Care?
- Why Should Parents Be Concerned?
- Why Should Workers and Business Leaders Take Interest?
- Why Should Seniors Care?
- Why Should Teachers Care?
- Why Should Students Care?
- Why Should Elected Officials Care?
- How Can the Problem Be Solved?

Each brochure creates an exigence: something must be done about inequitable funding levels for public school districts. Each targets a specific audience and tries to accomplish a different persuasive goal with each one. As you might guess, each of these brochures shows a compelling picture and tells a true, engaging story about why this particular set of readers should think that all schools deserve a better funding base and should do something to make this wish come true.

 ## In-Progress Task

If you are thinking about writing a question-and-answer brochure for your final composition, visit as many student support services office on your campus as you can find. Go to the Writing Center, the Career Placement Office, the Women's Center, the library, the Counseling Center, the Organizations Office, the Campus Ministry or chaplain's office—any office of this sort you can find. Ask for a copy of any brochure the office distributes. Examine carefully the structure of the brochures you collect and determine whether the structure is primarily question-and-answer or problem-then-solution.

The alternative to question-and-answer is a problem-then-solution brochure. A superb example is the Web page/electronic brochure that Jeanette Doane produced for the final composition in her Inquiry Contract on the issue of the different treatment of boys and girls in schools. Here is the text-only portion of Jeanette's brochure:

Fostering Self-Esteem in Young Women:
A Guide for Parents

Although feminists have made considerable progress in the struggle for equal rights, gender bias is still quite evident in today's educational system. In the formative grammar school years, children learn to read with textbooks that portray women in traditional gender roles; both parents and teachers tend to enforce strict gender roles during playtime. While boys carry sports equipment and operate electrical equipment, girls are often encouraged to set up art supplies and put out food during snack times. Male children learn to be strong and rambunctious, while female children learn to be quiet and respectful.

During the difficult adolescent years, traditional gender expectations have far-reaching effects on young women. Trying to discover their own identities, many are often torn between their desires and the characteristics that society expects from them. Adolescent girls quickly learn that their value lies in being docile, dependent, pretty people pleasers. For this reason, many young women begin to doubt themselves and "sell out" to societal expectations. Eating disorders, sexual promiscuity, low motivation, and poor grades begin to manifest themselves in late middle school and early high school years.

Unfortunately, these problems do not subside once a young woman reaches late high school. If anything, the problems tend to become worse. Girls are afraid to be as smart as the boys in their classes for fear of not being attractive; self-esteem and self-confidence sink to deplorable levels during this time. High dropout rates, high levels of teen pregnancy, and low levels of ambition are directly related to this lack of self-esteem. These, in turn, affect the matriculation of women into higher education and their success in the professional world.

If we are to help confident, well-spoken, ambitious young women enter the business world, something MUST be done to reverse the current trend. While teachers, peers, and the media have considerable influence in young women's lives, this influence is often negative. Unfortunately, gender reform in today's schools is progressing too slowly to be considered a viable option for fostering self-esteem in female students. However, parents and families have the potential to positively affect the lives of female family members; they have the strongest influence on the self esteem and life choices of young women. The following is a list of suggestions for parents interested in raising healthy, ambitious, confident, and happy daughters.

Suggestions for Parents

- Praise girls for skills, accomplishments, and ideas; do not concentrate on appearance.
- Discuss media portrayal of women with your children. Are the portrayals accurate and realistic?
- Encourage girls to experience things that are normally reserved for boys (woodworking, playing with reptiles or insects, athletics).
- Avoid rescuing female children: encourage them to get dirty and make mistakes.
- Encourage girls to explore the technical world; expose them to computers at an early age.
- Remember that words and actions are very powerful. Be careful to "practice what you preach."
- Encourage daughters to participate in a wide range of extracurricular activities; emphasize the importance of leadership. Encourage girls to try out new interests and acquire new skills; participation in debate, journalism, athletics, arts, and government is character-building.
- Dissuade girls from excessive dieting. Concentrate on healthy eating, positive body image, and exercise activities for the entire family.
- Talk to your daughter about school experiences; let her know she can talk to you about her concerns.
- If feasible, visit your daughter's school and discuss the interaction of teachers and students with her. Consider all-girls schools.
- Encourage young women to take advanced level math and science courses and applaud their efforts.
- Celebrate the accomplishments of women in your household. Help your child choose books that portray women as strong, positive role models.
- Introduce career awareness at an early age; discuss benefits and drawbacks of both traditional and professional roles for women.
- Keep scholastic expectations high for all children; do not lower your expectations for girls.
- Be a positive role model for your own daughter.

■ Finally, and perhaps most importantly, let your daughter explore herself and the person she wants to become. Allow her some freedom, yet be firm in your adherence to rules.

Encourage girls to celebrate their femininity, not fall victim to it!

Links to sites for parents

■ Healthy Relationships
■ Encouraging Challenging Careers
■ Debunking the "Boys are better at math" Myth

Links to sites for girls

■ Girls and Women in Science Project
■ Girl Power
■ Girls Interwire
■ Girls to the Fourth Power

Recommended Reading for Further Information

■ Burchell, Helen and Millman, Val. *Changing Perspectives on Gender: New Initiatives in Secondary Education.* Philadelphia: Open University Press, 1989.
■ Kenway, Jane and Willis, Sue. *Hearts and Minds: Self Esteem and the Schooling of Girls.* Bristol: The Falmer Press, 1990.
■ Pipher, Ph.D., Mary, *Reviving Ophelia: Saving the Selves of Adolescent Girls.* New York: Random House, 1994.
■ Skelton, Christine. *Whatever Happens to Little Women? Gender and Primary Schooling.* Bristol: Open University Press, 1989.
■ Thomas, Kim. *Gender and Subject in Higher Education.* Bristol: Open University Press, 1990.
■ Weiner, Gaby. *Just a Bunch of Girls.* Philadelphia: Open University Press, 1985.   ■

Since you have read Jeanette's Contract Proposal and exploratory essay, you have a sense of the exigence that she is working to establish with in this brochure: the need to do something about the unequal treatment of the sexes in schools. In the brochure, she focuses on a specific audience. Her observations and reading have convinced her that the unequal treatment of children in schools is a problem that parents need to know more about. Particularly, parents of young girls need to know what they can do to help their children build self-esteem.

The problem-then-solution structure of Jeanette's brochure is clear. She establishes the problem in the first four paragraphs. Boys and girls are often treated differently in schools in ways that harm girls' self-esteem. This unequal treatment can lead to physical, emotional, and behavioral problems for young girls. These problems do not subside when the girls reach high school age. Following the fourth paragraph, she provides, in a bulleted list, the solution—sixteen specific things that parents can do to bolster their daughters' self-esteem. Jeanette's structure is problem, then solution.

Because it is a Web page/electronic brochure, however, there is more to Jeanette's composition than a fleshing out of this simple structure. After an admonition to parents to "[e]ncourage girls to celebrate their feminity, not fall victim to it," Jeanette takes advantage of the Web page/electronic brochure format by providing links to three other Web pages for parents and four additional ones for girls. Readers who are visiting Jeanette's site on the Internet can use their computer mouse to move the cursor over the label of one of these links and click the mouse button once or twice. When they do so, they then move to the electronic brochure that the link has developed. Jeanette closes the electronic brochure with a list of books on gender, self-esteem, and education that readers might want to consult.

Though it is a relatively flashy genre, Jeanette's electronic brochure nonetheless makes use of the traditional three appeals, the three ways to urge her readers to understand the exigence (i.e., the problem) and act on her persuasive goal (the solution). She appeals to her readers' emotions by portraying young girls—the children of her intended readers—as being in grave danger of the physical, emotional, and behavioral problems that come with low self-esteem. She appeals to her own credibility by offering a succinct, no-nonsense list of sixteen potential solutions to the problem and by showing she has done lots of homework on the subject, providing seven links and the titles of six books for further reading. Her *logos*, her appeal to her readers' reasoning, is largely bottom-up. The first paragraph offers a repeated pattern of examples showing things that happen in school that harm young girls' self-esteem. The second paragraph provides a repeated pattern of examples of problems that emerge in "the difficult adolescent years." With these specific details, Jeanette establishes the problem that she then proposes that parents solve.

Jeanette's Web page/electronic brochure works powerfully to educate parents (i.e., change their minds) about their daughters' self-esteem and to get them to treat their daughters in new, healthier ways (i.e., to change their actions). Your own brochure, electronic or printed, can be similarly powerful.

In-Progress Task

After you have read Jeanette's Web page/electronic brochure carefully, meet with your writing-as-inquiry group or with one or two other people who have read the composition. Concentrating only on the quality, organization, and development of Jeanette's ideas—not on her sentence structure, style, mechanics, punctuation, or grammar—make a list of two things Jeanette did well in her document. Then list at least two specific things Jeanette might have done differently as she planned and wrote this paper that would have improved it as a working document.

Appendix to Part One: Adapting the Inquiry Contract for Other Classes

The chapters in Part One illustrate a plan for completing an Inquiry Contract by writing a series of five papers: a contract proposal, a reflective reading response, an informative report, an exploratory essay, and a working document (an opinion-piece editorial column, an open letter, or a brochure). The chapters, in general, alternate between explaining the theory that underlies producing each of these genres and demonstrating how to organize and create them yourself.

While the writing-as-inquiry project explained in Part One is well suited for college and university classes that require extensive writing, you should not see the Inquiry Contract as a lock-step method. Indeed, since the mid-1980s, students and instructors at colleges and universities around the United States have been experimenting with variations on the Inquiry Contract, adapting the assignments to meet the demands of specific writing situations.

The purpose of this appendix is to describe possible alternatives to the sequence of compositions explained in Part One and to suggest, using an In-Progress Task, several examples of Inquiry Contracts that could be developed by writers taking classes in the humanities, the social sciences, and the natural and life sciences. As we move from one stage of the contract to the next in this appendix, notice how you can, with your instructor's consent and guidance, choose the alternative from each stage that is most appropriate to your specific writing situation. Thus, you can build your own structure for a four- or five-stage writing-as-inquiry project, submitting to your instructor (or project supervisor or thesis director) those papers that you and he or she agree should be assessed and evaluated. Notice that writing an Inquiry Contract requires *lots* of self-discipline on your part. In some writing situations, your instructor, supervisor, or director may only read and comment on one paper in the project, usually the last one. But you will write a *much better* project, one that you learn more by completing and one that will benefit you as a writer and independent thinker, if you write something—commit something to paper or diskette—at each stage of the Inquiry Contract that you decide to include.

One additional note: Even though this appendix refers to the different places you can produce a composition in the Inquiry Contract as *stages,* do not think that you can never return to an earlier composition and revise your thinking and writing—indeed, the overall design of your contract—as you move through the project. One major benefit of the Inquiry Contract is that later papers build on earlier ones, and often the work you do on later papers helps you see what you might have done differently earlier. With the guidance of your instructor, director, or supervisor, feel free to return to earlier papers in the project when it suits your purpose.

STAGE 1

In the Inquiry Contract developed in Part One, this stage calls for a Contract Proposal, a brief explanation of what subject you propose to write about, why this is an important subject for you to inquire into, what are two things you know about it already, and what are two major questions you think you will need to address.

When you create your own Inquiry Contract, some instructors, directors, and supervisors might expect you to be more definite and specific in this proposal. Since each of the compositions in the Inquiry Contract leads to the next, one could say that even though you might produce four or five compositions for your project, you are essentially working on one long paper—the final one. Thus, some situations might call for you to write a proposal that sets out what you hope to accomplish in the fourth or fifth paper, whatever form it might take. If you decide to write such a definite proposal, you should discuss with your instructor, director, or supervisor how much leeway you have to alter your plans for this final composition as you work on it. In some cases, it will be perfectly acceptable for you to alter your plans as you work on the project. In other cases, the proposal can be seen as a binding document, and writing a composition different from the one you propose to write might cause problems. The best advice: Discuss the nature of the proposal, and the nature of the commitment you make with it, with your instructor, director, or supervisor.

STAGE 2

In the Inquiry Contract developed in Part One, this stage calls for a reflective reading response for which you read something concerning your subject and then write about what you feel, think, believe, and know about the reading, or you paraphrase two important portions of it, or you write answers and reactions to questions that the reading raises.

The alternative at this stage is to write entries in a learning journal (which you may want to call simply a *reading journal* or a *project jour-*

nal) not once but many times and at regular intervals. With the guidance of your instructor, director, or supervisor, you might use one of the three methods of generating reflective reading responses described in Chapter 5. Alternatively, you may decide to be less structured in generating your journal entries. Let's say, for example, that you decide to write in your project journal twice a week. You might simply write in response to these three questions (or some variation on them that you create) each time:

- Since the last time I wrote in this project journal, what have I read, what have I experienced or observed, whom have I talked to about my subject and my project?
- What did I learn from this reading, these observations or experiences, or these conversations?
- What do I need to do next on the project? How and when am I going to do this?

Some instructors, directors, and supervisors might want to read your project journal and write comments back to you about its contents. In some projects, your project journal might be graded.

At this stage in particular, you will need to be a stern disciplinarian of yourself. If no one but you reads the project journal and you do not receive a grade for it, it will require lot of initiative on your part to produce it. But your discipline and effort will pay dividends. You will find it easier to write your final composition, and it will be better, if you can reread your project journal as you are working on the papers in your project.

STAGE 3

In the Inquiry Contract developed in Part One, this stage calls for you to conduct an interview, a "careful conversation," and to write an informative report explaining what you learned.

Two alternatives are possible at this stage. The first is what researchers in many fields call a *review of the literature*. (*Literature* here does not mean poems, plays, stories, and novels. It means published articles, chapters, and books on your subject.) If you pursue this alternative, either on your own or with the guidance of your instructor, director, or supervisor, you assemble a list of articles, chapters, and books on your subject that you need to read. After you read them, you write one of two kinds of compositions. The first is a called a *bibliographic essay* in some fields; in others it is called a *review paper*. In it, you summarize the thesis and central ideas of each piece of the literature you read and then explain what relationships, trends, and conclusions you see emerging from these points. The second is called an *annotated bibliography*. In this paper, you simply list the bibliographic information for each piece of the literature you read and then write a paragraph summarizing its thesis and central ideas. To list the bibliographic information, you should consult with your instructor, director, or supervisor about the format. Most projects in the humanities require you to list the bibliographic information using a format prescribed by the Modern Language Association (*MLA*) or the *Chicago Manual of Style* (often called simply *Chicago style*). In the social sciences, most frequently you use the format prescribed by the American Psychological Association (*APA*) or the *Chicago Manual of Style*. Many fields in the natural and life sciences, business, and engineering have their own formats for listing bibliographic entries. One format commonly used in the sciences is prescribed by the Council of Biology Editors. All of these formats are explained in detail in handbooks that your instructor, director, or supervisor might refer you to or assign you to read. As you write bibliographic entries, do not rely on your memory and do not guess about the format. Keep the handbook open while you are writing the entries and follow the rules exactly. Your readers will pay more attention to your writing if you do so.

The second alternative at this stage is a straightforward project that combines reading in the field and interviewing people with interesting perspectives on your subject. Here is how I have often asked students to complete this alternative:

- Read two articles or chapters on your subject.
- Interview two people about your subject.
- Write a paper in which you do the following: In the first paragraph, state what you read (providing complete bibliographic information at the end of the paper) and whom you interviewed. In two full paragraphs following the first, summarize the thesis and central ideas from each piece you read. Then, in two full paragraphs, explain the most important thing you learned in each of the interviews you conducted. Then, in one full paragraph, compare what you learned from the readings and interviews—say how the conclusions you drew from each are similar. Then, in one full paragraph, contrast what you learned from the readings and the interviews—say how your conclusions are different. Finally, in one full paragraph, explain what you think you need to do next on the project on the basis of what you learned by reading and conducting interviews.

STAGE 4

In the Inquiry Contract developed in Part One, this stage calls for an exploratory essay in which you propose alternative ways that people *could* think and act concerning your subject and then explain the benefits and drawbacks for *each* of the alternatives you propose.

There are two alternatives at this stage. The first comes into play frequently when writers, for any number of reasons, do not have the time to write all five compositions in the Inquiry Contract. The alternative is simply to skip this stage and move to the final project, in which you try to get readers to think or act in a new way concerning your subject. Obviously, I do not recommend following this alternative, but I understand why some writers must do it. If you must omit this stage, be sure when you write your final paper to give considerable thought to how readers might object to your thesis or central ideas—how they might not see or agree with your exigence, or how they might resist your persuasive goal. In the final paper, work carefully to address their concerns and counter their objections so they will think and act in the new ways you are working to present.

The second alternative at this stage is to write a composition, either in your learning journal or elsewhere, in which you play *devil's advocate* to the thesis and central ideas you are thinking about developing in the final paper. In such a composition, you consider your thesis and central ideas and instead of writing a paper that aims to get people to accept them, you write a paper that critiques them and tries to get people to see flaws and objections in them. The purpose of such a paper is not to dismantle the goals you hope to accomplish in the final paper. The goal is to help you predict how a careful, critical audience will read your last composition so you can determine the exigence and plan your persuasive goal and appeals accordingly.

STAGE 5

In the Inquiry Contract developed in Part One, this stage calls for you to produce a public-oriented working document—an opinion-piece editorial column, an open letter, or a brochure—about your subject.

As Chapter 11 indicated, the major alternative at this stage is to produce a more academically oriented composition, creating the genre that scholars in the field generally use to "do the work" of the discipline. In most fields of the humanities and many in the social sciences, this genre is called the *critical paper*, the *research paper*, or simply a *paper*. In some fields of the social sciences and most in the natural and life sciences, this genre is called a *research report* or sometimes a *technical report*. This paper might call for other genres also—for example, a *book review* or *performance review* in the humanities; a *case study* or *case report* in the social sciences, education, or business; or a *laboratory report* or *field report* in the natural and life sciences or engineering. If you need to produce one of these genres, your instructor, director, or supervisor can refer you to guidebooks in which you can read about them.

In-Progress Task

A SAMPLE OF POSSIBLE INQUIRY CONTRACTS IN SEVERAL FIELDS

In your writing-as-inquiry group or another group of classmates or colleagues, generate notes about Inquiry Contracts, each consisting of four or five papers, for as many of the following topics from different academic fields as possible. Be creative. Use the genres developed in Part One—the contract proposal, the reflective reading response, the informative report, the exploratory essay, and the working document—or alternatives described in this appendix. Try to describe as specifically as possible how a writer would plan and write each composition in the sequences you outline.

Humanities

- The moral influence of the city versus that of the country in American literature
- Myths of the American Plains Indians
- The Holocaust
- Religious communities in contemporary America
- Types and functions of music at the end of the twentieth century

Social Sciences, Business, and Education

- The roles women have played in the world wars
- The African diaspora in Latin America
- The child care dilemma: What is it, who provides it, who gets it, who pays for it?
- The European Union and monetary policy
- The People's Republic of China before and after Tiananmen Square, 1989

Natural Sciences, Life Sciences, and Engineering

- Cells, genes, and heritable diseases
- Controversies over ecological restoration
- The Manhattan Project and the nuclear age
- Uses of hypertext in mechanical and structural engineering
- The least a runner needs to know about exercise physiology

The Trim-and-Target Method for Rewriting Prose

As all the chapters in Part One assume, producing the papers in the Inquiry Contract requires not only that you know something about how writing works as a process but also that you are able to be flexible and adapt the process to fit the needs of specific writing situations. In other words, you know that all writing involves investigating, inventing, planning, drafting, consulting, revising, and editing, and for some projects you need to allow yourself a full span of time and space to engage in all those activities thoroughly. You also know, however, that you do not need, or necessarily have, the luxury to undertake all these process tasks for every paper you write. In the course of writing the Inquiry Contract papers, for example, you might find that your work on the Contract Proposal involves mostly investigating and inventing, while your work on the Clarification Project is largely limited to investigating and drafting. However, your work on the Information, Exploration, and Working Documents Projects, when you are producing full-bodied essays and "real-world" papers, may require you to investigate, invent, plan, draft, consult, revise, and edit.

The Inquiry Contract, thus, is about writing, and Part One provides guidance on how to draft the major compositions that grow out of the Inquiry Contract. Part Two is about *rewriting* those compositions, plus other papers that you must produce for your classes, job, or personal correspondence. The goal of Part Two is to offer a checklist of rewriting activities you can do to produce writing that is clear, correct, and easy to read. Stating what successful writers have known for centuries, James Thurber once said succinctly, "The only good writing is rewriting."

In Part Two, we will work through ten activities, collectively known as the *Trim-and-Target Method,* that you can do to rewrite and improve a draft. To illustrate this method, we will examine how one student's paper from her Inquiry Contract changed as she rewrote it following these ten steps.

As you work with Part Two, constantly keep two ideas in mind. First, this section does not provide an all-inclusive, exhaustive guide to rewriting. It does offer a ten-step procedure you can follow to guide your attention to parts of a draft that would be improved by rewriting. The sections here do not point out every problem in the sample paper; the tasks that follow the explanation of each step ask you to look in the draft and find additional examples of features that could be improved by rewriting. Second, everything in Part Two assumes you have a draft of a composition to work on. These ten activities are not about drafting; they are about rewriting—the only good writing, after all.

MEET JEANETTE DOANE—AGAIN!

As we learn about the ten strategies for rewriting a paper, we will examine the early first draft of a paper you have seen before, in finished form, at the end of Chapter 9. It is the exploratory essay written by Jeanette Doane, an undergraduate biology major at DePaul University. Not only did you have the chance to read Jeanette's exploratory essay, but you also examined her Contract Proposal and her working document—her Web page/electronic brochure.

As you recall, in Jeanette's Inquiry Contract, she investigated the concept of gender equity and equal treatment of the sexes in schooling. For the Contract Proposal, Jeanette set out the scope of the problem as she saw it, explained two things she knew already about treatment of the sexes in schools, and posed two questions that she believed she would need to answer as the contract proceeded. For the Clarification Project, she read three chapters from books about gender equity in schooling and created reflective reading responses using the *writing dialectically* method described in Chapter 4. For the Information Project, she interviewed two teachers, asking them to share their observations about the treatment of the sexes in classrooms, and she wrote an informative report, comparing and contrasting what she learned from these interviews with what she had learned from reading the three book chapters. For the Exploration Project, she wrote an exploratory essay that sets out *status quo* thinking on gender equity in schooling, explains the problems inherent in this thinking, proposes alternatives to the *status quo,* and then critiques the benefits and drawbacks of the alternatives. Finally, for the Working Documents Project, she created a Web site/electronic brochure with numerous links, for parents who are curious and concerned about the ways their child's gender is affecting the nature and progress of his or her schooling.

AN OVERVIEW OF THE TRIM-AND-TARGET METHOD

Before reading Jeanette's draft, read this quick preview of the ten steps of the Trim-and-Target Method of rewriting. The remainder of Part Two will explain each step:

1. Reread your composition. On a separate sheet of paper or in a separate file, write *one phrase* that says what your paper is about. Then write *one sentence* that says what your paper is about. Then write *one paragraph* that says what your paper is about.
2. Look at every sentence and determine what possibilities it holds for you to write with *active verbs.* If it seems appropriate, rewrite the sentence using such verbs.
3. Look at every sentence and determine what possibilities it holds to have a human being or some human collective or force as the agent, or doer, of the action. If it seems appropriate, rewrite the sentence putting those agents in as the subjects of verbs.
4. Test every sentence for completeness and boundaries. If you encounter any sentence fragments, ask yourself whether you can justify their use on stylistic grounds. If so, do nothing. If not, rewrite them as complete sentences. If you encounter any spliced or run-on sentences, rewrite them as separate sentences.
5. Write a gloss for each paragraph.
6. Create a target chart for each paragraph by charting the number of topics introduced and the depth and direction of their development.
7. Reread the composition for deadwood and redundancy, and eliminate their sources.
8. Edit your paper thoroughly. Read your paper aloud. Read your paper backward.

9. If your paper is on a computer disk or hard drive, run the spell checker program, but do not hit the replace key indiscriminantly. Then run any grammar checker program you have access to. *Consider* the advice that the grammar checker program offers, but do not feel as though you *must* take the actions it recommends.
10. Repeat step 1.

JEANETTE'S EXPLORATORY ESSAY— FIRST DRAFT

Note: Lines have been numbered for ease of reference. Jeanette did not submit this draft with the lines numbered.

GENDER BIAS: AVENUES FOR CHANGE

1   Although the treatment of women has improved dramatically over the years, one

2   must admit that society does not place equal value on the both sexes yet. This lack

3   of equality is particularly evident in educational settings. In terms of attention, fund-

4   ing levels, and amount of praise given, young women are not up to the same status

5   as their male counterparts. Why is the dropout rate higher for women than it is for

6   men? Why do male athletic programs receive more money than those for women?

7   Why do teachers ask males more questions and spend more one-on-one time with

8   their male students than female? Most gender bias is due to society's reluctance to

9   change antiquated views. What can be done by teachers, parents, and administra-

10   tors to alleviate the problem?

11   While many people sense and recognize the need for gender reform at all ed-

12   ucational levels, most do not know how to go about changing the system. In addi-

13   tion, many do not even want the system to change. It has been my experience that

14   many feminist attempts are being labeled and written off as "femiNazi extremist

15   measures." I cannot tell you how many times that both men and women have come

16   to an agreement that change is not only necessary but vital. Only to dismiss every

17   suggestion for reform as being completely unrealistic and not worth the effort. This

18   attitude is precisely the problem in so many areas of concern today; people and so-

19 ciety unwilling to change the traditional roles of men and women. Young women will

20 only cease to be docile, dependent, pretty puppets once society convinces them

21 that their ideas, thoughts, and insights have as much intrinsic value as those of their

22 outspoken, independent, confident male counterparts. This will only occur once

23 people realize that change is imperative and necessary now.

24 Current thinking on gender issues in schools is split halfway between those

25 who believe that change is necessary now and those feeling that feminists are

26 spending too much time and energy trying to reform a system that doesn't need

27 change. After all, it was good enough for them, wasn't it? Conversations with many

28 family members and classmates have convinced me that despite their politically

29 correct appearances, a lot of people are in complete congruence with the thinking

30 of the past that now seems archaic. Unfortunately, the past is not good enough any

31 more. The proper preparation of young girls must start right now. If women on a

32 whole are ever going to achieve complete and total equality.

33 In this day and age, with more women entering the workplace than ever before,

34 it makes sense to teach young girls the characteristics necessary to succeed in the

35 professional world. However, young women are torn between two worlds. Academia

36 says that females are as intelligent and capable as men, the media portray women

37 as pretty, thin, dependent, well-behaved individuals, with the self-esteem of ants.

38 Consequently, *Reviving Ophelia* author Mary Pipher says, society is turning out more

39 troubled girls than ever before. What will happen when these young women, riddled

40 by eating disorders, sexual promiscuity, and lost identities enter the workplace? Un-

41 fortunately, many of these girls will never finish high school, let alone proceed, ma-

42 triculate, and complete degrees in post-secondary settings. Those who do manage

43 to become successful still experience a growing lack of self-confidence and feel

44 enormous pressure to be perfect. These problems are not limited to race or class,

45 but they are almost exclusively female-oriented. As the real world becomes more

46 and more harsher, it will be even more difficult for adult women to sort out the prob-

47 lems of their adolescence. This will most likely cause problems in their interpersonal

48 relationships with others, especially those of the family. In order to ensure that

49 healthy, well adjusted women enter the workplace and become productive mem-

50 bers of working society, it is necessary to start preparing them at an early age.

51 One method of preparation, and perhaps the most extreme, is to completely

52 separate boys and girls in terms of education. In addition, the school itself would not

53 hold to traditional gender roles, administrators and teachers of advanced subjects

54 could be female instead of almost exclusively male. Cafeteria workers, cleaning

55 staff, groundskeepers, and secretarial staff would be equally divided in terms of

56 gender. Students would wear some sort of uniform (preferably pants) in order to

57 take the focus off of designer labels and physical appearance. Family members

58 would be encouraged to take an active part in the educational process.

59 At an early age, girls would be the ones to run the VCR or slide projector. They

60 would carry the sports equipment as well as set out the milk for lunch and mix the

61 paints for art class. Both traditionally male and female toys would be available to

62 them. Textbooks and library books would cast their portrayal of women in a posi-

63 tive light. Elementary school teachers would encourage girls to develop their ram-

64 bunctious, outspoken personalities rather than chiding them for not being quiet and

65 lady-like.

66 Such development in personality would continue throughout the traditionally

67 difficult middle school and high school years. Special classes would focus on sexu-

68 ality, self-confidence, and positive body image. Students and teachers would discuss

69 the portrayal of women by the media, they would also conduct explorations of their

70 families expectations of them in terms of their adherence to traditional gender roles.

71 Class selection would be determined on the basis of interest and ability rather than

72 on stereotypical gender roles. Both concentrations in the humanities and those in

73 sciences would be considered perfectly acceptable. Most importantly, students

74 would be encouraged to determine what type of person they want to be, they would

75 learn the importance of forming strong, healthy relationships with both the men and

76 women in their lives.

77   The curriculum of such a school would concentrate on forming a strong base of
78 knowledge in all areas, with the opportunity for students to take elective courses in
79 the fine arts, industrial arts, and home economics. Discussion based seminars in
80 which the students are active participants and make decisions regarding the struc-
81 ture of the class are wonderful for culturing self-esteem and confidence, they also pre-
82 pare young women for their high school and post-secondary education. Health
83 classes would educate young women about eating disorders, alcohol and drug
84 abuse, and the dangers of early sexual activity, but the real focus would be on main-
85 taining a positive body image and a healthy lifestyle. Young women would be en-
86 couraged to retain their active, imaginative, energetic personalities rather than
87 succumbing to the personality of the traditional well-behaved, respectful, docile lady.
88 Of course, they would still be taught to be respectful and polite, but they would be en-
89 couraged to develop their personalities rather than stifle them. This would eliminate
90 many problems most psychologists agree that typical problems of adolescence stem
91 from the child's struggle to become their own person while realizing that they need
92 to please others in order to be accepted and loved. Often, they feel that acceptance
93 will be offered only if they are in conformance with traditional gender roles. After all,
94 everyone loves a well-behaved, quiet, polite girl who doesn't cause any trouble.

95   Segregated education has many benefits, the most important is that young
96 women are encouraged to develop and maintain distinct personalities and huge lev-
97 els of self confidence. Class participation and input into course development will
98 prepare girls for education at the university level, as will increased levels of self-
99 esteem. Young women will generally be a lot happier, they will pursue education and
100 careers in subjects they are interested in rather than those they feel pressured to
101 like. In addition, rates of teen pregnancy, dropout, committing suicide, and eating
102 disorders should drastically decrease. It is no secret that these problems are directly
103 related to low confidence and self-esteem levels.

104   One major drawback of segregated education is that men and women are not
105 segregated in the real world. How can women claim to be equal to men when they

106 cannot be educated with them? In addition, one might claim that girls taught in seg-

107 regated environments might get the impression that men are bad, which could lead

108 to the formation of negative affective dissonances with males the rest of their lives.

109 However, I don't think that this would be a substantial issue; girls will only learn that

110 they are equal by experiencing the same things that their male counterparts do. Un-

111 fortunately, this simply cannot happen in today's boy/girl schools. I have numerous

112 friends who attended all-girls Catholic schools, and they had nothing but praise for

113 them. However, I have heard some of them say that they wish they would of attended

114 single sex elementary schools as well, for this is when traditional sex roles begin to

115 become firmly implanted. Girls' and boys' schools could have mixers, joint field

116 trips, and dances in order to facilitate interaction between the sexes. Teachers could

117 emphasize that men are in no way bad and encourage healthy relationships be-

118 tween males and females.

119   Another method for installing gender reform in today's schools would be to

120 completely wipe out everyone's mind and start fresh. Elementary school classrooms

121 would be completely integrated. Boys and girls would never be ridiculed by being

122 forced to sit together or pitted against each other in singing contests. In addition,

123 schools would attempt to be more gender sensitive. Textbooks and library books

124 would portray women positively. Students would discuss how traditional gender

125 roles function and their potential inaccuracy. Both boys and girls would have equal

126 opportunities to use equipment and have one on one time with the teacher. Health

127 classes stressing healthy lifestyles and positive body image would be required for

128 all students.

129   A benefit of simply revising the existing system is that it would teach boys and

130 girls to actively socialize and get along at an early age. On the other hand, antisexist

131 schools and classrooms that attempt to make everything equal for men and women

132 haven't worked so far. The main reason for the failure of these systems and the rea-

133 son why I don't believe it will ever work is that society is not going to change easily,

134 in a system that is not radically different from one that is in place now it won't be

135   forced to. I concede that schools do not exist in a vacuum, and that students of an

136   all-girls' system would still be affected by media influences. However, it's worth a try.

137   The best alternative and most effective system feasible at this time.

138   In short, a lot of the same changes I would institute in an all-girls' school would

139   be in place in traditional boy/girl schools. However, the fundamental problem with

140   this system is that most people are reluctant to change their views on certain issues.

141   Unfortunately, gender is one such issue. In order for such a change to work, the

142   media, government, and most importantly families, must make a commitment to the

143   education of our young women and the preparation of them to be happy, healthy

144   adults. How can a little boy realize that women are not inferior to men when he sees

145   his father beat up his mother or refuse to let him play with dolls? How can a small

146   girl learn that she is as capable and intelligent as boys are when she watches her

147   older sister starve herself in order to be more attractive to teenage boys and sees

148   her mother meekly obey her father's unreasonable whims? The answer is simple:

149   they can't. It is only with efforts from all sides that we can save the young women of

150   the future from falling into the same trap that so many girls before them have.

Step 1: After rereading the composition, on a separate sheet of paper or in a separate file, write *one phrase* that says what your paper is about. Then write *one sentence* that says what your paper is about. Then write *one paragraph* that says what your paper is about.

In any rewrite, your most important goal should be to clarify your meaning for your readers. To achieve this goal, you have to be sure your meaning is clear to you. While you may think that you know exactly what your paper is about, it is always helpful to perform this first step, just to be *certain* you know. In addition, you will return to the work you do in this first step later in step 6 when you create a *target index,* a graphic chart that enables you to see how you introduce and develop topics in your composition.

Here's how Jeanette completed step 1:

- *Phrase:* Treatment of boys and girls in school
- *Sentence:* The ways that teachers treat boys and girls in school reinforces traditional gender stereotypes, so we need to explore alternative methods of schooling to counteract this treatment.

- *Paragraph:* The ways that teachers treat boys and girls in school re-inforce traditional gender stereotypes, so we need to explore alter-native methods of schooling to counteract this treatment. One method would be would be to create more single-sex elementary schools that would encourage young girls to become independent and strong-willed. A second would be to reform the current system of schooling thoroughly so that boys and girls are treated equally in terms of classroom expectations and rewards. In both methods, young students would be taught specifically about gender relations and the development of male and female identity.

Notice how Jeanette expanded her phrase into a sentence and her sen-tence into a paragraph. Doing so allows her to see what the essay is about in three stages, and this effort will help her focus the meaning as she rewrites the piece to clarify its meaning.

In-Progress Task

Reread the draft version of the paper you are rewriting. Then write a phrase, a sentence, and a paragraph that say what the paper is about.

Step 2: Look at every sentence and determine what possibilities it holds for you to write with *active verbs*. If it seems appropriate, rewrite the sentence using such verbs.

Verbs are the words in a sentence that express action or condition of being. They are potentially a source of clarity and strength in your writ-ing, but many writers fail to capitalize on the power of verbs. These writ-ers downplay the action in sentences, often by trying to convey it using modifying words and long, supposedly impressive-sounding words called *nominalizations*—nouns that are "built out" from verbs. Putting the ac-tion into modifiers and nominalizations can make the writing seem dull and lifeless. Putting the action into active verbs can invigorate the writing.

Keep in mind two important definitions and related concepts as you do this step:

ACTIVE VERBS

Active verbs are those that show that some person or force does some-thing to, with, or for some other person or object. Active verbs contrast with *passive verbs*, which show that some action *is done* rather than some person or force *does* the action. Consider, for example, this sentence from the second paragraph, lines 13–15, of Jeanette's essay: "It has been my experience that many feminist attempts are being labeled and written off as 'femiNazi extremist measures'." The second half of this sentence is dominated by two multiword, passive verbs: *are being labeled* and *(are being) written off.* Listen to the difference when you rewrite the sentence using simple, active verbs: "It has been my experience that social critics label feminist attempts as 'femiNazi extremist measures' and write them off." This version shows who is doing what to whom, rather than simply saying something is done.

Of course, you cannot—indeed, you should not—avoid using passive verbs completely. But you should look for opportunities to rewrite passives into actives. Here's a tip for recognizing passive verbs: They are always formed (and I have just formed one!) by combining some form of the verb *be* as a helper with a past participle—that form of a verb that would sensibly follow *have* or *has.* If there is a doer of the action expressed in a sentence with a passive verb, the doer is placed in a phrase beginning with *by* and placed after the verb. Compare "I studied the material" with "The material was studied by me."

FINITE VERBS

A *finite verb* is the word in a clause that shows the action or condition of being; a *verbal* is a form of a verb, usually ending in *ing* or *ed,* that is the main word in a modifying phrase. Both finite verbs and verbals can have active and passive forms. Look for the opportunity to rewrite both finite verbs and verbals as active. Consider this sentence from Jeanette's essay: *"Boys and girls would never be ridiculed by being forced to sit together or pitted against each other in singing contests."* Jeanette could rewrite this sentence and change both the finite verb and a verbal from passive to active: *"Teachers would never ridicule boys and girls by forcing them to sit together or pitting them against each other in singing contests."*

In terms of using active verbs, Jeanette does not need to rewrite her draft significantly. In a few places in the paper, however, her prose could be stronger if she used more active verbs. Look, for example, at lines 85–89 in the draft:

> Young women would be encouraged to retain their active, imaginative, energetic personalities rather than succumbing to the personality of the traditional well-behaved, respectful, docile lady. Of course, they would still be taught to be respectful and polite, but they would be encouraged to develop their personalities rather than stifle them.

Would Jeanette's prose sound stronger, more direct, and therefore more effective in this passage if it were rewritten using simple, active verbs? Consider this rewritten version:

This new type of school would encourage young women to retain their active, imaginative, energetic personalities rather than succumbing to the personality of the tradition, well-behaved, respectful, docile lady. Of course, their mentors would still teach them to be respectful and polite, but they would encourage the girls to develop their personalities rather than stifle them.

 ## Two In-Progress Tasks

(A) Practice rewriting using active verbs by rewriting lines 92–93 and the paragraph beginning with line 119 in Jeanette's essay. (B) Select several passages from the draft you are working on and rewrite them using active verbs.

Step 3: Look at every sentence and determine what possibilities it holds to have a human being or some human collective or force as the agent, or doer, of the action. If it seems appropriate, rewrite the sentence putting those agents in as the subjects of verbs.

Step 2 assumes that readers find a composition to be more direct and therefore more effective if it uses active verbs as much as possible. Step 3 complements this view by assuming that readers find prose more direct and effective if it casts real human beings, or human collectives or forces, as the *doers* of the action in those verbs. Passive verbs, as we have seen, tuck the doer of the action into the end of the clause, in a phrase that begins with the word *by*, and when you rewrite these clauses using active verbs, you have to put someone or something before the verb as the doer of the action. But it is also possible to write a sentence with an active verb in the first place and not have a human being, collective, or force in the doer position. Consider this passage, from about lines 51–58 in Jeanette's draft:

> One method of preparation, and perhaps the most extreme, is to completely separate boys and girls in terms of education. In addition, the school itself would not hold to traditional gender roles, administrators and teachers of advanced subjects could be female instead of almost exclusively male. Cafeteria workers, cleaning staff, groundskeepers, and secretarial staff would be equally divided in terms of gender. Students would wear some sort of uniform (preferably pants) in order to take the focus off of designer labels and phys-

ical appearance. Family members would be encouraged to take an active part in the educational process.

This is not bad writing, but it does not convey much sense of who is doing what to whom. Consider how a rewritten version, with human beings or forces in the doer positions, would sound stronger:

> One method of preparation, and perhaps the most extreme, is for educational leaders to separate boys and girls completely in distinct schools. In addition, these leaders could counteract traditional gender roles: they could hire only females to be administrators and teachers of advanced subjects, and they could employ only males as cafeteria workers and secretaries. Leaders would direct students to wear some kind of uniform (preferably pants) in order to take the focus off of designer labels and physical appearance. Administrators and teachers would encourage family members to take an active part in the educational process.

A complementary rewriting strategy is to look carefully at the use of *this* in the doer position. *This,* used alone as the subject of a verb, can cause confusion for readers, who might sensibly ask, "This what?" Consider, for example, lines 19–23 of Jeanette's essay:

> Young women will only cease to be docile, dependent, pretty puppets once society convinces them that their ideas, thoughts, and insights have as much intrinsic value as those of their outspoken, independent, confident male counterparts. This will only occur once people realize that change is imperative and necessary now.

What exactly does *this* refer to in the second sentence of this passage? Wouldn't the passage be stronger if the second sentence began with *"This convincing"* or if it read *"This message will only be conveyed once people realize that change is imperative and necessary now"*?

 Two In-Progress Tasks

To practice rewriting with human beings, collective, or forces as doers of the action, (A) rewrite the paragraph beginning with line 95 in Jeanette's essay, and (B) rewrite a passage of whatever draft you are currently working on. Be sure to look carefully at instances of *this* standing alone as the doer of an action, and think about adding another word after *this* to clarify the meaning.

Step 4: Test every sentence for completeness and boundaries. If you encounter any sentence fragments, ask yourself whether you can justify their use on stylistic grounds. If so, do nothing. If not, rewrite them as complete sentences. If you encounter any spliced or run-on sentences, rewrite them as separate sentences.

Of all the problems involving standard written English, the two that seem to annoy readers most severely are incomplete sentences, better known as fragments, and sentences with no boundary markers, better known as comma splices and run-ons. Both of these problems involve violations of the basic definition of sentence—a group of words that contains a subject and a finite verb and expresses a complete thought. A fragment may have a subject and some kind of verb, usually not finite, but it rarely expresses a complete thought. Both comma splices and run-ons contain two sentences. A comma splice places a comma between the two sentences rather than a period and a capital letter. A run-on simply runs one sentence into the next with no punctuation between them.

These definitions, as simple as they sound, are also relatively difficult to grasp. Rather than simply looking at a group of words and trying to determine, with relatively vague directions, whether it is a fragment, comma splice, or run-on, you can use one of the following three tests to determine whether you should rewrite it or not:

THE TAG-QUESTION TEST

Every declarative sentence—that is, every sentence that is not a question or an exclamation—can be followed by a *single* tag question, a question essentially asking for confirmation of the sentence's content, that potentially makes sense. Here is an example of a sentence with a tag question added to it:

> This book is entitled *Inquiry and Genre,* isn't it? [The tag question is *isn't it?*]

When you try to follow a sentence fragment with a single tag question, it usually does not make sense. When you try to follow a comma splice or run-on with a single tag question, you see that you have at least two sentences that could be converted into a tag question, which signals that you should rewrite them as separate sentences.

To see this test at work, let's examine two passages from Jeanette's essays. The first comes from lines 16–17:

> Only to dismiss every suggestion from reform as being completely unrealistic and not worth the effort.

The second comes from lines 35–37:

Academia says that females are as intelligent and capable as men, the media portray women as pretty, thin, dependent, well-behaved individuals with the self-esteem of ants.

When we try to add a tag question to the first passage, it doesn't make any sense:

Only to dismiss every suggestion for reform as being completely unrealistic and not worth the effort, isn't it?

This passage is a fragment. We can rewrite it by attaching it to the preceding sentence, as in the following:

I cannot tell you how many times that both men and women have come to an agreement that change is not only necessary but vital, only to dismiss every suggestion for reform as being completely unrealistic and not worth the effort.

You could follow this long but successful sentence with the tag question "haven't they?" and it would make sense. You could also rewrite the sentence by adding a doer of the action, ideally a human being, collective, or force, and changing *to dismiss* into a finite verb.

These men and women then dismiss every suggestion for reform as being completely unrealistic and not worth the effort.

You could follow this sentence with the sensible tag question "don't they?" and it would make perfect sense. Try the tag question test with the second passage, the one from lines 35–37:

Academia says that females are as intelligent and capable as men, the media portray women as pretty, thin, dependent, well-behaved individuals with the self-esteem of ants.

Do you add tag question "doesn't it?" to reflect "Academia says," or do you add the tag question "don't they?" to reflect "the media portray"? Seeing that you need two tag questions, you conclude that you probably have two sentences fused together by a comma, better known as a comma splice. You rewrite them by putting a period after *men* and capitalizing the beginning of *The* before *media*. In other words, you make two sentences.

THE YES/NO QUESTION TEST

You can conduct a similar test for fragments, comma splices, and run-ons by trying to convert them into a yes/no question. Every declarative sentence can be transformed into a yes/no question that makes sense. Many sentence fragments cannot. Let's look at the corrected version of the fragment from our earlier discussion:

These men and women then dismiss every suggestion for reform as being completely unrealistic and not worth the effort.

Here is the same sentence converted into a yes/no question:

Do these men and women then dismiss every suggestion for reform as being completely unrealistic and not worth the effort?

This version makes sense. But now try to convert the original fragment into a yes/no question. You can't do so and make sense, so you see again that your fragment needs to be rewritten.

When you try to cast the original comma splice as a yes/no question, you see again that you have two parts that need recasting:

Does academia say that females are as intelligent and capable as men?
Do the media portray women as pretty, thin, dependent, well-behaved individuals with the self-esteem of ants?

Once again, you see that the passage should be rewritten as two sentences.

THE "I REFUSE TO BELIEVE THAT" TEST

It is possible to add "I refuse to believe that" to the beginning of a complete declarative sentence and thereby create an even more emphatic sentence that makes a complete thought. (Whether you actually do refuse to believe the content of the sentence is beside the point. This is just a test for fragments.) When you add "I refuse to believe that" to the beginning of a fragment, however, you can plainly see its incomplete, fragmentary nature. When you add "I refuse to believe that" to the beginning of a comma splice or run-on, the addition points us the dual nature of the passage, showing you once again that you need to rewrite it as two sentences:

Fragment revealed: I refuse to believe that only to dismiss every suggestion for reform as being completely unrealistic and not worth the effort.

Sentence: I refuse to believe that these men and women dismiss every suggestion for reform as being completely unrealistic and not worth the effort.

Comma splice revealed: I refuse to believe that academic says that females are as intelligent and capable as men, the media portray women as pretty, thin, dependent well-behaved individuals with the self-esteem of ants.

Two sentences: I refuse to believe that academic says that females are as intelligent and capable as men. I refuse to believe the media portray women as pretty, thin, dependent well-behaved individuals with the self-esteem of ants.

Two In-Progress Tasks

To practice recognizing and rewriting fragments, comma splices, and run-ons, (A) examine and rewrite lines 31–32, 73–76, 79–82, and 132–135 of Jeanette's essay; (B) conduct the tests and rewrite passages in the draft you are working on.

Step 5: Write a gloss for each paragraph.

A gloss is an explanatory note written in the margin of a text. When you write a gloss for each paragraph, you write a note (it need not even be a complete sentence) that explains what the paragraph accomplishes in terms of the overall development of the essay. Writing paragraph glosses helps you to see whether your composition introduces and develops material in an appropriate and accessible way for your readers. The glosses also prepare you for the next step in the Trim-and-Target Method, in which you determine whether your draft develops material in sufficient depth.

Jeanette's essay has thirteen paragraphs. Here are glosses of the first ten:

- Paragraph 1, lines 1–10: Provides general background about unequal treatment of the sexes in schools; poses questions
- Paragraph 2, lines 11–23: Establishes widespread unwillingness to change inequalities
- Paragraph 3, lines 24–32: Argues that attitudes focusing on the past are not appropriate
- Paragraph 4, lines 33–50: Explains that the world of work calls for women who have worked out the problems of adolescence
- Paragraph 5, lines 51–58: Introduces alternative of schools segregated by gender
- Paragraph 6, lines 59–65: Gives more details of segregated schools plan
- Paragraph 7, lines 66–76: Emphasizes how segregated schools would assist personality development
- Paragraph 8, lines 77–94: Discusses the curriculum of segregated schools
- Paragraph 9, lines 95–103: Explains the benefits of segregated education
- Paragraph 10, lines 104–118: Suggests the drawbacks of segregated education, but dismisses them

Two In-Progress Tasks:

(A) Write glosses for the remaining three paragraphs in Jeanette's essay. Then look back over Chapters 8 and 9 and determine which exploratory strategy Jeanette used to develop her essay. (B) Write glosses for the paragraphs of the draft you are working on.

Step 6: Create a target chart for each paragraph by charting the number of topics introduced and the depth and direction of their development.

Step 6 brings together the "target" aspect of the Trim-and-Target Method of rewriting. In step 6, you create a chart for each paragraph and place in it a topic, the word or phrase that seems to be most important, for each sentence in the paragraph. These charts enable you to see whether you are "on target" in the paragraph—that is, whether you are focusing on the material that your paragraph gloss, from step 5, suggests is central to the paragraph.

For each topic you place in the chart, you decide whether it is a reiteration of a topic previously introduced or a new topic. After charting a paragraph, you examine the chart carefully and decide whether you have introduced too many topics or need to develop any of the topics more fully by reiterating them. Paragraphs in which each sentence introduces a new topic and topics are seldom developed by reiteration can seem breezy and superficial to a reader.

In completing this step, consider the topic of a sentence the *most important* word or phrase in the sentence that says what the sentence is about. In some cases, the topic will be the main word or phrase in the grammatical subject of the main clause in the sentence. In other cases, the topic might come in a phrase that begins the sentence. In still other cases, you may find the topic near the end of the sentence, away from the main subject. The decision about what you want to call the topic of each sentence is yours since you are the one who must use the chart to guide any rewriting you choose to do.

A target chart lists numbers beginning with 1 horizontally across the top, then places each sentence's topic under the appropriate number, depending on whether it is a reiteration of a previous topic or a new topic.

To practice creating target index charts, let's reexamine a rewritten version (the rewrites having been guided by the first five steps in the Trim-and-Target Method) of Jeanette's essay:

1   Although the treatment of women has improved dramatically over the years, one
2   must admit that society does not place equal value on the both sexes yet. This lack
3   of equality is particularly evident in educational settings. In terms of attention, fund-
4   ing levels, and amount of praise given, young women are not up to the same status
5   as their male counterparts. Why is the dropout rate higher for women than it is for
6   men? Why do male athletic programs receive more money than those for women?
7   Why do teachers ask males more questions and spend more one-on-one time with
8   their male students than female? Most gender bias is due to society's reluctance to
9   change antiquated views. What can be done by teachers, parents, and administra-
10   tors to alleviate the problem?

11   While many people sense and recognize the need for gender reform at all
12   educational levels, most do not know how to go about changing the system. In ad-
13   dition, many do not even want the system to change. It has been my experience
14   that many feminist attempts are being labeled and written off as "femiNazi ex-
15   tremist measures." I cannot tell you how many times that both men and women
16   have come to an agreement that change is not only necessary but vital, only to dis-
17   miss every suggestion for reform as being completely unrealistic and not worth
18   the effort. This attitude is precisely the problem in so many areas of concern today;
19   people and society are unwilling to change the traditional roles of men and
20   women. Young women will only cease to be docile, dependent, pretty puppets
21   once society convinces them that their ideas, thoughts, and insights have as much
22   intrinsic value as those of their outspoken, independent, confident male counter-
23   parts. This message will only be conveyed when people realize that change is im-
24   perative and necessary now.

25   Current thinking on gender issues in schools is split halfway between those
26   who believe that change is necessary now and those feeling that feminists are
27   spending too much time and energy trying to reform a system that doesn't need
28   change. After all, what was good enough in the past is good enough for today's stu-
29   dents, right? Conversations with many family members and classmates have

30 convinced me that despite their politically correct appearances, a lot of people are

31 still caught up in the archaic thinking of the past. Unfortunately, the past is not good

32 enough any more. The proper preparation of young girls must start right now if

33 women on a whole are ever going to achieve complete equality.

Here are target charts for these three paragraphs:
Notice that the first paragraph introduces three topics:

1. *Society*
2. *Lack of equality* and other variations on that general term in the paragraph: *attention, funding levels,* and *amount of praise given* in sentence 3 are really reiterations of *lack of equality,* as are *dropout rate* in sentence 4 and *gender bias* in sentence 6.
3. *Teachers,* introduced in sentence 5 and expanded to include *teachers, parents, and administrators,* all people in positions of authority over students, in sentence 7.

The first paragraph is well developed, and the target chart shows it. Two of the three topics are developed by reiteration.

The target chart for the second paragraph shows a similarly thorough development. Five topics are introduced, but the first two are developed with reiteration. The last three are not developed, but their single-mention introduction serves as a bridge to the third paragraph, which introduces four topics and develops one with reiteration.

So far, then, the target charts show Jeanette introducing topics either to develop them with reiteration or to provide transition to a new paragraph. Notice, however, a partially rewritten version of the next-to-last paragraph and the target chart for it:

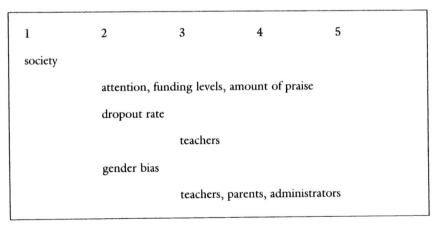

1	2	3	4	5
society				
	attention, funding levels, amount of praise			
	dropout rate			
		teachers		
	gender bias			
		teachers, parents, administrators		

FIGURE II.1   Jeanette's essay, Target chart, paragraph 1

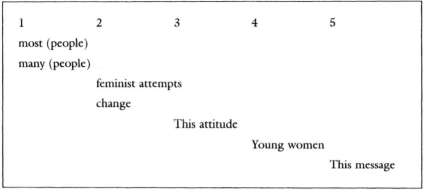

FIGURE II.2   Jeanette's essay, Target chart, paragraph 2

114 A benefit of simply revising the existing system is that it would teach boys and
115 girls to actively socialize and get along at an early age. On the other hand, antisexist
116 schools and classrooms that attempt to make everything equal for men and women
117 haven't worked so far. The main reason for the failure of these systems and the rea-
118 son why I don't believe it will ever work is that society is not going to change easily,
119 in a system that is not radically different from one that is in place now it won't be
120 forced to. I concede that schools do not exist in a vacuum, and that students of an
121 all-girls' system would still be affected by media influences. However, it's worth a try.
122 It is the best alternative and most effective system feasible at this time.

The target chart suggests that this paragraph, near the end of the
draft, might benefit from rewriting. Because each of the first four sentences introduces a new topic and none is reiterated with a repeat or a reiteration, this paragraph might strike a reader as superficial.

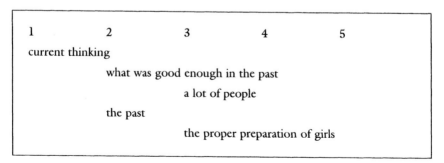

FIGURE II.3   Jeanette's essay, Target chart, paragraph 3

Three In-Progress Tasks

(A) Rewrite paragraph 12 of Jeanette's draft, charted as follows, to develop one or more of the topics more fully. (B) Select another paragraph besides 1, 2, 3, or 12; create a target chart; and decide whether the paragraph needs additional development. (C) Create target charts for the paragraphs of the draft you are working on and determine whether the paragraphs are "on target" with your paragraph glosses and whether any of the topics need further development.

1	2	3	4	5
benefit				
	antisexist . . . classrooms			
		The main reason		
			schools	
				It
				It

FIGURE II.4   Jeanette's essay, Target chart, paragraph 12

Step 7: Reread the composition for deadwood and redundancy, and eliminate their sources.

Deadwood is a writer's term for any extraneous words that can be cut to make the meaning of a composition clearer. *Redundancy* is the term for any repetitive words or phrases that can be trimmed because they say the same thing. Deadwood and redundancy have many causes. Let's concentrate on three of the most evident:

■ Using "be" or "condition" verbs followed by a modifier, rather than simply using a single verb. Examine lines 29–30: "a lot of people are in complete congruence with the thinking of the past that now seems archaic." Notice how this clause can be trimmed: "a lot of people agree with the archaic thinking of the past."

■ Engaging in "elegant variation," a collection of synonyms or near-synonyms in the same passage. Look, for example, at lines 19–22: "Young women will only cease to be docile, dependent, pretty puppets once society convinces them that their ideas, thoughts, and insights have as much intrinsic value as their outspoken, independent, confident male counterparts." Notice the three strings: "docile, dependent, pretty," "ideas, thoughts, insights," and "outspoken, independent, confident." The first and the third strings are not really redundant. The meanings of each of the three terms are different enough to warrant keeping the phrase intact. But "ideas, thoughts, and insights" mean the same thing. A rewrite would cut one of those terms.

- Using two or more words when one will do. Examine line 33: "In this day and age." Say "today" or "now." Look at line 43: "experience a growing lack of self-confidence." Say "lose self-confidence." Your prose will sound stronger.

 ## Two In-Progress Tasks

(A) Read Jeanette's draft carefully for other instances of deadwood and redundancy and rewrite to eliminate them. (B) Look for and eliminate deadwood and redundancy in your own draft.

Step 8: Edit your paper thoroughly. Read your paper aloud. Read your paper backward.

Many students do not edit their papers carefully enough before submitting the final draft. Read your paper aloud and read it backward. Doing so will enable you to catch any words you have left out, any misspelled words that the checker didn't catch, and any words or phrases that you have accidentally repeated.

Step 9: If your paper is on a computer disk or hard drive, run the spell checker program, but do not hit the replace key indiscriminantly. Then run any grammar checker program you have access to. *Consider* the advice that the grammar checker program offers, but do not feel as though you *must* take the actions it recommends.

At the very least, if you have used a word processor, you should run the spell checker program before producing the final version. Do not, however, hit the replace key indiscriminantly when running this program. Hit the replace key only when the program is offering the correct spelling of the word you actually intend to use. The computer does not know how to spell many words, including many personal nouns and important academic terms, and it might replace them with words similar in spelling but very distant in meaning. A personal example: I was writing about the institution where I teach, DePaul University, and I mistakenly hit the replace key in the spell check program. Throughout my paper, my school was referred to as "Dapple University." I am glad I caught the "correction" before I submitted the paper.

Most grammar checker programs will alert you about commonly misused words, overusing the passive voice, avoiding one-sentence paragraphs, and recognizing redundancies and deadwood. The most valuable of these functions is the first. A good grammar checker will stop when it encounters words that sound the same, like *its* and *it's*, *here* and *hear*, and *there*, *their*, and *they're*. The most common error in this category involves *its* and *it's*. Be sure that you use *its* as the possessive pronoun *("Every dog has its day")* and *it's* as the contraction of *it is ("It's getting easier to detect problems in our papers.")*. Search for every example of the word *of* to make sure you are not using it as part of a verb, in place of *have*, as Jeanette has done in line 113.

Beyond the advice about commonly misused words, be selective in doing what the grammar checker proposes. Look at each sentence that uses the passive voice, and ask yourself whether you *should* use it to make the prose flow smoothly. It is generally a good idea to avoid one-sentence paragraphs since it is difficult to develop an idea fully in one sentence. Remember, though, that many newspaper stories rely on one-sentence paragraphs, and *occasionally* writers use them in essays and other working documents to achieve a dramatic, startling effect. In summary, consult your grammar checker, but do not be a slave to its advice.

Step 10: Repeat step 1.

See whether your paper is still about what you thought it was about at the beginning of the rewriting process. Determine whether you need to return to any of the eight steps for further rewriting.

Index

Credits